CHSP
HUNGARIAN STUDIES SERIES
NO. 21

EDITORS
Peter Pastor
Ivan Sanders

A Joint Publication with the
Institute of Habsburg History, Budapest

Public Space in Budapest

The History of Kossuth Square

ANDRÁS GERŐ

Translated from the Hungarian by
THOMAS J. AND HELEN D. DEKORNFELD

Social Science Monographs, Boulder, Colorado

Center for Hungarian Studies and Publications, Inc.
Wayne, New Jersey

Distributed by Columbia University Press, New York

2009

EAST EUROPEAN MONOGRAPHS
NO. DCCL

Originally published as *Térerő. A Kossuth tér története*

47 Cecilia Drive, Wayne, New Jersey
07470–4649
E-mail: pastorp@mail.montclair.edu

This book is a joint publication with the
Institute of Habsburg History, Budapest
www.Habsburg.org.hu

Public Foundation for
Habsburg Studies
Institute of
Habsburg History

Library of Congress Control Number 2009939023
ISBN 978–0–88033–648–2

Printed in the United States of America

CONTENTS

PREFACE vii

◁ **THE PHYSICAL TOPOGRAPHY OF THE SQUARE** 1

The Name 2

Dimension and Awareness 5

The Buildings on the Square 9

The House of the Nation 16

◁ **THE SYMBOLIC SQUARE** 29

The Manifestations of Power 30

Manifestations of Protest 34

Moments of Political Mercy 37

Political Piety 39

Unclassifiable Tragedy 41

The Non-Political Square 43

◁ **THE SPIRITUAL SQUARE** 47

The First Step—The Andrássy Memorial 49

Intermezzo 62

The Second Step—The *Kossuth* Statue 63

A Sidestep—The *István Nagyatádi Szabó* Statue 68

Another Sidestep—The Martyrs of the Nation Memorial 70

The Third Step—The Count István Tisza Memorial 71

The Fourth Step—The Ferenc II Rákóczi Memorial 74

A New Situation—Damage, Destruction, Purging 77

Kossuth to Replace Kossuth 79

A New Element—The National Banner 83

Tisza Replaced by Károlyi 84
Andrássy Replaced by Attila József 86
Spiritual Explosion—Spiritual Fragments 88
A Grimace of Spirituality 93

◁ **Postscript** 97

◁ **Press Reports** 103

Political Position of the Selected Dailies 105

Biographical Notes 245

Photographs 307
The Physical Topography of the Square 309
The Symbolic Square 313
The Spiritual Square 323
Press Reports 331

Name Index 365

About the Author 377

Books Published by CHSP 378

PREFACE

There are many squares in Hungary named for Lajos Kossuth, including three in Budapest. One of these is usually referred to with a capital letter as "The" Kossuth Square. It is the square around the Parliament. Nobody confounds it with any other square by the same name. This book records the history of The Kossuth Square. Yet I must immediately correct this claim. This book deals with those human wishes and actions which shaped the importance of the square and filled it with a symbolic and spiritual content.

I have, therefore, aimed to describe the history of the square and interpret it in a fashion which allowed me to introduce and demonstrate the changing but ongoing human intentions and endeavors.

The dimensions of the narrative determine the various starting points of the story. In a physical-topographic sense the story begins in 1885 when the foundations for the Parliament building were laid down. In a symbolic sense the starting point is 1896. It was at that time that the first major political program was initiated here, even though the building had not been completed. In a spiritual sense the starting point is 1906. It was then that the first memorial was erected on the square. It was the Gyula Andrássy statue that has since been removed.

Not only the starting points differ but, I believe, that a similar difference exists in the end points as well. In a physical sense 1972 is the end of the story. This was when the last empty space on the square was filled. In a symbolic sense there is no end to the story. In a spiritual sense the end point is 2002 when the last monument on the square was dedicated.

The diverging threads of the story, the various starting and ending points and the never-ending progress of the square made it necessary to present the square in its unique individuality and complexity. This was the only way to solve its strange and worldly mysticism.

The diverging dimensions demand that they be approached by varying methodologies. The historical interpretation of the events cannot be modeled according to the architectural evolution of the buildings. Description of the various monuments must differ from the collective approach taken toward the events.

Any approach toward such a complexity, in which the nature of the dimensions is so variable, cannot be adapted to a single theoretical framework. To use a descriptive narrative method would be absurd when relating the physical history of the square. Because of the context of the memorials a description according to the theoretical framework of memorial architecture would be of only limited value. The often widely divergent meanings of the events which have taken place in the square make it impossible to discuss them by trying to confine them to a theoretical construction. I attempted to resolve this problem by using expressive and relevant concepts. This might or perhaps does have theoretical criteria but which, dogmatically, are not threaded on a single theoretical scheme. To put it more simply, let me paraphrase some words of Mephistopheles from Goethe's *Faust*: "Every theory is grey, and green is the golden tree" of history.

The square-centered approach in a number of dimensions raised some serious obstacles. What I wanted to say always had been constrained by the chosen program. I tried to indicate this in the text.

It is seemly in a preface to explain why this book was written. This is a personal matter and there are two reasons. In 1990 my book about Heroes' Square was published in both English and German, under the titles of *Heroes' Square* and *Der Heldenplatz*, and was published by Corvina in Budapest. Since that time I continued to think about the square because symbolic politics have become one of the major concerns of my scholarly endeavors. I knew in 1990 that the Kossuth Square had to be studied. The more I became involved in the history of symbolic politics the clearer it became that the history of the Kossuth Square should not and could not be avoided. I also realized that to date nobody had done this with any completeness.

Now then the square and I have met. On my part it is the realization of an old and fervent desire.

Even though I do not compare the two squares in this volume, I have to make a one-sentence comment. Both squares play a key role in Hungarian symbolic political history. Heroes' Square has a national essentiality, which is interpreted politically, and which is a point of national grandeur and glory. In fact it is the altar of the nation. Kossuth Square has a power-political essence, which is placed in a national context. There are many other differences between the two squares, but the above is the most significant.

There was another reason for my interest in Kossuth Square. I will speak to this in the postscript of this volume.

* * *

This work was the result of the research project of the Public Foundation for Habsburg Studies and of the Institute of Habsburg History. Daniel Borovi, Ádám Paár, and Attila Rácz contributed to the gathering of the material. Emőke Tomsics had a key role in selecting the illustrations. The Budapest City Archives staff assisted in the selection of the maps. Éva Beleznay, the chief architect of the city of Budapest, was most helpful in providing information about the future of the square.

Special thanks are due to the officials of Studio 73, Ltd., landscape architects Sándor Mohácsi and Péter István Balogh, Sr., who advised me about the details of their prize-winning designs.

* * *

I sincerely hope that this book will provide a documented and reasoned explanation why Kossuth Square deserves its honorific adjectives and the elevated role and character in Hungarian culture which it had held and still holds.

THE PHYSICAL TOPOGRAPHY OF THE SQUARE

In its first approximation the square is a physical-topographical concept. It is a wide public space surrounded by buildings.

Thus, to be able to describe the square we have to take its physical determinants as the base. The reason for this is that for all the other dimensions of the square, symbolic, spiritual, and sacred, only the physical concept can serve as a base. Every other content sketch must, or must not, be derived from this.

In order to describe the large public square surrounded by buildings it is not necessary to discuss the history of every building. If we were to do that, we would not write the history of the square but we would write, and practice, architectural history. In my view, and because of the topic I have chosen, there is no need for this. The history of the square is not the history of the buildings surrounding it.

Yet, albeit briefly, reference must be made to what constitutes the boundaries of the square. It must be done by rendering the functionality of the physical dimensions but not with any artistic, architectural or urban history details.

This is true for the building, namely the Parliament, which has given the square a supra-physical dimension right from the beginning. If the Parliament were not there, the history of the square would have been quite different and there would not have been a symbolic or a spiritual history. This does not mean, however, that the entire history and inner structure of the building has to be discussed. For us, and for me, the important matters are only those which affected the history of the square.

The Name

The official name of the square today is Lajos Kossuth Square. For the sake of simplicity I will call it the Kossuth Square all throughout its history. The history of how the name was given suggests that the physical-topographic field had undergone a change and that the name of the square moved from the concrete to the realm of symbolism and spirituality.

The square, or more accurately, the area which is largely today's square was known after 1853 as the Stadt Schopper Platz, meaning the City Calking Square.[1] The name reflected the use to which the square was put at the time. Prior to that, ever since the 1820s, the area was known as a river port and shipyard area. The German names of the times, Städtischer Auswind Platz (City Port) and Schiffauswindsamst Platz (Ship Unloading Office Square) reflect this. It was also known as Flotillen Platz (Flotilla Square). The port also had a shipyard attached to it and this led to the Schopper Platz, i.e. Calking Square designation which became widely accepted in the middle of the nineteenth century. The *Schopper* was the shipwright who calked the planks in the sides and bottom of the vessels. Acceptance of the calking (filling) name was promoted by the fact that the uneven area was originally used as a

---

[1] For the architectural history of the square which went through a series of names, see Attila Déry, *Belváros-Lipótváros: V. kerület, Budapesti építészeti tipográfidája* [The Fifth District: Town Center-Leopoldville, The Architectural Topography of Budapest] (Budapest: Terc, 2005), vol 2; Erzsébet Farkaslaky and Mihály Ráday, eds., *Adalékok Lipótváros történetéhez* [Sources to the History of Leopoldville], 2 vols. (Budapest: Budapesti Városszépítő Egyesület, 1988); András Ferkai, ed., *Pest építészete a két világháború között* [The Architecture of Pest between the Two World Wars] (Budapest: Budapesti Városépítészeti Egyesület, 2001); Mihály Pásztor, "A százötvenéves Lipótváros" [The 150-years old Leopoldville], *Statisztikai Közlemények* 93, no. 4 (1919); László Siklóssy, *Hogyan épült Budapest? 1870–1930* [How was Budapest Built? 1870–1930] (Budapest: Fővárosi Közmunka Tanács, 1931); *Budapest lexikon* [Budapest Encyclopedia] (Budapest: Akadémiai Kiadó, 1973); and *Budapest teljes utcanévlexikona* [The Complete Encyclopedia of the Street Names of Budapest] (Budapest: Dinasztia Kiadó, 1998). For specifics about the city's history, see Károly Vörös, ed., *Budapest története* [The History of Budapest] (Budapest: Akadémiai Kiadó, 1974), vol. 4; András Gerő and János Pór, eds., *Budapest. A History from Its Beginnings to 1998* (Boulder, CO: East European Monographs, 1997); Catherine Horel, *Histoire de Budapest* (Paris: Fayard, 1999); and Vera Bácskai, Gábor Gyáni, and András Kubinyi, *Budapest története a kezdetektől 1945-ig* [The History of Budapest from the Beginnings to 1945–1945] (Budapest: Budapest Főváros Levéltára, 2000).

dump, but that the depressions were increasingly filled, i.e. calked. The square retained this name until 1898 even though the calking of ships had decreased markedly.

In 1896 the Parliament was being built and the entire square was named Országház Tér, i.e. Parliament Square. For the previous thirty years one part of the square had been known as the Vízmű tér (Waterworks Square) because such a structure did occupy this area.

The emotional motivation for the name of the square was the fact that it was here that the Parliament building was being erected. This, however, does not explain the date. The construction of the Parliament began substantially earlier, namely in 1885. By 1896 the central dome was already almost complete.

The date of 1898 was not chosen due to the stage of completion but by the fact that it was the fiftieth anniversary of the 1848 revolution. It was at this time that April 11, the anniversary date of the April Laws of 1848, was sanctified as a national holiday (Act V of 1898). The enactment occurred within the framework of seventeen years during which the Parliament was erected and the naming of the square emphasized the government action, which otherwise had little if any impact on public interest.[2]

Assigning this name also indicates that the decision makers of the day took it for granted that the area in front of and around the Parliament building would be known as the Parliament Square. They insisted that buildings enclosing the square on one side provide the topographic designation. In this they followed an old tradition which always favored physical-topographic characteristics in assigning names.

The Parliament was being built during the years when the slow dissolution of the Austro-Hungarian Monarchy was taking place and after the defeat of Hungary in World War I, the republic was proclaimed in November 1918. Just prior to this, still in November, the other two losers, Germany and Austria, underwent a constitutional change and became republics. To emphasize the change, Parliament Square was

---

2 For the role of 1898 see Péter Hanák, "1898—a nemzeti és az állampatrióta értékrend frontális összeütközése a Monarchiában" [The direct clash of the values of national and official patriotism], in *A kert és a műhely* [The Garden and the Workshop] (Budapest: Gondolat, 1988), pp. 112–129; and András Gerő, *Imagined History, Chapters from Nineteenth and Twentieth Century Hungarian Symbolic Politics* (Boulder, CO: East European Monographs, 2006), pp. 235–251.

renamed Köztársaság tér (Republic Square). This suggests that the square had earned the right to be elevated into a symbolic-spiritual dimension. It was no longer simply an area where a particular building could be found, but it could now be used to indicate a particular concept. It was the first time in its history that at the level of its name it rises above itself.

The new name was still in use in 1919 for a while, but public usage never accepted it because the previous name was already twenty years old and fitted in perfectly with the obvious characteristic of the square. After the short-lived 1919 Soviet Republic the counterrevolutionary system reestablished the Parliament Square designation. One of the principal reasons for so doing was that it defined itself intellectually as opposition to the revolution. It was, therefore, opposed to the concept of a republic and Hungary again became a kingdom, albeit without a king. Consequently there was no need for a Republic Square.

The rechristening was not long-lived. It lasted only for eight years. The counterrevolutionary system considered itself to be national, Christian, and conservative. Thus, in principle, it had no use for the traditions which diverged from this triad of values. On the other hand, following World War I, Hungary lost much of its territory and a significant percentage of its population, including more than three million Hungarians. In the politics of the counterrevolutionary system the revision of the peace treaty of Trianon, ending the war for Hungary, became a matter of primary importance. In order to accomplish this revision it was necessary to mobilize all those traditions that were nationalistic or could be so interpreted, even if their relative values differed from the values of the counterrevolutionary system.

The eightieth anniversary of the 1848 revolution offered the opportunity to make the day of the revolution, March 15, a national holiday and to establish a nationally sanctified memorial to Lajos Kossuth, who personified the revolution and who had been a cult figure in Hungarian society. To be sure, in 1848–49 Kossuth was a liberal and a democrat, but he also represented the case for the territorial unity of Hungary.

In November 1927 two laws were enacted. Act XXXI of 1927 made March 15 a national holiday and Act XXXII of 1927 recognized the lasting merits and memory of Lajos Kossuth. At the northern end of the square in front of the Parliament a memorial statue of Kossuth was dedicated on November 6, 1927. This made it possible to again rename Parliament Square which henceforth was known as Lajos Kossuth Square.

Since it has been so named several political systems have ruled Hungary. None of them, however, wanted to change the name which suggests at least two issues. It seems that Kossuth is the shining star of Hungarian national consciousness and was thus important for every political system. To a different degree and with different content it became not only important but inevitable.[3]

It is equally important that a symbolically significant designation could culturally define the topographic content. This is often generally true, but in Kossuth's case it can be incontrovertibly demonstrated. Simply because over the years the square became increasingly the site for events and features the contents of which had no relationship to the Parliament building even though without it they would not have taken place there. The existence of the Parliament gives a varying context to the events, which elsewhere would not be the same. They gain symbolism and spirituality from the presence of the Parliament building without which they would have a different symbolism and a different spiritual content.

The symbolic name designates a physical space, even though this given space is not simply a wide public area surrounded by buildings.

Dimension and Awareness

In shaping the Kossuth Square everything was subject to the fact that the Parliament building was being erected here. In this respect it did not matter that some other buildings were completed earlier, they were all remodeled to preserve the desired structure of the square and the proposed system of streets.

The law about the building of the Parliament (Act LVIII of 1889) was signed by Francis Joseph on December 14, 1880. Even prior to its enactment Prime Minister Kálmán Tisza asked the Capital Public

3 For the Kossuth cult, see ibid., pp. 37–60.

Works Council to take a position concerning the site. It recommended the Calking Square and justified the choice by the following statement:

> This 4,410 square fathom group of parcels is owned by the state, it faces the Danube and is surrounded on four sides by relatively quiet streets. In front there are two parks which provide recreation and fresh air and which look out over the Danube. It meets all requirements for comfort and health and is particularly well suited for peaceful activities. In the overall city plan this area had been selected for the Parliament. It is in a quiet and elegant district of the city and its surroundings will develop at the same time as the Parliament is being erected and will provide space for magnificent palace-like structures all the way to the Margit híd [Margaret Bridge]. It is substantially less expensive than any other area and, at fifty forints the square fathom it comes only to barely 300,000 forints. The other areas would be one and a half or two million forints which sum would represent a substantial part of the entire expense of erecting the Parliament. The wide area along the Danube is of particular advantage and so are the two parks which will form an integral part of it.[4]

The potential square was mentioned here already, at least in a way which represented the two parks as an advantage. Yet this served only to argue in favor of the area and not to discuss the environment to be created for the Parliament. About this issue a position was taken in 1881:

> The grandiose building demands to stand by itself and that a suitable environment be created around it. Its majestic front should face the regal Danube and the other three sides shall be girded by a wide square. The outer segment of the square shall be divided so that beautiful palatial buildings might be erected there, keeping in mind the erection of public buildings. The principal entry into the square will be along the Alkotmány utca [Constitution Street] and

---

[4] Quoted in Siklóssy, *Hogyan épült Budapest?*, p. 282.

> the Parliament building will be positioned so that the axis of its eastern projection will parallel the axis of the Alkotmány utca.[5]

Further comments addressed the other streets leading into the square but for us this is less important. We are interested in the square and not in the network of streets.[6]

According to the original concept, therefore, a plan was evolved which saw a square around the Parliament and which would have found it desirable to see it lined with public buildings.

The proposed design of the square was accomplished, but, as we will see, the plan to line it with public buildings was only partly successful. For this reason, in 1927 when plans were made to enclose the northern and southern end of the square with new buildings, the Public Works Council added the following to Paragraph 129/a of the Building Regulations concerning the buildings to be erected:

> On the northern end of Lajos Kossuth Square, the entire area between the extension of Falk Miksa utca [Miksa Falk Street] and Személynök utca [Court President Street] and on the southern end of the square between the extensions of Nádor utca [Lord Lieutenant Street] and Akadémia utca [Academy Street], regardless of whether there are one or more parcels of land, the buildings have

---

[5] Quoted in ibid., pp. 283–284.

[6] The planning of the system of streets around the square is linked to the name of Ferenc Devecis Delvecchio. For us the final arrangement of the streets is of importance only as a point of reference. Therefore, I list the names from north to south on the basis of the *Complete Encyclopedia of Street Names of Budapest*. The present names are followed in parenthesis by the names used prior to 1914.
Széchenyi Embankment (Rudolf Embankment)
Balassi Bálint Street (Személynök Street)
Szalay Street (Szalay Street)
Báthory Street (Báthory Street)
Nádor Street (Nádor Street)
Akadémia Street (Akadémia Street)

It is not my goal to deal with street names at this point and I just mention that the present names usually agree with the names used at the beginning of the twentieth century. This was not always the case and it was only after 1990 that a number of streets were given back their old name.

> to be erected so that they constitute a single, continuous and homogenous front. Furthermore, on the entire width of both the northern and southern ends of the square, the buildings facing each other along the entire lengths, must have identical frontages, the same architecture, the same height and the same roof construction.
>
> The frontage of the buildings must be designed forcefully and monumentally, with serene, horizontal, corbelled cornices and without crenellations. The frontage has to be of natural or artificial stone and the flat wall surfaces may be covered with weather-resistant mortar. No strong colors may be used. There may be no open courtyard toward the street. In addition to the ground floor the buildings must consist of five stories. The trussed rafter roofs must be constructed so that at the juncture of the buildings no free-standing firewall needs be created. The attic spaces toward the street may not be used for any purpose. On the street level no mercantile spaces are allowed and this area may be used only for coffee houses, restaurants or offices. There may be no retail doorways, and no billboards or electric advertisements on any of the buildings.[7]

The architectural unity of the square leaves much to be desired, even in retrospect. This is mostly due to the fact that part of the area is occupied by buildings other than public ones.

The original concept, however, remained intact and around the Parliament a wide, symmetrical, tripartite square was created. The total symmetry of the square is vitiated by the central portion of the Parliament being across the Constitution Street and not at right angles with it. Similarly, the streets entering the square on the eastern side are not parallel to the long axis of the Parliament. Thus the square is somewhat irregular but may still be considered as a reasonably symmetrical structure.

The present surface of the square is 65,000 square meters which can be considered as permanent. The surface changed over time

---

7 "A Fővárosi Közmunkák Tanácsa tanácsülési és bizottsági jegyzőkönyvek" [The minutes of the council and committee meetings of the Capital Public Works Council], vol. 59, "Az FKT ülése, 1927. március 1." [Meeting of the CPWC, March 1, 1927], 2154/1927, Budapest Fővárosi Levéltára [The Archives of the Captal City of Budapest] (hereafter cited as BFL).

because in the middle of the 1880s a surface area of 95,000 square meters was still being discussed. While preserving the concept of the three-part structure of the square, this area was reduced by changing the entrance arrangements of the streets, doing away with the original funnel-shaped entrances, and also by increasing the ratio of buildings to open space.[8] The original concepts about the park-like arrangement of the open spaces was preserved unchanged. It was also preserved that the owner of the square is neither the fifth district (Leopoldville), nor the state, but the capital city.

The Buildings on the Square

As we have already seen, the perspectives of the planned and future Parliament envisaged as the House of the Nation to be surrounded by public buildings.

Ministries having had a brief period of existence in 1848 after the revolution made their first significant appearance after 1867. But it was in 1867 that, for the second time, a responsible government was established which surrounded itself with the structures of government administration and power. The ministries were integral parts of these structures.

The responsible government and the ministerial systems were political and administrative in nature and did not represent the evolution of a sound infrastructure. The creation of a responsible and effective infrastructure for the ministries became a task to be confronted during the years after 1867.[9]

Immediately after the Compromise the problems were managed by enlarging existing older buildings and renting space in privately owned apartment buildings. Clearly these approaches were considered to be temporary and inadequate expedients. Considering Kossuth Square as a

---

8 The exact area is important for estimating the demonstrating crowds on the square. It is figured that for every square meter one could count four persons.

9 Beáta Fabó, "Építkezés a reprezentáció szolgálatában: Középületek és tervek" [Construction in the service of representation: Public buildings and Plans], in *Az egyesített főváros. Pest, Buda, Óbuda* [The United Capital City. Pest, Buda, Óbuda], ed. Gábor Gyáni (Budapest: Városháza, 1998), pp. 171.

suitable area for public buildings it was natural to assume that one or more ministries would be established there.

According to a government decision, the Ministry of Agriculture, Industry and Commerce was chosen. The decision was buttressed by two considerations. The Ministry of Defense, important symbolically for Hungarian statehood, but of very limited importance under the political structure of the Compromise, had been placed in the Castle Hill area ever since 1881. The second, symbolically and factually important ministry was the one mentioned above. Its sphere of activity covered the principal economic sectors of a basically agricultural country. Another important consideration was that the ministry, up to that time, was located in highly unsatisfactory conditions. Its main office was at 5 Ferenc József tér (Francis Joseph Square, now Roosevelt Square) in the Nákó building, which had been mentioned as a potential site for the Parliament. A number of the offices of the ministry were scattered around town and located in rental spaces in apartment buildings. The latter factor was the strongest motive for building a special building for the ministry. The importance of its economic role justified the proposal that the building be located in the vicinity of the Parliament.

In 1881 the government bought the lot and in March 1885 the law authorizing the building and financing of the ministry was passed (Act IV of 1885). The design of the building was entrusted to Gyula Bukovics. The corner stone was laid on January 2, 1886, and by August of that year the framework was up. In view of the fact that the building cost more than anticipated the original act had to be amended (Act IV of 1887) and August 1, 1887, was designated as the day of completion and occupation. In fact, this took place on July 17. The building was modernized and partially rebuilt starting with 1906,[10] but this process was completed only between the two wars when a fifth and sixth floor were added. Starting in the 1970s, the arcades of the building facing the

---

10 For the plans of the never carried out reconstruction, see "A földművelésügyi minisztérium tervpályázata" [The architectural bids for the Ministry of Agriculture], *Építőipar* [Construction Industry], April 7, 1907, 135–137; "A földművelési minisztériumi palota pályatervei" [The competitive designs for the palace of the Agricultural Ministry], *Magyar Pályázatok* 5, no. 6 (1907): 1–13; and Eszter Gábor and Mária Verő, eds., *Schickedanz Albert (1846–1915). Ezredévi emlékművek a múltnak és jövőnek* [Millennial Monuments for the Past and Future] (Budapest: Szépművészeti Múzeum, 1996), pp. 230–231.

Kossuth Square were being used for the placement of statues honoring the outstanding scientists and practitioners of Hungarian agriculture.[11]

The building was erected in classical style and it has preserved this character in spite of all modernization and rebuilding. Since it was built, the name and sphere of authority of the ministry has undergone numerous changes but, to this day, it is the home of the government agency responsible for agriculture and the agrarian activities. Its formal address is 11 Kossuth Square.

The second building designed as a public building and functioning in this capacity ever since, albeit in a variety of roles, is located at 12 Kossuth Square. This building was erected before the Parliament was finished, but with the understanding that there would be a square here dominated by the Parliament. It was originally built as the Palace of Justice. When completed it housed the Hungarian Royal Supreme Court, the Budapest Royal Court of Appeals, and the offices of the Royal Prosecutor and of the Crown Prosecutor. Common parlance did not use the term Palace of Justice, did not list the various offices the building contained and always referred to it simply as the Curia.

Need for such a building became evident immediately after the Compromise. The ideas originated with Boldizsár Horvát, the minister of justice, but the final resolution of the matter was not reached for several decades. It was not until 1892 that Dezső Szilágyi, the minister of justice asked the most prominent architect of the day, Alajos Hauszmann, to prepare a design for the Curia building.

The proposed site was the lot directly across from the Parliament. The space was originally occupied by a military cart depot. There were three reasons for selecting this space. Firstly, it seemed to be a generally good idea, secondly it would strengthen the symbolism of the square and thirdly that the highest judicial organizations should be located in the vicinity of the legislative body. An office of the executive branch, the Ministry of Agriculture was also in that area. The ideas seemed to make economic sense as well because the Ministry of Justice had to acquire the lot from the state. Finally, the great representative event of the Hungarian nation and of the country, the millennial celebration, the hypothetical one thousandth anniversary of the conquest of the country

---

11 For the statues on the square, see chapter two.

was approaching. It seemed appropriate that the building representing constitutionality be completed by the anniversary and that it be located in the vicinity of the Parliament building under construction.

The legislation authorizing the building and its financing was passed in 1893 (Act XIII of 1893). Construction began in that same year and the completed edifice was turned over to the state at the beginning of the millennial year, on May 1, 1896. The building shows both neoclassicist and neorenaissance components, which Hauszmann called Roman style. The building has four floors: a lower and upper mezzanine and a second and third floor. The principal façade, facing the square, is 125 meter long. The principal entrance consists of three sections. The statuary on the façade was prepared by György Zala. Above the statues a victory chariot can be seen, which is the work of Károly Sengei. The chariot is driven by the Genius of Enlightenment. On both sides of the chariot there are statues representing legislators carved by János Fadrusz. Between the ionic columns of the façade there are twelve statues representing art, science, and commerce and which are the work of students of the Strobl school. There are two statues each at the ends of the building. On one side a convicted and liberated captive, the work of József Róna, and on the other side, a defendant and his attorney by Gyula Donáth.

The building was officially dedicated by Emperor Francis Joseph on October 20, 1896. Three years after its completion another law was passed authorizing the pay-off of the expenses (Act XXVI of 1899). The building was severely damaged during World War II and was repaired on the basis of the plans of Elemér Csánk. After the repairs were made the function of the building changed and after 1950 the Munkásmozgalmi Intézet (Labor Movement Institute) took over. From 1957 to 1973 much of the building was taken up by the Hungarian National Gallery. The Párttörténeti Intézet (Party History Institute), which replaced the Labor Movement Institute, was limited to the upper stories of the building on the Alkotmány Street side. In 1973 the National Gallery was replaced by the Ethnographic Museum. After the change of regime, the Party History Institute became the Institute for Political History. The name changed but the location did not.

The ornamental chambers of the Palace of Justice can be leased for ceremonial occasions.

We may recall that, according to the Public Works Council, the spaces around the square were to be used for public buildings. The enthusiasm for public buildings lasted only until the largest of the public buildings, the Parliament was completed.

All the other buildings on the square were built from private funds. This does not mean, of course, that they might not fit in well with the character of the square. It does mean, however, that the original plans, focusing on public buildings, did not materialize. Among the blocks of buildings surrounding the square and divided by access routes, four, i.e. two thirds of the blocks are not public buildings.

To keep to our plan, let us now look at the private buildings forming a large part of the square.

At the southernmost part of the square there is a block of buildings, 4 Kossuth Square, where two buildings were joined to serve as the office of the prime minister. The lot on which the building facing the Kossuth Square stands initially belonged to the Capital City of Budapest and, after 1900, to the Capital Public Works Council. The lot was purchased in 1911 by architect Alfréd Wellisch and his wife, Vilma Ullmann. The building was erected in 1911. On the two wings, facing the square there were domes which were destroyed during World War II.[12] The building was designed as an apartment-office building and consisted of a small hotel, apartments and offices. Prior to World War I, there was a store facing the street where ribbons and strings were sold. The offices, above the ground floor, were occupied by companies dealing in chemicals, metals, and industrial products. In 1934 the Hungarian Revisionist League, the organization endeavoring to revise the Trianon peace treaty, established its headquarters there. After World War II the building was nationalized and was taken over by the Ministry of Housing and Public Construction. At that time the building was connected architecturally with the building behind it. The latter originally was the headquarters of the Magyar Általános Kőszénbánya, Rt. (Hungarian General Coalmining Company). A seventh floor was added at this time. Today it serves as one of the offices for the prime minister. It was a private property which was converted into a public building.

---

12 Simultaneously with the completion of the construction, a detailed article with photos of the building was published in *Magyar Építőművészet*, no 11 (1911): 21–42.

The erection of buildings on the southern side of the square, between the Akadémia and Nádor Streets (nos. 6, 8, 9, and 10), began at the same time as the northern side and started from the Nádor Street. The uniformity of the façades on both the north and south side of the square became a matter of importance for the Public Works Council. This was the reason why, in 1927, Paragraph 129/a of the Act was accepted and Dezső Hültl was charged with designing a unified façade. It was according to the Hültl design that in 1928–1929 the building of 10 Kossuth Square was erected, to be followed in 1937–1938 by building no. 9. As we will see the unified façade plan was only partially realized.

Ten Kossuth Square was designed as a domiciliary building. It was financed by Miksa Blitz and his wife, Malvin Albrecht, and designed by Sámuel Révész and József Kollár. The street level was almost entirely occupied by the Országház (Parliament) Coffeehouse which was designed by István Gerő. Later, during the Communist era, it was converted into a hall for civil marriage ceremonies. Today it is again a coffee house called Parlament Café. I mention it only as a matter of curiosity that after 1929 this building housed the editorial offices of the *Magyar Detektív* (The Hungarian Detective) journal and that the president of the Rimamurány-Salgótarján Steel Company once lived there.

The building of 9 Kossuth Square was financed by the Rimamurány-Salgótarján Steel Company and was designed by Tibor Hübner and Lajos Gyenes. Its street level was occupied by a coffee house but is now the home of a large delicatessen.

The third lot, toward the Akadémia Street, was built only in the late 1960s and early 1970s.

Six and 8 Kossuth Square violates the Hültl design and is a modern office building, completed in 1972, according to the design of Béla Pintér and his associates. Under this building the Kossuth Square Metro station is located. The building was erected for the use of the Magyar Kereskedelmi Kamara (The Hungarian Chamber of Commerce) and of the Műszaki és Természettudományi Egyesületek (The Technical and Natural Sciences Associations). It is in a marked disharmony with the adjacent buildings.[13]

---

13 Béla Pintér, "Az építész cikke az épületről" [The article of the architect about the building], *Magyar Építőművészet*, no. 1 (1974): 9–17.

On the northern side of the square the block between Miksa Falk and Bálint Balassi (formerly Személynök) Streets was built according to the plans of the Public Works Council and has preserved its original appearance to this day. The façade is unified, even though it is composed of three buildings, 13, 14, and 15 Kossuth Square. The block was erected in 1927–1928 for the Magyar Általános Kőszénbányák Rt. (Hungarian General Coalmines, Inc), according to the design of Béla Málnai.[14] The wrought iron gate is the work of Gyula Jungfer. The buildings were designed for business activities. They accommodated the offices of the company which financed the building construction, known as M.Á.K. and also the offices of Beremend Portland Cement and Lime Works, Rt., the Nyergesújfalui Cementgyár (Nyergesújfalu Cement Works) and other cement works. They also accommodated several electrical companies. Prior to World War II, the street level was occupied by the Elysée Coffee House.[15] One of the upper stories held a guest house. After the war the building was nationalized, it was used for offices, apartments and temporary accommodations. On the street level there was a Bulgarian restaurant,[16] a travel agency and an insurance company. The restaurant has been replaced by a bank.

House nos. 16–17 is next to the Málnai building, but its façade does not face Kossuth Square but looks toward the west. It was designed as an apartment building by Sámuel Révész and József Kollár in 1911. It also accommodated some offices, including a paper-goods wholesaler.

At the northernmost point of the square, between Bálint Balassi Street and the Széchenyi, (formerly Rudolf) **Quay**, the block of houses facing the Kossuth Square, 18 Kossuth Square, was designed by Alfréd Wellisch, Gábor Preisich, and Mihály Vadász. The building was erected in 1938, in Bauhaus style, as an apartment house, by the Baux-

---

[14] An article about the architect, and another about the building was printed in *Magyar Építőművészet*, no. 4 (1934).

[15] In fact, there were two Elysée cafés in the same building. The big one, which later became the Bulgarian restaurant, then a bank, was designed by Béla Málnai. The small one was designed by Lajos Kozma. The latter's illustrated article about the café was printed in *Tér és Forma* 6, (1933): 95–97.

[16] About the restaurant, see Sándor Mikó, "Szófia étterem. Budapest" [Sofia Restaurant, Budapest], *Magyar Építőművészet* 6, no. 1 (1968): 48–49.

it Ipari Rt. (Bauxite Industries, Inc.). It also accommodated some corporations, including the Ford Motor Company, the Bauxit Ipari Rt. (Bauxite Industrial Corporation), and the Victoria Vegyészeti Rt. (Victoria Chemical Corporation). After World War II it was the home of the Magyar-Szovjet Olaj Társaság (Hungarian-Soviet Oil Company) and, for a short period of time, of the United States Consulate General.

Before the war, on the side of the building facing the Danube, there was the Biarritz Café.[17] It was closed for a long time but was resuscitated recently on the Balassi Street side. In addition to the café, the street level accommodates a bank, a real estate agency, and a flower shop.

These buildings border the square in the east, south, and north. As we have seen there is no unified style or general function. The esthetic quality of the square is not greatly affected by this because the symmetry and shape of the square satisfactorily balance the variations in style.

One side, the western one, has not been discussed yet. Yet this is the most important one because the building on this side governs and defines the square. It could be said that that this side gives the square its symbolic and spiritual content, far beyond the purely physical one.

The House of the Nation

The entire west side of the square is taken up by the Parliament building, 1–3 Kossuth Square.[18] The completed building is so emphatic that it sets the characteristic image not only for the square but for the entire Pest side of the city. The Parliament, the House of the Nation, can be viewed as the standing symbol of all of Hungary.

From my perspective, at least so far as the square is concerned, the entire history of the Parliament, its internal arrangement, artistic description and interpretation are of limited interest. For us only those areas are of interest which formed, or could have formed, a part of the history of the square.

---

[17] For an illustrated report about the Biarritz Café, see *Vendéglátóipari Szemle*, July 1, 1938.

[18] The ensuing text about the Parliament is based on the essays in Eszter Gábor and Mária Verő, eds., *House of the Nation. Parliament's Plans for Buda-Pest, 1784–1882* (Budapest: Museum of Fine Arts, 2000).

The first question is why the Parliament was built on the former Tömő and current Kossuth Square?

The House of Representatives on Sándor Street (today Sándor Bródy Street) was clearly a temporary expedient and serves today as the Italian Cultural Institute. Replacing it with a permanent edifice became a major concept as early as 1871. The prime minister of the day, Menyhért Lónyay, recommended that the country purchase and remodel the so-called Nákó building. The size of this palace was considerably larger than the House of Representatives in Sándor Street. The Nákó building was in the longitudinal axis of the Lánchíd (Chain Bridge), on the present Roosevelt Square, at the site of the Gresham Palace, which has currently been remodeled into a luxury hotel. Nothing came of this idea even though the building was impressive, had an 80 meter frontage and sat on a lot of 3,700 square meters.

Eight years later the idea of building a permanent House of Representatives emerged again. The government, under the leadership of Kálmán Tisza, submitted to the representatives its proposal for the erection of a permanent Parliament building. The proposal recommended Tömő Square as the site for the building but also listed three other options.

Let us look at these options first. The second potential site after the Tömő Square was the lot of the Károly barracks, facing the inner boulevard. It had an area of 19,400 square meters and was owned by the Military Treasury. Today this area is part of Károly körút (Károly Boulevard) across from the Imre Madách Square, on the other side from the City Hall.

The third area was not far from there. The lot of 7,300 square meters was bordered by Erzsébet Square, Deák Square, Kiskörút (Small Boulevard, today Bajcsy-Zsilinsky Avenue) and Marokkói Street (today József Attila Street) and was privately owned. The area is still an open space, even today. In 1997 a start was made to build the National Theater on this site, but only the foundations were dug when the project was abandoned and the foundation was converted into an underground parking area and cultural center.

The fourth option, according to the proposal, was an inner city lot owned by the Piarist fathers. One part of this 7,300 square-meter lot was occupied by a Piarist monastery. Today this area is part of Petőfi Square and is occupied by the Sapientia Theological College which was built in 1917 and which is once again owned by the religious order.

The alternative sites would have been much more expensive than Tömő Square which covered an area of 15,600 square meters. Other arguments also favored Tömő Square.

There was little if any parliamentary debate about the site. Whoever is familiar with the workings of the Hungarian parliament in the Dualistic era knows that whatever the government and Prime Minister Kálmán Tisza wanted between 1875 and 1890, would be carried out (Act LVIII of 1880).

The next question, critical from the perspective of the square, was where and how to position the building on the square.

After the act was passed in 1881, Tisza appointed a committee which was referred to in the language of the time as the "Large Committee." Its task was to coordinate the various activities relative to a permanent Parliament building. It was also the responsibility of the committee to decide in favor of one of a number of applications and to define the requirements of the proposals. There was also a "Small Committee" and several other committees.

On the basis of the work of these committees two general concepts emerged. According to one of them the applicants were supposed to submit a plan with the future building of the Parliament being at right angles to the Danube. The building was to be a square one with the main entrance facing the Danube. The building would have been adjacent to the present site of the Akadémia Street.

According to another concept, expressed jointly by the now retired prime minister and by the Joint Minister of Foreign Affairs Count Gyula Andrássy, "The permanent Parliament should not be built according to the presently proposed plans but in such a fashion that its principal façade, with a terrace-like structure in front of it, face the Danube directly. The lower quay should be covered by an arched passage allowing the continued movement of traffic. Behind the building a park-like square should be developed."[19] Andrássy's ideas viewed the principal entrance to the Parliament facing the Danube.

---

[19] "Jegyzőkönyv az állandó országház építése érdekében működő országos bizottság kebeléből kiküldött albizottság 1881. évi, december 8-i (III.) üléséről" [Minutes of the December 8, 1881, meeting (the third meeting) of the Subcommittee of the National Committee for the Construction of a Permanent House of the Nation], no 21, Országház, Műszaki Osztály [Parliament, Technical Department], Terv- és Irattár [Archive of Plans and Documents].

Eventually the proposals were solicited without defining the position of the building. It was left to the applicants to recommend that the axis of the building should be at right angles to or parallel with the Danube. In order to assure appropriate creativity, it was decided to purchase the lots along the Danube for the future Parliament building.

The submissions were solicited in 1882 with a deadline of February 1, 1883. Twenty submissions were received of which several were praised and two were purchased. The results were announced on April 23, 1883.

Among the major submissions only one, by Alajos Hauszmann, envisaged the building at right angles to the Danube. All the others positioned it with its long axis parallel to the river.

Those who proposed that the building be parallel with the Danube rapidly realized that it was practically impossible to place the principal entry facing the river. Their submissions were not among the praised ones.

The major recognized submissions included one offered under the code-word Alkotmány I (Constitution I), which was the work of Imre Steindl. The submission suggested a design which was close to the one eventually accepted except that it proposed a building considerably lower than the one eventually erected.

The committee, acting for the government, decided to award the contract to Imre Steindl and asked him to submit the final plans. This decision meant that the Parliament building would be parallel to the Danube and that the principal entrance would face the square to be designed in front of it.

The precise location of the building was still not decided and the revisions of the Steindl plans took five years. The final plans were submitted in 1888.

The three revisions of the plans, 1884, 1885, and 1888, are not of equal or even great interest to us. The first one made the building both longer and taller. It was moved seventy-two meters north which significantly contributed to the eventual shape of the square. This move also made it possible that the long axis of the building be truly parallel to the river, because now the bend in the river, in the back of the building became minimal. All these modifications took place in 1885 and the same year saw the beginnings of site preparation. In 1888 the entrance way toward the square was made more impressive and Steindl designed a set of steps flanked by a pair of lions. The Parliament faced the square and the city.

The building is in neo-Gothic style, which was the original idea. More accurately, the combination of style and monumentality could have produced an effect which according to the ideas of the Capital City Engineer's Office in 1884, would have, "Made it possible to create an environment for the Parliament and for a square in front of it that was in proper proportions to the façade of the new Parliament and to surround it with blocks of buildings and to easily create a suitably wide system of roads connecting the inner boulevard with the square around the Parliament."[20]

This proposal was partially realized, since Constitution Street, in fact, connects Kossuth Square with the inner boulevard. So far as the ideas of the monumental square being filled with neo-Gothic blocks of buildings were concerned, the Office of the Capital City Engineer was in for a major disappointment. Other than the Parliament building, there is not a trace of neo-Gothic anywhere on the square and the only building which came close to having a façade of comparable proportions was the Palace of Justice.

Nevertheless, the size, the harmonic and symmetrical structure of the Parliament, and its neo-Gothic style significantly affected the history of the Kossuth Square.

Both the ones placing the order and the one submitting the plan tried to express something. They wished to convey a symbolic and spiritual content to the people. It is therefore essential that we explain precisely what they wished to say.

Naturally the first issue is that there was a need for a Parliament and that it was good to have a square around it.[21] In fact, they did have other things to say.

---

[20] Bf. Szfv. Tanácsi Iratok [Document of the Council of the Capital City of Budapest], vol. 4, 1785/188 k.cs., BFL.

[21] The second half of the nineteenth century was predisposed to the construction of parliamentary buildings. Not only were the German Reichstag and the Austrian Parliament built at this time, but also the American Capitol building was completed during the period.

The sponsor, namely the Hungarian state, and the successive governments representing it, as well as the politicians, frequently indicated what they expected the new building to express. The Economics Committee of the House of Representatives wrote in 1869, about a new permanent Parliament as follows, "Let its form and structure be simple but such that it is appropriate to the dignity of a constitutional nation. Let it be of a size to accommodate both houses of parliament, their offices and the offices of its officials."[22]

Let it thus be simple and purposeful and let it express the dignity of a constitutional, free nation.

When, in 1880, the intent to erect a permanent Parliament building became more acute a government proposal stated, "Let there be built a permanent Parliament, purposefully furnished and sufficient to accommodate both chambers. It should be noted that even though the Parliament is built more modestly than the wealth of the nation would permit, it must be memorable so far as its size and shape are concerned."[23]

The purpose remained important but simplicity had to yield to the memorability of the proportions and shape. The statement emphasized that it was the intent of the government that the building be memorable and leave a lasting impression on viewers.

The memorability was a definite demand by 1884. This had to be because it became evident from the second modification of the Steindl design in 1885, according to which the cost of the building would be more than twice as much as was originally budgeted when, in 1882, the applications had been invited. The new design was accepted. Justifying this decision the Large Committee stated, "The building must be ornamental and monumental not only for artistic and architectural reasons, but it must be large, ornamental and monumental for national reasons, and because for the stated reasons, the Committee consid-

---

22 *Az 1869–1872-es országgyűlés képviselőházának irományai* [Papers of the House of Representatives of the National Assembly, 1869–1872] (Pest: Deutsch, 1869–1872), vol. 2, p. 239.

23 *Az 1878–1881-es országgyűlés képviselőházának irományai* [Papers of the House of Representatives of the National Assembly, 1878–1881] (Budapest: Magyar Királyi Állami Nyomda, 1878–1881), vol. 17, p. 376.

ers it essential that the building be endowed with the monumental nature of the present era."[24]

It is evident that the times demanded and the decision-makers desired to erect a memorial for themselves. Terms like nation and constitution and other similar expressions all tend in the direction of monumentality. The Transportation Committee of the House of Representatives took the following position in 1884 after the first revision of the design: "The Parliament must correspond in a major way to the ancient constitution and to the elevated concepts of the state and must be a suitable counterpart to the Royal Castle and to the Danube."[25]

The great national enthusiasm and the support of grandiose design did not generate unanimous support. One of the leaders of the parliamentary opposition, Ignác Helfy, the head of the Independence Party, stated the following during the debate on the construction of a permanent Parliament:

> The honorable government was not instructed to plan a Parliament that would increase the beauty of the capital that would be the architectural representation of the Hungarian statehood idea, and even to a lesser degree, to link the construction to the millennial celebration. It is a simple fact that because we cannot remain for long in our present structure, the government was instructed only to make arrangements in a timely fashion to build a decent Parliament that is suitable and that is appropriate for the dignity of the nation.[26]

---

[24] "Jegyzőkönyv az állandó országház építése érdekében működő országos bizottság 1884. február 24-i (XII.) üléséről" [Minutes of the February 24, 1884, meeting (the twelfth meeting) of the National Committee for the Construction of a Permanent House of the Nation], no. 13, Országház, Műszaki Osztály [Parliament, Technical Department], Terv- és Irattár [Archive of Plans and Documents].

[25] Az *1881–1884-es országgyűlés képviselőházának irományai* [Papers of the House of Representatives of the National Assembly, 1881–1884] (Budapest: Magyar Királyi Állami Nyomda, 1881–1884), vol. 20, pp. 321–323.

[26] *Az 1881–1884. évi országgyűlés képviselőházának naplója* [Proceedings of the House of Representatives of the National Assembly, 1881–1884] (Budapest: Képviselőház, 1878–1881), vol. 17, p. 376.

Lajos Tisza, younger brother of the prime minister and government party representative responsible for construction, came out in favor of the expensive grandiosity. According to him, "It is the task of the Parliament building to represent the incontrovertible strength of the Hungarian concepts of statehood and of the Hungarian constitution."[27]

It appears that in the eyes of the government the Parliament building had grown beyond its basic functions. It was no longer just a place providing a permanent home for an essential establishment, but had become a symbol of the constitutional Hungarian state.

Evolving during the first half of the 1880s the building appears to have become increasingly expensive, precisely because it was interpreted as an ambitious symbol. Originally 4.5 million forints were budgeted for it. When construction began on October 12, 1885, the budget was already 9.5 million and when it was finally completed in 1904, it had cost 18.5 million forints.[28] The representatives had moved into the new palace along the Danube in 1902.

Imre Steindl, who did the designs, agreed with those who hired him. Being an architect, however, he had already conceptualized the square surrounding the Parliament and the way it was going to be arranged. In 1885 when he did his first major review of the design, and when it was decided that the building would be erected further north and that it would be both longer and taller, then he committed his thoughts about the square to paper. Because of his detailed ideas about the square, I cite the document in considerable length:

> *Situation.* The permanent Parliament is planned to be erected in the fifth district of Budapest, the Lipótváros, on a square known as Tömő Square and on riparian lots adjacent to it, so that the principal wall of the façade, facing the Danube, will rise directly from the upper parapet of the quay. Behind and on the sides of the building there will be a square consisting of three parts.

---

27 Ibid., vol. 13, p. 84.

28 By the time Parliament was completed the name of the currency had been changed in 1892 from forint to korona (crown). One forint equaled two koronas. The final cost of the building amounted to thirty-seven million coronas.

The entire complex, which presently consists of a largely bare lot with a few small, insignificant buildings, will be arranged so that the building to be erected will be accessible from all the roads leading into the square and that the building, qua building, be appropriately significant.

For this reason the bend of the Nádor Street, between the corner of the Újépület (New Building) and the Markó Street, will be straightened out. Removing this strip will allow the area between the Báthory and Szalay Streets to join the square to be set up.

The lots along Akadémia Street would also be arranged so that some areas toward the city would be removed. Thus the area between the Zoltán Street and the Markó Street would form a straight line in front of the Parliament building. The square surrounding the proposed Parliament will be of approximately twenty-two hectares.

There will be three major access roads to the square, the Danube quay, the Nádor Street and the Alkotmány Street. The latter, leading toward the Váci Avenue, would also have to be rebuilt. In addition, Akadémia, Báthory, and Szalay Streets all open into the square.

The Parliament would be erected on the redesigned square in such a fashion that the longitudinal axis would be parallel to the Danube and the cross-axis would face the axis of the Alkotmány Street, widened to twenty-eight meters. The building would be approximately at the midpoint of the quay between the Margit Bridge and the Lánchíd (Chain Bridge).

The lower level of the quay will remain open to traffic in almost its entire width and pedestrian traffic will continue on the edge of the upper level of the quay.

Dimensions. The building is a lengthy parallelogram, broken up by extensions. The entire length is 260 meters. Its greatest width is 115 meters. Its area is 16,274.44 square meters. The actual building sits on 14,159.12 square meters and thus the courtyards occupy an area of 2,116 square meters.

General concept. When I designed my plan I started from the assumption that the permanent Parliament did not only have to be

> functional from a practical perspective but that it also had to be the dignified expression of our country, our constitution, and our statehood. The building, to be erected by the will of the people, in the heart of the country, for the purpose of legislation, across the river from the Royal Castle, had to be grandiose and true in all its parts and details. There is no place for niggling economies and other considerations and I have endeavored to design my plans so that a dignified and appropriate form would be given to all those concepts which are consistent with the Parliament of the country.
>
> The two chambers of the legislature were to be expressed in the exterior of the building as well but in a fashion that allowed the unity of the legislative process to remain the dominant concept and be unmistakable. This unity and the untouchable nature of the constitution are expressed by the dome which rises from the center of the building.
>
> The dome and the large joint space covered by it are organically attached to the meeting chambers of the two "houses" the roofs of which are raised by square towers at the corners, indicating the site where the legislative bodies of the country performe their task.

He continues with a description of internal arrangements which are of no interest to us. Concerning the cost of the ornamentation he states,

> I cannot deny that the items in the "Supplement" were calculated so that funds made available be suitable to have the internal decorations appropriate to the dignity of the building and even be executed in a spectacular style. It is true that some economies could be implemented, but, on the other hand, I cannot deny my absolute conviction that when the country erects a ten million forint temple of the constitution for its legislature, it cannot be right to withhold the necessary funds from the final decorations just so as to save 150,000 forints. I consider this even more inappropriate because this was the modest sum which was designated to the support and promotion of the domestic arts and crafts.[29]

---

[29] The paper by Imre Steindl was published in *Építési Ipar*, no. 9, (1885). It is reprinted in the Museum of Fine Arts catalog. The quotation is from pages 243–244.

Steindl uses the argument of supporting domestic industry when he seriously underestimates the potential excess expenditures. In doing so he uses a composite term which describes the spirit of his original work. He calls the Parliament the temple of the constitution. This shows unmistakably that the architect was thinking not only in simple political categories, not only in symbols, but in terms of sanctity.

The conceptual encounter of the architect and the sponsor fundamentally affects the tone of the square and can be detected in yet another area. This is the neo-Gothic style which strongly suggests the church-like nature of the edifice.

We must limit what we say here. The debates on style are not important from our perspective and we do not care who assessed what from a national perspective.

The only thing that is important for us here and now, is the way in which the sanctity was reflected on the square by the statehood concept and the constitution and how the external configuration of the building, and thus the square itself, could demonstrate it.

In nineteenth century Hungary the nobility and aristocracy, trained in common law, were convinced that the Magna Charta in England in 1215 and the Golden Bull in Hungary in 1222 were the foundation of the British and Hungarian constitutions. This also meant that the British constitution, considered to be a model at the time, was coeval with the Hungarian one. This belief, more of a political myth than an intellectually valid conviction, played a dominant role in the worldview held by the liberals holding power in Hungary after 1867, who were mostly of noble origin. When the applications for the erection of a new Parliament were sent out in England in 1835, it was stated emphatically that the style had to be gothic or Elizabethan. Charles Barry and A. W. N. Pugin, the architects of Westminster Hall met the request for a Gothic building.

For the reasons mentioned above, the English model had a major effect on the Hungarian decision. The plans for the German Parliament, the Reichstag, built about the same time had no effect on the Hungarian decision even though the Hungarian government did acquire the German plans. The personal representative of the British example was no less a person than Count Gyula Andrássy, prime minister from 1867 to 1871 and joint minister of foreign affairs from 1871 to 1879. At a session of the Upper House in May, 1884 he said, "We are the only ones, beside England, who can trace their constitution back such a long time."[30] Andrássy had a great influence not only in the Upper House but in all bodies which were in a decision-making position on all matters pertaining to the Parliament building. He used this influence to its fullest extent.

Fortunately all this coincided well with Steindl's tastes. As a pupil of Friedrich von Schmidt, he was fully committed to the Gothic and in his designs for the Parliament he used the plans of his former master, used in the building of the Viennese City Hall or the church of Maria von Siege in Fünfhaus.

The meeting of the minds between the sponsors and the architect, albeit coming from different directions, did result in the dominance of the Gothic style on the Kossuth Square.

* * *

The Gothic building, the Hungarian Parliament, completed by the beginning of the twentieth century is the temple of the constitution. The legislature began its work here in 1902 and the building was officially opened in 1904. Partly before this date and partly following it, Kossuth Square was built up. Not precisely as planned, but not very differently.

The physical-topographic square came into existence over time and was completed in 1972. The question was, how the people were going to use it? Would it be a square like all the others where one could stroll, look around, and go to work or would it be used, in addition to the above, for other purposes as well. Would it be a different square from all the others? Would it be more than a public space surrounded by buildings?

---

30 *Az 1881–1884. országgyűlés főrendiházának naplója* [Journal of the Upper House of the National Assembly, 1881–1884] (Budapest: Magyar Királyi Állami Nyomda, 1881–1884), vol. 2, p. 328.

THE SYMBOLIC SQUARE

It is evident that there is a Kossuth Square, because there is the Parliament. The Parliament not only created the square but, by its dimensions and mass, gave it a structure.

According to the architect, Imre Steindl, the building is the temple of the constitution, but in reality it is also something else. Its image raises the specter of political power regardless of whether the power is constitutional or not. This symbolic power was potent from the beginning. It made the actual site of the political power meaningless. Both within and without politics a peculiar dual feeling developed in people. They recognized the Parliament as a symbol of centralized political power even though they knew that, in fact, the center of power was elsewhere, When the building was erected everybody knew that without Francis Joseph there could be no meaningful political decisions. Yet the ruler saw to the affairs from Vienna and never worked from the Parliament building. Between the two wars everybody knew that Miklós Horthy, the regent of independent Hungary, lived in the Buda Castle and had generally the same sphere of authority as Francis Joseph. During the Communist era everybody knew that the essential power resided at the Party headquarters, which was located, during the 1950s, one hundred meters south of the Parliament on Akadémia Street. After 1956 it was three hundred meters to the north of it on the Széchenyi Embankment. (Actually the important decisions were not made there, but in Moscow). The known power center could be in the Buda Castle or in the capital of the Soviet Union, the Parliament still became fixed as a building of symbolic power.

We might think about it as a political magnet, deposited in the center of the city, which could attract every intention which wished to manifest itself in the world of politics. In order for this to happen, it has the square surrounding it.

It is this that made the Kossuth Square particular and different. Naturally it endured everything that an ordinary square had to endure but it attracted what did not and could not take place on any other square the way it did here.

In this shorter chapter I will review the events that the square attracted. I could say that I will investigate the political magnet effect. I will not study all of them but only those which were particularly characteristic and significant. I will not spend a great deal of effort on them because I have two other means of information available. What I do have are photographs and documentary reports from the contemporary press. Both of these are parts of this volume.

I consider it my duty to interpret the events which took place here in the context of a square representing politics and power. It was because of this characteristic of the square that the events took place here and the principal reason was that the organizers of the events attributed symbolic significance to the area.

The Manifestations of Power

Kossuth Square, precisely because of the presence of the Parliament, almost automatically provided an opportunity for the political-power establishment to present itself. In contrast to the interior of the building, the square is public, can be seen directly and thus the self-presentation of the establishment is available there for a larger audience. The need for the power structure to show itself off is not a new and/or transient phenomenon. The manifestation and self-representation usually follow ritual activities and one of their strongest features is that they must be impressive. This can be achieved by involving large groups of people, by their active participation and/or by the ritual choreography of formal elements which can be identified with the power establishment.

In the case of Kossuth Square we can find examples for all of the above. We can see the starting point of the square's symbolic history in such a power structure self-representation on June 8, 1896, a day the contemporary press called the "Day of Homage." At that time, in the year of the millennium and on the anniversary of the 1867 coronation, a so-called "Mounted Parade" was held and an important part of this was the "activation" of the newly created square. The goal of the show of power through self-advertising was to indicate that all of Hungarian history validates the given political system. In effect, the contemporary power elite demonstrated itself, in the form of a legitimizing action through the use of history, in accordance with a predetermined choreography.

It was this "starting event" from which everything representing one line of the square's symbolic history of events was derived. All of it had been already potentially contained in the conceptualization of the square.

The manifestation of power changed over the years, but even though there were variations, the basic, common elements remained the same. The starting event, the buttressing of the existing power establishment by historical justification, continued even under different systems of power. One of the characteristic elements of the Hungarian political structure during the interwar years was the elevation of Christianity to a political concept. At the end of May 1938, the nine hundredth anniversary of the death of St. Stephen, the main entrance of the Parliament was converted into an altar and the Holy Crown and the mummified extremity of the king, the Holy Right Hand relic, were paraded in the square.

A similar function of legitimizing manifestations of power was accomplished in the square by the dedication ceremonies of statues and memorials, erected by different political systems, to the memory of individuals ranging from Andrássy to István Nagyatádi Szabó and from Kossuth to Béla Kovács. Historical legitimization was important for all political systems, it being the least important for the democracy. Since, however, the history of Hungary during the twentieth century was dominated by anti-democratic regimes, it was no accident that such acts were organized as a symbol of power.

The second set of the manifestations of power were those events on the square when an announcement was made to the people declaring: "we are the new power, we are the new world." These manifestations of power were functions directly justifying politics.

The 1918 liberal democratic revolution declared its victory on this square to a large assembly of people. It was also here and again before an enthusiastic crowd, that in November 1918, it was announced that the country had a new form of government, it had become a republic. It was here that the Communists held the celebration of the initiation of the rule of the Hungarian proletariat after they had assumed power on March 21, 1919. It was here that Zoltán Tildy was honored on February 1, 1946, on the occasion of being elected president of the republic. This was the second republic that was proclaimed on this square. It was also here that on October 23, 1989, the third Hungarian republic was proclaimed, on the basis of a parliamentary decision. So far there have been three republics in Hungary and all were proclaimed on this square, These were formally very emphatic events and it was no accident that they were associated with the presence of a very large assembly of people. The presence of the "people" fulfilled a politically justifying function. It assisted the new power to proclaim itself and emphasized its existence or appearance.

The power which happens to rule at the time likes to gather masses of people on this square so that they can demonstrate their loyalty to the existing polity. An example for this was when the first government of the new democracy summoned its supporters at the end of October 1990, at the time the taxi drivers started a movement announcing and producing major traffic blocks. At the time of the 2002 elections, the prime minister of the day, who because of losing the elections would have to vacate his position, also organized a mass meeting of his followers on this square.[1]

So far we have seen two types of activities in the history of the square which demonstrated either the historical and/or the immediate political justification of the powers in being. Now I am going to show the third subset and discuss the manifestations of a national character by the powers.

---

[1] The number of people is an important factor at all events which tend to emphasize the power of protest manifestation. The greater number the greater the emphasis. For this reason, in many instances, the organizers or the press exaggerate the numbers. The most striking exaggeration occurred in connection with the government party's mass meeting during the 2002 election campaign. The organizers talked about 1.5–2 million demonstrators, when the square with only 65,000 square meters of usable space can accommodate no more than 260–300 thousand.

The Parliament building was designed and erected as a structure of power, ready to serve as the representation of the state. In the prescribed, protocol-determined ritual of this activity the main entrance to the Parliament and the square in front of it had a major role. On such occasions the steps leading to the entrance are covered by a red carpet. The foreign guests arriving here are greeted on the square by honor guards appropriate to the rank of the visitor or to the nature of their visit. This is the way it is done everywhere in the world.

The history of the Kossuth Square, however, includes additional functions as well. It is the site of the National Banner and from 1965 to 2006, on August 20, the anniversary of Hungarian statehood and constitution, the newly graduated military officers took their oath of allegiance there.[32] The oath taken and the presence of the National Banner emphasized the existence of the system in power at the time. During the communist era Soviet generals participated in the swearing-in of the new officers indicating that the Parliament and the Kossuth Square were not really the centers of the prevailing powers. Their presence was suitable, however, to demonstrate the true legitimacy of the communist system.

There were instances in the history of the square that on national holidays major official ceremonies were held here. An example for this is that at the beginning of the 1990s, on October 23, anniversary commemorations of the 1956 revolution were held here. The large, official arrangements for national holidays were not linked tightly to the square and their appearance here was sporadic. On various national holidays displays are usually set up in the square. Placing wreaths before the statues and monuments on the square has become a part of the square's function.

The events followed their protocol, became an organic part of the square's history and remained within their official forms and framework. So far as I know, only one foreign statesman spoke to the people here. On July 11, 1989, George Bush, the president of the United States, spoke to the people in the square, forgoing all rules of protocol.

Whichever subset we examine, it cannot be denied that the manifestations of power had become an organic component of the symbolic use of the square.

---

[2] In 2006 the banner staff was given a new base. After 2007 the new officers were sworn in at the Heroes' Square.

Manifestations of Protest

The square attracted manifestations of protest precisely for the same reason it attracted manifestations of power. The effects of the political magnet produced the one just as it did the other. In 1896 the square opened its activities with a demonstration of power but nine years later, with the legislature already busy in the building, the first major protest meeting took place there. This first one was followed by a large number of such events up to the present time.

The term "protest" is used here as a generic concept. It means that some people do not want something and would prefer something else. What this something else might be is frequently confused and difficult to understand. It is usually clear what they do not want and that it is this emotion that brings them to the square. Thus, just like the manifestations of power, the expression of protest represents a variety of components which can be readily categorized. This is why I believe that their use is legitimate.

September 15, 1905, was the day which initiated the manifestations of protest in the history of the Kossuth Square. The contemporary press called the day "Red Friday." The demonstration was organized by the Social Democratic Party. The purpose of the protest was the matter of the universal, secret franchise. This was one of the principal demands of the period and this is why, contrary to its positive statement, it may be considered a manifestation of protest, because the powers of the day were not inclined to grant it. With the prolongation of the debates on electoral rules and in connection with several parliamentary crises, there were several attempts to hold such protest meetings on the square.[3]

The next notable occasion was a protest against the republican government which had obtained its power after the 1918 revolution. It was organized by the Communists at the beginning of February 1919, on behalf of the unemployed. I must note that the first dual protest

---

[3] A demonstration in May 1912, which came to be known as "Bloodred Thursday," was unable to reach its announced target, Kossuth Square. For an analysis of the events, see Gábor Gyáni, *Identity and the Urban Experience: Fin-de-Siècle Budapest* (Boulder, CO: East European Monographs, 2004), pp. 144–151.

meeting in the history of the square also took place in February 1919. The Social Democrats, favoring the government, and the Communists in opposition to it demonstrated at the same time and not far from each other.

The protest actions of the Social Democrats were linked tightly with the Kossuth Square. After the Soviet Republic was replaced, they organized a demonstration here to have the trade unions participate in the government.

They were also the ones who used the square for protest activities during the Horthy era. In 1927 they protested against the regime using the name of Lajos Kossuth for its own purpose. It was again the Social Democrats who, in the name of the construction workers, protested in 1946 against the government led by the Smallholder Party.

During the decades of the Communist dictatorship the square was dormant as far as protest meetings were concerned. It is in the nature of dictatorships that they do not allow public protest activities and from this perspective it made no difference whether the dictatorship was a benign or malignant one. It was only during the 1980s that the square began to reenergize itself. On the occasion of the commemoration of the Hungarian Revolution of March 15, 1848, the opposition organized small groups to place flowers before the statue of Kossuth. In 1988 even a speech was delivered on this occasion.

It was in the autumn of 1988 that the square really came back to life. Two protest meetings were held at that time. One of them, on September 12, protested against the Nagymaros-Gabčikovo hydroelectric dam project and the other one, between October 6–8, demanded the release of the 160 young men who were incarcerated as conscientious objectors. The crowd called for the establishment of alternatives to military service. The former one was organized by the Duna Kör (Danube Circle) and the latter one by the East-West Dialog Network Circle (Hálózat Kör).

Following these events the use of the square for protests increased sharply. Taxi drivers demonstrated here, smallholders with and without tractors, students about tuition, meat processing workers, teachers, firemen, policemen, large estate owners, people harmed by economic transactions, investors, supporters of the Democratic Charter, and all others who had some issues to air.

Protests, linked to this square, became a general practice. It was here, in 2006, that the prime minister who lost out in 2002 organized a major gathering at the end of his electoral campaign. It seemed to prove through one person and one political party, that the square, that political magnet, was equally suitable for the manifestations of power and for protests. It is a matter of the two sides of a single principle.

In 2006 the longest protests in the history of the square took place. Continuous, way of life demonstrations lasted from the middle of September to the eve of October 23, demanding the resignation of the prime minister.

The novelty was not in the protest. We have seen that for protests there was a long tradition in the history of the square. What was new is what I referred to as a way of life demonstration. In a cultural-anthropological sense this means that it had a different shape from all previous protest demonstrations. Because of its duration of more than a month, a tent camp was set up by the *Rákóczi* statue on the square. "National rock music," i.e. rock music with a nationalistic text was played continuously, a mobile goulash kitchen functioned for a while, clothes were hung between the tents to dry, and in the evening there were speeches. The whole event gave the impression of a reunion of campers in the wilds. The legislators and the enforcers of the law watched the event helplessly. The movement was the living denial of the social science theory, according to which the behavioral patterns and rules of the private and public spheres differed from each other.[4]

After 1988, one of the statues on the square also "participated" in the protest movement. The *Mihály Károlyi* statue, commemorating the controversial leader of the 1918 revolution, was repeatedly doused with red paint.[5]

4 One of the principal theoreticians of the utilization of squares, Richard Senett bases his theories on the belief, that it is a basic characteristic of the changes in public activities, that the private lives become mystified because they can no longer be made public and can no longer be part of public life. Senett's arguments have some validity but it is likely that he ignored the vital demonstrations representing the conscious publicity of a whole form of life. See Richard Sennett, *The Fall of Public Man* (New York: Vintage Books, 1978).

5 On the right of the political spectrum Mihály Károlyi came to be known as the "Red Count" for his left-wing sympathies. He has been falsely accused of paving the way for the humiliating Peace Treaty of Trianon. His statue has been repeatedly doused with red paint. On October 31, twice during the last week of July 2003, and on February 26, 2007. On April 26, 2007, it was doused with acid.

The use of the square for protests started from the left wing, but became general after 1988. It seems that if the Hungarians have a problem, they definitely favor the Kossuth Square to express their complaints more or less violently. Therefore, not only manifestations of power, but protests as well, became integral traditions of the square.

Moments of Political Mercy

Because the Kossuth Square became totally politicized, there were some moments in its existence when events took place there which were clearly political in nature but which could not be defined as either manifestations of power or protests. When they occurred the participants were not yet in a position of power but were just at its gates. They could be confident that the power would be theirs momentarily. These events were related to the revolutionary and counterrevolutionary changes in Hungarian history. Because the history of the square, being a political magnet, illustrated these changes, they usually took shape in the events taking place in the square.

In essence we are talking about a few moments which signify the most exciting and erotic sides of political activity. Every indicator points toward completion but the act had not taken place yet. It is almost certain that power will be acquired, but it has not yet. We must remember that political passions just like all passion-based activities seek gratification.

The first such event in the history of the square was the popular meeting on October 28, 1918. The event was about the government powers descending upon the National Council, about Mihály Károlyi becoming prime minister, and about the transformation of the still existing but moribund political system. Three days later it happened and the revolution, known as the "Fall Aster Revolution" was victorious.

The second similar event took place, almost exactly one year later, when on November 16, 1919, The National Army, under Miklós Horthy's leadership, marched into Budapest. The terminal point of the march was the square in front of the Parliament. Horthy was not regent yet, the power was not yet his, this would only come on March 1, 1920, but it was almost certain that he would achieve what he wanted.

In the marching-in ritual of the National Army's political eroticism, the moment of male-dominated victory, was reasonably overt. A delegation of Hungarian women presented Horthy, riding a white stallion, with a banner. The writer Cecil Tormay declared, "Take it! The hands of women have blessed it and consecrated it to glorify your manly hands." Then sixty-three women with black veils marched in, representing the sixty-three counties and presented flowers to Horthy. Cecil Tormay called them the daughters of the dismembered and occupied Hungary.[6]

Then "beautiful girls in Hungarian national dress" marched in, with the daughter of the prime minister at their head, presenting a bouquet of chrysanthemums to the commander in chief. It can be felt that the ritual has a barely concealed, distinct, sphere of interest related sexual-erotic content: the male leader is entitled to unconditional female submission.

The third such moment occurred on October 23, 1956. At about nine in the evening the reform communist Imre Nagy spoke to the people assembled in the Kossuth Square. At the same time, in a different part of the city, the *Stalin* statue was torn down and the radio station was occupied. The masses gathering in the square demanded Imre Nagy. He was the one they wanted to hear. In the political atmosphere of the day it was obvious that after the dictatorial Rákosi-type of leadership, Imre Nagy must follow and that he was the man of the hour. Imre Nagy spoke to the multitude. He stated that the legitimate demands of the young people would be heard, that reforms would come promptly but that all problems would have to be resolved through the Party. Less than twenty-four hours later he was the prime minister. Barely a week later, on October 31, he again spoke on the Kossuth Square. He announced that he negotiated the removal of the Soviet troops from Hungary, the withdrawal of Hungary from the Warsaw Pact and that October 23 would become a national holiday.

The three moments show considerable differences in their political orientation and choreography. Yet all three took place on the square and it is a common feature of all three that they were preliminaries to the assumption of power. They were moments of mercy.

---

6 Cecil Tormay's text is published as, "A nemzeti hadsereg ünnepe az Országház téren" [The feast of the National Army on Parliament Square], *Az Est*, November 18, 1919, pp. 3–5.

POLITICAL PIETY

Memorial events and acts of piety represent a separate chapter in the history of the square. These were also linked to the actual political powers because they were the only ones who could use the square and the Parliament as an area for a funerary activity. Yet, I am reluctant to include them as manifestations of power. The reason for this is cultural in nature. Death and the related ceremonies and rituals can, naturally, be used for political and power purposes, but here we are dealing with a larger picture. Death and piety are placed in such a sanctified value system that while the political issues and the conflicts battled over in life do not disappear, after death they are temporarily placed in abeyance. Stating it differently, death and piety can, for a short time, culturally overshadow political logic. I believe that political piety might be a better term than manifestation of power.

The starting point of these types of events was in February 1919. On the 20th participants in a large meeting of the Central Committee of the Unemployed were persuaded by the Communists to march to the editorial office of the Social Democratic Party newspaper, the *Népszava*. There was gunfire and six of the defenders of the editorial office were killed. Their catafalque was set up in the Dome Chamber of the Parliament. Then, the coffins were taken out onto the steps of the main entrance. The memorial ceremony and the speeches were held in the square.

Not much later there was another occasion to use the square for piety. On June 24, 1919, with the assistance of some gunboats on the Danube, a revolt started against the ruling Soviet Republic. The revolt was defeated but a number of soldiers of the Red Army were killed in the firefight against the insurgents. At the end of June, the bodies of eighteen soldiers were placed on a catafalque in the square. They were the "martyrs of the proletarian state."

During the Horthy era a number of noted funerary rituals took place on the square. It was from here that in February 1936, the body of Count Albert Apponyi, the "Grand Old Man" of the political life of the day, was taken to the cemetery. Gyula Gömbös, the prime minister died on October 6, 1936. He was put on a catafalque in the Parliament and the square became a part of the funerary ceremonies. Count Pál

Teleki was also the prime minister when he committed suicide on January 27, 1941. He also was placed on a catafalque in the Parliament and the square was an integral part of the funerary ceremonies.

The next occasion was the funeral of István Horthy, the vice regent of Hungary. The son of Miklós Horthy, he crashed his plane on August 20, 1942, near Alexeyevka, on the Russian front. He also was placed on a bier in the Parliament and the square was once again an important part of the ceremonies.

The acts of political piety, related to the square and being now considered a matter of tradition did not come to an end with the Horthy era. Almost immediately after the end of the war, at the end of May 1945, a catafalque was set up in the square for Endre Bajcsy-Zsilinsky, whom the Arrow Cross partisans executed on December 24, 1944, in Sopronkőhida. He was considered to be worthy of this honor as a martyr of Hungarian antifascist activity.

Mihály Károlyi, the first president of the first Hungarian republic died in his exile in France on March 19, 1955. Seven years after his death his remains were brought back home and were taken to burial from the Kossuth Square on March 19, 1962.

János Kádár had no catafalque in the Parliament or on the square and yet the square became an act of piety for him. The catafalque was set up in the Party headquarters on the Széchenyi Embankment, (today an office building for the parliamentary representatives), but the long lines of mourners were reaching the Kossuth Square. Thus, during the summer of 1989, during the rapidly progressing change in the regime, Kossuth Square became indirectly involved in the manifestation of piety rendered to the leader of the post-1956 Communist regime.

The last manifestation of piety to date occurred in December 1993. This was when József Antall, the first prime minister after the change of regime died. The traditional example of Gömbös, Teleki, and István Horthy was observed, and the departed prime minister had his catafalque in the Parliament and his funerary ceremonies in the Kossuth Square.

These acts of political piety are the best testimony to the original intent that Imre Steindl had in mind for the Parliament building. The deaths and the piety had political emphasis and their sanctified content was well suited to the aura of the temple of the constitution.

Unclassifiable Tragedy

The most tragic event on the square occurred on October 25, 1956.

According to later and somewhat biased descriptions:

> In the morning a huge protest group gathered on Kossuth Square. The Soviet tanks guarding the Party headquarters on Akadémia Street peacefully watched the demonstration. Suslov and Mikoyan were negotiating with the demonstrators in the building when fire was opened by machine guns from the roofs of the adjoining buildings on the peaceful demonstrators and on the Soviet tanks and their personnel fraternizing with the demonstrators. The bloody assault resulted in eighty dead and one hundred and fifty wounded. The persons involved in the bloody assault and their leaders have not been identified definitely to this day.[7]

> Between 10:00 and 11:00 [in the morning], eight to ten thousand people marched from the Astoria Hotel to Kossuth Square in front of the Parliament, demanding to hear Imre Nagy. The soldiers manning the Soviet armed vehicles and tanks protecting the Parliament and the Soviet soldiers stationed in the square fraternized with the demonstrators. At about 11:15 A.M. additional Soviet tanks arrived in the square. At approximately the same time, according to eye witnesses, unknown riflemen opened fire on the demonstrators from the attic windows of the Ministry of Agriculture. Some of the Soviet armed vehicles also fired on the demonstrators while others returned the fire from the ministry. The firing claimed sixty to seventy dead and one hundred to one hundred and fifty wounded. The precise sequence of events is still not entirely clear but public opinion uniformly attributes the bloody assault to the AVH.[8]

---

7 Mihály Bihari, *Magyar politika, 1944–2004: politikai s hatalmi viszonyok* [Hungarian Politics, 1944–2004: Political and Power Relations] (Budapest: Osiris, 2005).

8 András B. Hegedűs, ed., *1956 kézikönyve. Kronológia* [Handbook of 1956: Chronology] (Budapest: '56-os Intézet, 1996), p. 92.

A large number of people were killed on the square It is no accident that I call this an "unclassifiable tragedy." It is an unclassifiable tragedy because it is the only instance of mass murder in the square. Unfortunately in the twentieth century history of the country the murder of unarmed victims was far from a unique event but in the life of the square it never happened, except on October 25, 1956.

It is also unique because the demonstration on October 25, while unmistakably political, did not fit into either the pro- or antipower category. It did not fit because after October 23 there was a series of events which had led by the 25th to the situation that there was a prime minister who became prime minister by the will of the uprising and of the insurgents, but there were still the Stalinists in leadership positions both in the Party and in the military, against whom the uprising was directed and against whom the demonstration in the square was organized. In addition, another duality, there was no unity between the leadership of the military and the police and segments of the polity. Lastly, it is unclassifiable because tragedies always are.

It is not my purpose or my duty to give the details of the events, which, actually, are far from being accurately known.[9] It only complements the above to say that, according to other sources, the demonstrators were fired upon from the Ministry of Construction, from the lower windows of the Parliament, and from the direction of Akadémia, Nádor, and Báthory Streets.

The participants in the shooting, the mass murders, included the border guards and the formation responsible for guarding prominent structures who were part of the AVH security police system, the so called "partisans" who were former antifascist fighters recruited for the support of the Rákosi leadership, and the Soviet military formations.

The demonstrators came to the square to emphasize four specific demands. It is an odd twist of fate that one of their demands, the discharge of the Stalinist Ernő Gerő from his position as first secretary of the Communist Party, actually took place, at the time of the massacre,

---

[9] For the events on the Kossuth Square, see László Varga, *Az elhagyott tömeg: tanulmányok 1950–1956-ról* [The Abandoned Crowd: Essays about 1950–1956]] (Budapest: Cserépfalvi, 1994), pp. 99–126; László Eörsi, "A véres csütörtök" [Bloody Thursday], *Századvég* 6, no. 1 (1990): 241–251; and András Kő and Lambert J. Nagy, *Kossuth tér, 1956* (Budapest: Teleki László Alapítvány 2001).

only one hundred meters away at the Party headquarters. The representatives of the Soviet leadership chose János Kádár to replace Ernő Gerő.

There is no agreement yet as to the number of victims of the massacre.[10] Nobody can tell for certain.

It is not a matter of debate, however, that the event was tragic. It is also not a matter of debate that the massacre was largely caused by Hungarian armed units loyal to the Stalinist system and by Soviet formations. Who was responsible, to what degree, is still a matter of debate. Finally, even though the precise number of the victims is not known, there is no question that a politically motivated massacre had been committed on the square.

It is no accident that in the eventful history of the square this is the day to which memorials have been erected.

The Non-Political Square

We could sense from the series of events that the symbolism of Kossuth Square favored its political role. It was the continuity of political events which made the square into what it is. This is what gave the square its uniqueness and its specific character.

In addition to the dominance of the political role, there was a non-political, or mainly non-political, trend which was not characteristic, which could have happened anywhere, but which is still a part of the whole picture.

The non-political events on the square took place mostly after the regime change in 1989–1990. Such events included the erection of a Christmas tree, the occasional erection of a skating rink, the occasional establishment of a pontoon bridge between the Kossuth Square and the opposite side of the Danube, mass meditations in the square, charity handball tournaments, giant photograph displays, concerts, and a square music and film festival where movies are projected onto giant screens for all to see. It is also part of this series of events that at one time the new public transportation buses were first shown in the square.

---

[10] Varga gives seventy-four names. Eörsi estimates the number of dead at two hundred.

The civilian and non-political use of the square occasionally included surprising events. Such an occasion occurred on May 6, 2003, when thirty blind or vision impaired people marched to the *Kossuth* statue and placed white canes at its pedestal. This was to express their displeasure with the insoluble personality conflict in the National Institute for the Blind between the female director and one of her section heads.

Yet, even the surprising and unusual actions express the realization that the square, in addition to its political dominance, entered so deeply into public consciousness that it was used for events which had seemingly no relationship with its political symbolism. I use the term "seemingly" intentionally because I feel it is justified by the fact that the notable political-symbolic role automatically attracts other activities seeking public notice.

It is also a part of the non-event-centric public use of the square that people walk through it going to and coming from work, sit on the benches in the park-like portion of the square and, in other words, use it just like they would use any other partly park-like public areas.

The public use leads from time to time to the question whether the square should not be made more public oriented. Since the change ofregime the political activities on the square increased. Ever since 1988 it is almost a daily discussion item that the square should be made more suitable for public use.

A contributing factor is that since the Parliament was erected many things had changed. Mass automobile use in Hungary took place after 1956, but because during the communist era the House of Delegates met only for one or two days four times each year, parking was not a problem for the representatives. Following the change of regime, disregarding recess, the legislature meets for two session days and one committee day each week. If the square is not to serve as an open air parking area, something has to be done.[11]

[11] In 2002 a bicycle path to the square was being discussed and, according to the May 27, 2002, issue of *Népszabadság*, an underground garage is also planned. In 2003 the plans for public toilettes were considered. The press reported on April 14, 2004, that on August 20 the square would be remodeled. In 2005 the underground garage was again the main topic. It was announced on June 25, 2005, that the government would remodel the Kossuth Square. Nothing of the above was ever realized.

Security issues have also changed. From 1902 until the beginning of the 2000s anybody could walk up to the building or, at least, get quite close to it. Today the Parliament is encircled by a security zone, in an esthetically rather undemanding way. From the beginning of the last century, because of the public use of the square and the daily use by the people, there was always an attempt to establish parks. At the beginning of the twenty-first century this might have to be reconsidered.

* * *

So far as the symbolic use of the Kossuth Square is concerned the elements showing a temporal continuity were established between 1896 and 1919. The later periods only followed what had been established in the above period. The "political magnet," the radiation emanating from the Parliament was functioning perfectly. It attracted even acts of political piety. Consequently the political nature of the square underwent a complete transformation and the series of symbolic political events became a characteristic feature. The character so established was reinforced by the politically motivated massacre of 1956. The tragedy on the Kossuth Square became an integral component of history. In the mean time the daily public activities on the square continued and are part of the square's history albeit in a subordinate and not dominant role. Some elements of the square's public history were, and still are, influenced by the force of its political symbolism.

The symbolic use of the square was not always of the same intensity or of the same dimensions. The more civil rights were available in a period of time, the more the square was used for political protests. From 1956 to 1988 the square was totally silent in this regard. Its most intensive period began in 1988.

It was always available for the manifestations of power and every ruling power took advantage of this opportunity. Kossuth Square has been the principal square of Hungary.

THE SPIRITUAL SQUARE

The Parliament building, that Gothic structure, was thought of as a temple of the constitution. I could say that, in accordance with the view shared by the sponsor and by the architect, a secular dome was created which served political goals.

The demand for sanctity, attached to the political temple, could not stop at the walls of the building. It was surrounded by a square and the secular temple characteristic, in reflection, could be buttressed if the square was also adapted to the character attributed to the building. Naturally this can be approached from another side as well: the square could appear as the emission zone of the temple of the constitution.

In order for this function to be realized, the physical square had to be converted into a spiritual one. The term spiritual means that it is physical and intellectual. This means then that the physical-topographical square had to be converted into a physical-intellectual square if the force of its civic/political sanctity and its reflection on the temple was to become real.

The problem, namely the physical transubstantiation and conversion of the square, is not an insoluble one. Beginning in the second half of the nineteenth century, it was promoted by the statuary and the memorials, the world of special plasticity, which, in Central Europe, became an increasingly acceptable worldly motif.[1]

---

1 For Budapest and the statues in the public square, see György Rajna, *Budapest köztéri szobrainak katalógusa* [The Catalog of Statues in Budapest's Public Space] (Budapest: Budapesti Városszépítői Egyesület, 1989); Endre Liber, *Budapest szobrai és emléktáblái* [The Statues and Memorial Plaques of Budapest] (Budapest, n.p., 1934); László Prohászka, *Szoborhistoriák* (Budapest: Önkormányzat. Főpolgármesteri Hivatal, 2004); Endre Gádor, *Budapest szobrai* (Budapest: Képzőművészeti Alap Kiadóvállalata, 1955); János Potó, *Az emlékeztetés helyei. Emlékművek és politika* [The Realms of Memory. Memorials and Politics]

Because the temple is both lay and political, there was no reason why the Kossuth Square could not be gradually filled with the heroes of politics. That is with those whom the decision-making political powers considered to be important in spiritualizing the square.

Logical rationalization does not mean equality with historic thought processes. Historical logic contains many possibilities and much doubt. It includes all the human frailties of the decision makers and the battles between diverging interests. Thus logic, by itself, does not redeem history.

It is a fact, however, that the political dome, with all its internal decorations, was completed by 1904. It is also a fact that the first political memorial was dedicated in the square in 1906 and that the last one, to date, was unveiled in 2002. It did happen, essentially from its first days to the present that the square was to be spiritualized.

In this chapter I want to describe the history of the spiritualization of the square. The limitations of the explanation are linked inescapably to the selection process. The perspective of art history can, in my opinion, be safely ignored. So can the proposed and eventual costs of the various monuments. For me the important issue is to find out where and how the various decision makers, at different times, planned to spiritualize the square; when and what contents did they wish to implement and express according to their intentions. And also, naturally, how much of this was eventually brought to life.

(Budapest: Osiris, 2003); György Szűcs, "Memoriae, ars oblivendi. Emlékművek térben és időben" [Memoriae, ars oblivendi. Memorials in time and space], in *Történelem—Kép. Szemelvények múlt és művészet kapcsolatából Magyarországon* [History—Picture. Selections from the Ties between History and Art], ed. Árpád Mikó and Katalin Sinkó (Budapest: Magyar Nemzeti Galéria, 2000). I have used these works continuously and therefore I will make no further reference to them. I view them as compulsory reading for this subject. For the artistic perspective of the statues on the square, see Tibor Wehner, "A leleplezés napján...együtt volt az egész nemzet...A Parlament körüli szobordísz változásai" [On the day of the unveiling the whole nation was together...Changes in the decorative statues around the Parliament], in *A hazugság és a hiány emlékművei. Előadások, tanulmányok, cikkek, röpiratok, feljegyzések a magyar szobrászatról 1986–1999* [Memorials of lies and shortages. Presentations, essays, pamphlets, and notes about Hungarian Plastic Art] (Budapest: Új Művészet Kiadó, 2001), pp. 13–20.

The First Step—The Andrássy Memorial

Count Gyula Andrássy died on February 18, 1890, at the age of sixty-seven. He was the first Hungarian prime minister after the Compromise and later the minister of foreign affairs of the Austro-Hungarian Monarchy. He was committed to the improvement and development of Budapest and, as we have seen, to the building of the Parliament.

With the approval of Francis Joseph, the government, one day after Andrássy's death, initiated a law which the legislature endorsed on March 4, 1890. According to Act III of 1890, Paragraph 1, "In recognition of his services to the country and to the Throne a monument shall be erected, at government expense, to honor Count Gyula Andrássy." Paragraph 2 added: "The ministry is charged with implementing this act."

The truth is that there was no need to justify the proposal or the law. Andrássy was an emblematic figure of the given dualist system. During his long political career, he had a characteristic role in the 1848–49 period, he was sentenced to death in absentia, and had a major role in the shaping of the Compromise. In the political preparations for the Compromise, there was only one Hungarian figure who played a more important role than Andrássy. This was Ferenc Deák. Deák died in 1876 and a statue was erected in his honor in 1887 at the Pest bridgehead of the Chain Bridge, on the present Roosevelt Square. It was evident that a statue had to be erected for Andrássy to honor one of the successful proponents of the present ruling political system.[2]

It also seemed obvious where the statue should be placed. Giving a voice to public opinion, the paper *Fővárosi Lapok* wrote:

> Concerning the statue of Gyula Andrássy, everybody takes it for granted that it should be erected on Andrássy Avenue. This was

2 The history of the *Andrássy* statue, the first step in the spiritualization of the square, is well documented and followed in the organized material of the prime minister's section of the Magyar Országos Levéltár (Hungarian National Archives, hereafter cited as MOL). I refer to the parts that were important for me. About the sculptor, György Zala there is a relatively recent monograph. See György Borbás, *A Millenium szobrásza: Zala György, 1858–1937* [The Sculptor of the Millenium: György Zala, 1858–1937] (Budapest: Kossuth Kiadó, 1999).

> his most glorious contribution to the beautification of the city and the main avenue, noted throughout Europe, already carries his name as an expression of Budapest's gratitude. The bronze memorial of the country's gratitude should be there. There is no doubt about this. The only question is which point should be selected: the middle, on Octagon Square (Oktogon tér), or the end of the avenue, before the artesian well. There are no buildings in this area and thus, in order for the statue to have a proper environment, a large set of structures would have to be erected which would increase the costs significantly.
>
> We assume that the Octagon Square will be chosen. This site is not at the edge of town where a monument would really be seen only during warm weather, because in the winter nobody goes there. The purpose of the monument is to be seen by the largest number of people and for these people to be inspired by it.[3]

Public opinion was one thing, the sponsor Hungary and the government acting for it were another matter. The right of making a decision did not rest with public opinion.

A memorial committee, charged with the responsibility of having the statue erected, was under the leadership of the prime minister of the day. The committee held its first meeting on July 16, and it took a position concerning the site, which was almost identical with the one proposed by public opinion. It thought that the most suitable site would be the Városliget (City Park) end of the Andrássy Avenue. "This site owes its existence to the initiative of the late, great statesman and represents one of the permanent memorials of his many-sided, success-filled activities. The avenue by its dimensions and position would provide a dignified framework for the placement of the memorial for its creator."[4]

One of the members of the committee, Baron Frigyes Podmaniczky, the real leader of the Public Works Council, barely one month after the committee had taken its position, stated his views about the proper site for the monument. According to the newspaper reporting his

---

3 *Fővárosi Lapok*, March 27, 1890. pp. 617–618.

4 K 26, 1906–xxx–128 (1890–III.–541), fol. 533–535 (IMG 3449–3451), MOL.

speech, Podmaniczky only considered two locations in Budapest to be suitable for the statue. Starting at this point, the article stated:

> One area is the end of the Andrássy Avenue and this was the pick of the committee. The other is the square to be in front of the Parliament now being built. Both sites are tightly linked to the life of the late statesman. He planned the Andrássy Avenue, he expedited its completion, he rejoiced in its development, and he loved to drive, ride, or walk on it. His statue would proclaim from here the undying laurels he gathered in the beautification of the capital.
>
> Yet, at the end of the avenue, the baron cannot conceive of a simple statue without it being surrounded by an elaborate set of buildings. Such an artistic framework would raise the grandeur and the effects of the entire arrangement, would place a crown on the completion of the Andrássy Avenue, but would inevitably demand larger sums than those assigned to the project.
>
> The area in front of the Parliament would also be an appropriate location for his statue because Count Gyula Andrássy exerted considerable influence on the decision to erect the most monumental building of the country, on the selection of the site, and on deciding upon the application to be accepted. (He was the most creative, leading statesmen of the new Hungary, but the place before the Parliament should rightfully be assigned to the creator of the Compromise, the "Country's Sage." His statue, in fact, has been erected in another location and cannot be moved to the Parliament Square, even though this had been suggested recently.)
>
> The Parliament will take a long time to complete and, according to the baron, the statue should be erected there only if the building and the statue can be presented at the same time. If this is the site selected for the statue, it would be best if the committee charged with building the Parliament were entrusted with the preparation of the memorial, in order to assure complete harmony between the two.[5]

---

5 *Fővárosi Lapok*, July 28, 1890, p. 1518.

The intention of placing the statue on the future Kossuth Square appears here in a modest way. There was still a long way from the completion of the Parliament, and it was still only a very hesitant idea that the square surrounding the Parliament be designed in some form of spirituality.

The Executive Committee of the Memorial Committee held a meeting in December 1890. Even though it was still committed to the end of Andrássy Avenue, an area which incidentally was also considered as the site of a memorial group in honor of the 1848–49 War of Liberation, it did recommend the square to be placed in front of the southern side of the Parliament as an alternative site. According to their opinion, "The reasons for erecting a statue...are Andrássy's outstanding national achievements among which the principal action of the great statesman was to convert Ferenc Deák's great constitutional achievement, the Compromise, into practical reality. It would evidently be a dignified and proper place for his statue to be in front of the building which is destined to represent our statehood."[6]

In the meantime an alternative proposal was made public. In the *Budapesti Szemle* Ferenc Jakabffy recommended the other end of the Andrássy út, Deák Square as the site for the statue.[7] Dated July 1892, the request for applications for the statue design and production was published and the original site proposed was still the one in the submission package. The deadline for the application was October 1, 1893.[8]

Ten submissions were received. Nine saw the Andrássy memorial at the City Park end of the Andrássy Avenue, as specified in the request for applications. One would place the statue at the Parliament. This one came from Alajos Stróbl. He proposed a Gothic, sarcophagus-like base. It appears that the debate about the site did have an effect in spite of the unequivocal position taken by officialdom.

---

6 K 26, 1906–xxx–128 (1890–III–541), fol. 528 (IMG 3441–3445), MOL.

7 Ferenc Jakabffy, "Emlékszobraink" [Our memorial statues], *Budapesti Szemle*, no. 170 (February 1891): 228–241.

8 Not important from our perspective, but I mention that on recommendation of the family the submissions were for an equestrian statue. The decision-makers liked the idea because this was to be the first equestrian statue in Budapest.

The competition was won by György Zala. We now turn the story over to the writer in the Sunday paper, *Vasárnapi Ujság*:

> He planned to place his work at the end of the Andrássy Avenue. In order to give it an appropriate environment and simultaneously resolve the problem of finishing this end of the avenue he went into partnership with the architect, Albert Schickedanz, who designed a beautiful structure around the statue. This is a thirty-three meter diameter semicircle-shaped hall consisting of nine arches and eighteen slender columns. The columnar hall would be twenty meters high, made of Karst marble and appearing from a distance like a triumphal arch which would well represent a transition between the villas of the Andrássy Avenue and the City Park. This beautifully articulated, lacy structure would provide a magnificent completion for Andrássy Avenue, would provide a pleasant background for the statue and would be a fine starting point for the millennial exposition which would have its main entrance in this direction.
>
> Zala planned his equestrian statue to be in the center of this airy columnar hall. The artist solved his problem with consummate skill. He immortalized Andrássy at the height of his middle years, not in any theatrical pose, but with a calm and serene expression on his face, devoid of all gestures, bare-headed and on horseback. Looking at this statue we can perceive the wisdom of the statesman and the elegance of the diplomat. The entire figure is nobly simple and dignified and for this reason it has a very direct effect. Andrássy bestrides his horse elegantly and the horse is shown to be somewhat lively, to emphasize the serenity of the rider. The horse raises its right leg and puts its head down in order to display Andrássy's entire figure.
>
> The figure of Andrássy in coronation uniform and the stallion caparisoned with fancy harness were executed with remarkable plasticity. Andrássy's face is shown so finely and so accurately that Andrássy's widow, Countess Katinka Kendeffy, declared that she had never seen a better portrait of her husband.
>
> Andrássy's equestrian statue stands on a longitudinal square base. In the front there is the coat of arms of the Andrássy family

and on the two sides two relief carvings. On the left a coronation scene and on the right the Berlin Congress, the latter being based on Antal Werner's great historical canvas in the Berlin City Hall. The pedestal is 5.5 meters high, the statue is 6.5 meters and thus, including a slight elevation of the square, the statue would stand fifteen meters high, beautifully ruling over the majestic avenue.[9]

Zala, having won the competition began to be concerned about the site. On April 11, 1894, he realized that the planned site for the statue would serve better as the site for the Millennial Monument.[10] Five days after expressing his concerns the contract was signed but still with the end of the Andrássy Avenue as the designated site. Zala campaigned assiduously for a change in site and his persistence led to a change of mind among the decision-makers.

From the perspective of the spiritualization of the Kossuth Square, December 17, 1894, was a critical and determining date. It was on that day that the Executive Committee of the Memorial Committee held a meeting. They discussed the prime minister's directive, according to which the end of the Andrássy Avenue was designated as the site for the Millennial Monument. On this basis the committee recommended as a new site for the statue, the square to be built around the Parliament. György Zala had no objections. Henceforth the imagination of the committee became activated and they suggested that if the statue was placed in front of the eastern façade, then the boilerhouse, planned for the western side of Parliament, should be moved and make place for another equestrian statue.[11]

---

[9] Dénes Kovács, "Gróf Andrássy Gyula szobra" [The statue of Count Gyula Andrássy], *Vasárnapi Újság*, October 22, 1893, pp. 717–718. For a detailed contemporary review about the application, see József Fekete, "Az Andrássy szobor pályázat" [The *Andrássy* statue competition], *Magyar Szalon* 20, (October 1893–March 1894): 125–246; Kamill Fittle, "Az Andrássy szobor pályaművei" [Works submitted to the *Andrássy* statue competition], *Magyar Mérnök és Építész Egylet Közlönye*, no. 12 (1893): 189–205. Another publication with many data: Gábor and Verő eds, *Schickedanz Albert (1846–1915)*, pp. 108–111. For Heroes' Square, see Gerő, *Imagined History*, pp. 173–212.

[10] K 26, 1906–xxx–128 (1894–III–423), fol. 247 (IMG 3559), MOL.

[11] K 26, 1906–xxx–128 (1894–III–423), fol. 267–272 (IMG 3592–3595), MOL.

The Memorial Committee, under the chairmanship of the prime minister, accepted the recommendation of its executive committee on May 7, 1895, and decided that the statue "shall be erected on the southern side of the new Parliament, on the square to be set up along the Danube."[12]

It was clear from the first moment on that the memorial located there would attract other memorials and that the square would be and will be replete with structures designed to be spiritual. As soon as it was decided that the statue would be in front of the Parliament, the battle raged on the question why the square in front of the southern façade was the designated area? Zala again started a campaign because he wanted his statue to be placed in front of the main entrance to the Parliament, so that it would be located in the square just at the foot of the steps.[13]

The Memorial Committee and the executive committee proved to be inflexible. Yet, the possibility of spiritualizing the square in front of the Parliament, raised first in a spatial context, started a train of thought in that direction.

The Hungarian Architects and Builders Association held a meeting on November 26, 1900. Almost one hundred architects and builders attended. The principal topic was supposed to be the placement of the *Andrássy* statue which was the single item on the agenda. In fact, however, everybody present was thinking of how Kossuth Square could be "arranged" with memorials.[14] The most striking and forward-looking opinion was expressed by the architect and city planner Antal Palóczy. It is worth to quote him:

> We recently had the opportunity again to see how difficult it was to place a memorial statue properly on a square the planning of which did not consider its artistic arrangements.

---

[12] K 26, 1906–xxx–128 (1895–VIII–1563), fol. 213–216 (IMG 3592–3595), MOL.

[13] K 26, 1906–xxx–128 (1897–IV–1382), fol. 187–190 (IMG 3629–3632), MOL. Zala repeatedly argued against placing the statue in front of the southern façade.

[14] For a detailed report about the meeting, see "Az Andrássy szobor elhelyezése" [The placement of the *Andrássy* statue], *Pesti Hirlap,* November 28, 1900.

When our new Parliament building was positioned only the Danube side was attended to and, regretfully, they were not concerned with the fact that the façade facing the city was of equal importance when the Parliament was located in an essentially vacant area.

The plans show how unrelated the site of the Parliament was to its environment. The streets ending in the square do so arbitrarily and irregularly, the axes of the roads have no destinations and just disappear. The axis of the Alkotmány Street, does aim at a part of the new building but the encounter is at an awkward angle which cannot serve as a goal because it is at a side and far from the center of the building, the most important component of the building mass.

Yet proper alignment of the axes, symmetry and regularity are inseparable attributes of monumentality. It is a shame that the most important palace of the country was wedged into its environment so that the environment cannot provide it with the necessary emphasis for its monumentality. It cannot provide it although it cannot be said that they skimped in the planning of the square, a mistake they make with most of our public buildings. The square on the city side of the Parliament is large and could even be said to be too large. If there was a mistake in size, this is just the opposite from what we are used to.

The square is not artistically composed. There is no harmony in its measurements, it is irregular, and the greatest fault is that it is not oriented, arranged, and balanced vis-à-vis the orientation and position of the Parliament. The position of the Parliament does not fit properly into the Parliament square!

This fault cannot be corrected retroactively. It is precisely this fault which is responsible for the fact that the equestrian statue of Count Gyula Andrássy cannot be placed in the axis of the Parliament, in front of the main entrance, as it is demanded by the intention of glorifying the great statesman and by the patriotic piety of his memory.

The statue cannot be placed in this location esthetically or functionally. From an esthetic perspective the equestrian statue located along the axis of the building would emphasize the acute angle of the axis, make the unsightly obliquity even more offensive. From a practical perspective, the large base would be in the narrowest part of the square and would block the path of the traffic. It would cut the square in two and would significantly blunt the appearance of the entire square and of the Parliament building.

The configuration of the square is definitely elongated and its length rules over its width. The square is already split in two by the Palace of Justice and the Ministry of Agriculture placed at the right and left ends of the Alkotmány Street. This situation and the markedly projecting central part of the Parliament do not permit any other solution for the placement of the statue but the erection of a similar memorial directly opposite to it.

I mention parenthetically that at the meeting of the Architect Association one of the speakers referred to Zala, according to whom in the arrangement proposed by Palóczy, Lajos Batthyány, the first responsible Hungarian prime minister, executed on October 6, 1849, could be the "counter-statue."

Because in front of the principal façade of the Parliament, at both ends of the square there are fountains, they could be preserved and the two statues could be placed here. Palóczy continues:

> The previously mentioned excessive lengths of the square in front of the Parliament might be of assistance now and the existing fountains do not have to be disturbed if the two equestrian statues are placed in the same areas. It is made possible by the way the parks are arranged in these areas. This, in itself, is an indication that in its architectonic design the square suffers from its exaggerated measurements.
>
> We believe that a forum-like area in front of the Parliament would have been more appropriate than a park, which does not increase the monumentality and is only promoting nicety.
>
> But precisely because the square is so large it can be divided so that it forms a huge forum around the main entrance to the Parliament. On the right and left side of it, lower grassy segments of the square could accommodate two equestrian statues, with bushes providing a background for them. These bushes would extend

> to an area of the park, separated by readjusted roadways, where the fountains are.
>
> The fountains are totally indifferent as far as the center of the square is concerned, as though they did not even exist. They may well be hidden by the bushes. In this way they would assist in the focusing of the square and thus serve a beneficial purpose for the entire effect of the square.
>
> The two equestrian statues would be 110 meters apart, not entirely symmetrically with the center line of the square, but carefully adjusted so that they are closer to the Parliament and immediately reveal their intimate relationship to the building....
>
> The square must be regularly arranged around the equestrian statues, but because the length of the square was considerable, the façades of the buildings to be erected on the square could not serve as background for them. The natural background for the statues would be provided by the bushy grove.[15]

As we have seen, a statue at southern and northern end of the Parliament had been a consideration ever since 1894. After 1900 it was added that at the ends of the square, in front of the principal façade, memorials could be erected. Figuratively speaking, even before the Parliament was completely finished, there were four potential spaces where, with time and as the function of varying political desires, spiritualizing objects might be placed.

The story of the *Andrássy* statue henceforth followed the usual path. Slowly, and exceeding all deadlines, Zala completed the reliefs and Ernő Foerk completed the pedestal. There was a scandal about the cost of the casting procedure, in other words, the completion of the statue progressed steadily, albeit with minor jolts,

The statue was unveiled on December 2, 1906, sixteen years after the count's death and after the law about a memorial was passed.

The unveiling was a notable event. Emperor Francis Joseph was present and even spoke briefly. The principal speaker of the festivities

15 Antal Pálóczy, "Gróf Andrássy Gyula szobra és az Országház tere" [The statue of Count Gyula Andrássy and the square of the Parliament], *Építő Ipar* (1900): 33–34.

was Kálman Széll, prime minister from 1899 to 1903. He summarized the spiritual essence incorporated in the reliefs of the coronation and of the 1878 Berlin Congress, which, in his view, justified the erection of a statue to honor Andrássy. He said:

> Count Gyula Andrássy loyally served his king and his country. He lived to make his king and his country great. His critically significant activities gained glory for his country and for himself.
>
> In his Easter Address, Ferenc Deák had turned to the king and to the nation. The nation had begun to realize that after the continuity of laws and of the constitution had been reinstated, the conflicts had to be resolved and the relationships between the countries, living in harmony with Hungary's independence and under the joint rule of His Majesty, had to be reestablished so that the confidence between king and nation again be firmly in place. In this endeavor we find Andrássy side by side with Deák.
>
> Your Majesty's heart has sought out the heart of the nation. King and country have reached an understanding. The Compromise came into being. On a motion by Ferenc Deák, the National Assembly with enthusiastic unanimity, elected Gyula Andrássy to place the Crown of St. Stephen on the anointed brow of the king, in the name of the nation.
>
> The great task of implementing the Compromise and of reshaping the Hungarian state ensued. In the reestablished constitution Ferenc Deák gave the country's life a new framework. This framework had to be filled. The Hungarian state had to be reborn from the ruins, with poor organizations, and with slender resources.
>
> Ferenc Deák called Count Gyula Andrássy a man of destiny. Your Majesty's confidence placed him at the head of the government. There was no one more suitable for the great tasks to be accomplished. His statesmanship, his wide sphere of interest and knowledge, his mastery of resolving conflicts, his brilliant mind, his keen vision and his constructive forces brought this enormous task to successful completion.
>
> Your Majesty's trust soon called him to manage the foreign affairs. It was here in this wide sphere of activity that was able to demonstrate his marvelous strength and his great and brilliant skills

as a statesman. It seems as though he had never moved in any other sphere of activity.

He charted new pathways in our international relationship toward the West and the East. His great political concept was: intimate relationship with our great neighbor to the West and independence for the nations in the East and freedom from any outside interference. He reestablished the respect and the international position of the two-country Austro-Hungarian Monarchy which it earned by its past and by its grandeur.

The basic guidelines of his policies are just as valid today.

When he labored in the highest court of the nations with the other European statesmen in solving the problems of the East, he returned with a strengthened position for the Austro-Hungarian Monarchy. He brought back peace and the glory he earned reflected a glow on Hungary as well.

The crowning point of his accomplishments was the alliance with the great neighbor, the German Empire, based on the similarity of political interests and mutual security. For almost thirty years, enlarged to a triple alliance, this achievement has become the basis of security for European peace and for the international relations in Central Europe.

We have placed the statue here, by the curly waves of the blue Danube, on this beautiful site of the capital city which he wanted to be beautiful and great.

We have placed the statue here, near the building which the thousand year-old Hungary had erected to glorify its constitution.

We have placed it here, facing the Royal Castle, which Your Majesty had ordered to be erected on his recommendation. We have placed him here to show that loyalty to the king and patriotism are inseparable concepts in the heart of every true Hungarian, and as a symbol of what we have engraved onto the marble walls of Parliament, that the safety of the throne, the strength of the nation, and the happiness of future generations are possible only if there is full understanding between the king and the nation.[16]

---

[16] *Pesti Hirlap*, December 3, 1906.

The text is clear and unambiguous: Andrássy was given the memorial primarily because he played a leading role in the creation and implementation of the prevailing political system, and assisted in solidifying the great-power position of the Monarchy.[17]

The first step was thus taken in 1906. The idea had already evolved, however, that at the northern end and in two other sites in the principal parts of the square, three more statues were needed. The spir-

---

[17] The inscriptions on the statue:

I. On the front:
Gróf Andrássy Gyula
1823–1890

* * *

In accordance with Act II of 1890
Erected by the grateful nation
II. On the side of the coronation scene:
Serving his nation
he placed the crown on the head of his king
as Hungary's prime minister
Buda, June 8, 1867
III. On the side of the Congress scene:
Serving his king
he gave weight to the voice of the Hungarian nation in the council of the world
as the minister of foreign affairs of the Monarchy [at]
the Berlin Congress, July 13, 1878

The statue has its back toward the southern part of the Parliament and consequently looks toward the south. Its pedestal is 650 centimeters. Andrássy's equestrian statue is three times human size.Two opinions from the contemporary echoes questioning the equestrian format. In the unsigned critique published by the political and literary review, *A Hét*, we read: "Of all the problems of statuary the most difficult ones are with bronze or stone horses. The horse might be a noble beast but in form and mass it is beyond the monumentality of sculpture, particularly if burdened by a rider when the large mass resting on four slender legs completely upsets the equilibrium of the entire statue. Why György Zala thought of Gyula Andrássy on horseback will remain a mystery forever. Nothing in the life of the noble count ever came to public consciousness that could be associated with the idea of equestrianism." *A Hét*, December 2, 1906, p. 802.

The art critic Károly Lyka wrote: "We do not know why the bronze Andrássy had to sit on a horse, when nothing that made him famous has happened on horseback. Let us acquiesce in this caprice of the sponsors and let us remember that Velasquez was also represented on horseback even though he could do other things besides riding a horse. There would have been just as much justification for representing Dr. Semmelweis on horseback." *Új Idők*, no 50 (December 9, 1906): 578.

itualization of the square had begun and the only question remaining was: who would put whom and where?

Intermezzo

The erection of the statue in 1906 was not followed by any major surge in the desire to spiritualize. The Monarchy showed increasing signs of stress and could produce fewer and fewer examples of mutual understanding. Nothing happened on the square, at least not in this direction. It is true that in 1913 a plaque was affixed to the wall of the Palace of Justice. The inscription reads, "For Alajos Hauszmann, the designer of this building, in celebration of his forty years of educational and architectural activities, this memorial was erected by his loyal students." This cannot be considered as a continuation of the thought process which began with the erection of the *Andrássy* statue.

The war, known at the time as the Great War, was not a suitable time to populate the Kossuth Square with additional memorials. The revolution at the end of the war, and the communist assumption of power which followed, the new regime in its brief but frenzied activities wished to leave a memento in the square. In 1918, they only changed the name of the square, but in 1919, during the 133 days which was all the Soviet Republic had, the only statue in the square received a new adornment. May 1, the day of the labor movement, was selected, when the Communists who, in fact, controlled the city took symbolic and spiritual ownership. The *Andrássy* statue was surrounded and covered by a wooden structure in antique style, called the "House of the People." On each side the statue of a soldier was placed and on the square busts of Lenin and of Karl Liebknecht were erected, and also two large red globes.[18] This arrangement suggests the general direction

[18] See Boldizsár Vörös, "Károlyi Mihály tér, Marx szobrok, fehér ló—Budapest szimbolikus elfoglalása 1918–1919-ben" [Mihály Károlyi Square, *Marx* statues, white horse: The symbolic capture of Budapest in 1918–1919], *Budapesti Negyed*, nos. 29–30 (2000): 144–163. I note that Gyula Krúdy in 1918 recommended that the square be called Népszava (People's Voice) rather than Köztársaság (Republic). The May Day idea was explained by Communist leader, Tibor Szamuely, *Fáklya*, April 20, 1919.

in which the spiritualization of the square would have progressed if the Soviet Republic would have continued.

Neither the Soviet Republic, nor the structures erected by it in the square remained for long. All quickly disappeared.

The Second Step—The *Kossuth* Statue

For the second statue on the square the public had to wait until November 1927. It was then that the statue of Lajos Kossuth was unveiled on the segment of the square between the Parliament and the Palace of Justice.

The story of the creation of the *Andrássy* statue spanned a period of sixteen years, that of the *Kossuth* statue took thirty-three years.[19] It could have lasted for thirty-four years but toward the end there was a feeling of urgency because there was a likelihood that New York would have a *Kossuth* statue before Budapest.[20]

It is not important for us to detail the thirty-three year history. The only matter important for us is that the statue did arrive on the square, as the continuation of a process which had begun and which gradually reached completion.

Kossuth died on March 20, 1894, in Torino. The very next day the Capital Assembly met. Raising the statue was suggested and the proposal was accepted. A national committee was established. It was assigned the task of coordinating the various activities designed to further the Kossuth cult and to manage the financial contributions made for this purpose. The next meeting, following the enthusiasm of 1894, was held in 1902 and again took up the matter of the statue. In 1903 the Engineer's Office made a recommendation for the site of the statue. Of twelve possible sites, Freedom Square was considered to be the most suitable one with the area in front of the main entrance to the Parliament as the second choice and Octagon Square as the third one. From

---

[19] The history of the statue is given in detail by Liber, *Budapest szobrai*, pp. 327–341.

[20] József Ádámfy, *A világ Kossuth-szobrai* [The Kossuth Statues of the World] (Budapest: NPI, 1997). The statue in New York was dedicated in March 1928.

this point on, intermittently until 1926, the site was the matter of ongoing debates.

In September 1903, the text for the competition for the design of the statue was prepared and the part of the square before the main entrance to the Parliament was designated as its site. The deadline for the applications, in 1904, was extended by the city to March 31, 1905. Among considerable scandal, the competition was declared to be without any result. In the meantime there was an ongoing debate about the site, a process well known from the history of the *Andrássy* statue.

In 1906 specifications for another competitions was published, with the same site designation. The deadline for submission was February 28, 1908. Twenty-three submissions were received. There was another scandal but János Horvay was announced the winner.

Horvay went to work in 1909 and by 1911 the secondary figures were ready. It appears that in 1914, twenty years after Kossuth's death, a new memorial could be unveiled, in front of the main entrance to the Parliament, a site that was found unsuitable for the *Andrássy* statue.

Then came the war. After the conflagration the marble pedestal (180 square meters of finished marble from Ruszkica [Ruschiţa]) came into the hands of the Romanian authorities and the potential base of the Kossuth memorial was sold by them.

The silence surrounding the Kossuth memorial was finally broken by the original sponsor, the Capital City Assembly. The matter of the statue was raised at the November 6, 1925, meeting. In January 1926 Horvay began to carve the missing parts.

Erection of the statue became likely and this again triggered the debate about the site. It was primarily the Hungarian Engineer and Architect Association that argued against placing the statue in front of the main entrance to the Parliament, even though the city authorities continued to hold out in favor of this site.[21] Finally a committee was dispatched to designate the site for the memorial on the basis of the models erected at various parts of the Kossuth Square.

---

21 The debate can be followed in the various issues of the *Magyar Mérnök és Építész Egylet Közlönye* (1926): 117–118, 189–192, 195–196, and 222–224.

On July 1, 1926, the committee inspected the square and recommended that the statue be placed on the northern side of the main part of the square, in the axis of the MAK building, thirty meters from the building, and that Kossuth, just like Andrássy, should face south. The statue committee of the city accepted this recommendation in June 1927 and this was approved by the Capital Assembly. Thus the final site for the statue was settled.

On October 26, 1927, Mayor Ferenc Ripka announced that the statue was finished. It could be unveiled on November 6. Horvay's statue was completed in the Horthy era but its design was accepted during the rule of Francis Joseph. In fact most of the statue was completed at that time.

To acquaint the reader with the statue I call upon the contemporary Budapest monographer of the history of the statue.

> The nine statues, carved from marble from Ruszkica, stand on a wide and high limestone pedestal. The central figure, slightly ahead of the others, is Lajos Kossuth. The other eight statues are of the members of the first responsible Hungarian government, Kossuth's fellow ministers, appointed by King Ferdinand V. Wide steps lead up to the pedestal and the background for the statues is a high stone wall which rises like an altar. On the back of this wall there is a group of statues representing the devotion to freedom and to the sacrifices that had to be laid on the altar of the country. This group of high relief can be seen from the back of the structure. It is the work of János Horvay.
>
> The sculptor does not show Kossuth at the triumph of his career and in passionate activity but after the sad ending of the War of Liberation, in a long toga, as a sower of seeds who wishes to plant the seeds of independence in the soul of the nation. His face reflects serene determination and not disappointment. In the other figures vivid gestures express suffering about the fate of the nation and deep concern. On both sides two statues form a tight group. To the left of the principal figure, on Kossuth's right side as viewed from the front, Prime Minister Lajos Batthyány and Minister of the Interior Bertalan Szemere. Minister of Justice Ferenc Deák touches Minister of Defense Lajos Mészáros's arm with his

left hand. To the right of the principal figure, on Kossuth's left side as viewed from the front, is Minister of Public Works and Commerce Count István Széchenyi and Minister of Religion and Education Baron József Eötvös. At the edges Minister of Industry and Agriculture Gábor Klauzál and Prince Pál Eszterházy, minister around the person of the king, form individual groupings.

On the back wall of the statue we see the characteristics of the popular activities of the War for Freedom: saying good bye to wife and children, a man enthused by the events engaged in noisy demonstration, an old man carrying a battle flag with his son, a soldier ready to fight, and another who has already sacrificed his blood and is gravely wounded. Under the relief there is the first verse of Petőfi's poem "Élet és Halál" (Life and Death):

From the Carpathians to the Lower Danube
An angry scream, a wild thunderstorm,
With streaming hair and bloody forehead
Stands the Hungarian alone in the tempest![22]

Knowing in 1908 that the Horvay application had won, the Sunday paper, *Vasárnapi Újság*, opined: "Those who would have preferred to see the agitator Kossuth on the pedestal might have objections to the perception of the artist. Even they cannot change the fact that Horvay's basic concept is more monumental and grandiose than it would have been if he would have created a counterpart to the *Petőfi* statue, and provided posterity with a fiery demonstration of the awakened national conscience. The statesman perhaps would be more fitting in front of the Parliament."[23]

The loyal journalist addressed the crucial issue: if the winning proposal had represented Kossuth as a dynamic agitator, the question would have been asked immediately: against whom and why was Kossuth agitating? The answer would have been incontrovertible: Kos-

[22] Liber, *Budapest szobrai és emléktáblái*, pp. 327–328.

[23] *Vasárnapi Újság*, no. 16 (1908): 317. Károly Lyka speaks of a "sculptural disaster," in *Új Idők*, no. 17 (1908): 358.

suth's life work was to disavow the Hungary which had become a member of the Habsburg monarchy. Thus, there was no need whatever to represent Kossuth as a rebel.

It seems, however, that even after the Francis Joseph era was over the memorial required was just as Horvay designed it at the beginning of the twentieth century. The national context completely adapted itself, without any revolutionary élan, to the worldview of the ruling counter-revolutionary system.[24]

The unveiling of the statue took place with great splendor and in the presence of a large number of people. Naturally the regent, Miklós Horthy, was present. The Lord Mayor, Jenő Sipőcz, spoke for the city which sponsored the statue. The major address was delivered by Count Albert Apponyi. He said that Kossuth's life work consisted of two basic principles and a vigorous energy: "The two ideas, the two principles are that the well being of the nation rested on a solid foundation only if the entire nation was the beneficiary of the legal practices and of its benefits and it could be successful only if it was in sole control of its destiny, according to the guidelines of its own interests and not according to the aims of foreign goals. Stated briefly, the two ideas are the twin ideas of Hungarian national freedom and Hungarian national independence."

The source of the great energy was what reform activities and not revolutionary action provided. According to Apponyi, Kossuth, "Did not believe simply in the success of social reforms, if at the same time the independence of the country was not guaranteed, if the direction of the nation's affairs was not solely in our hands or if there was any doubt remaining that the increased national strength would serve the national autotelism."[25] The ceremony concluded with the singing of the "Hiszekegy" (Hungarian Credo) and of the national anthem.

---

[24] After its unveiling, J. Jenő Tersánszky wrote the following: "Thus, as a whole the statue is all right if it is looked at as a second-rate sculpture. The resignation of the uniformity of the motions of the figures rises to the point of the ludicrous. It would be excessive even for a tomb." See "Kossuth budapesti szobra" [The statue of Kossuth in Budapest], *Nyugat* 20, no. 22 (1927), http://www.epa.oszk.hu/00000/00022/00431/13487.htm.

[25] *Budapesti Hirlap*, November 8, 1927. For the history of the statue, see Lajos Vayer "A Kossuth kultusz a magyar művészetben" [The cult of Kossuth in the arts], in Ádámfy, *A világ Kossuth-szobrai.* For the part about Horvay's statue, see pp. 21–29.

After some uncertainties, the second step in the spiritualization of the square had been taken. According to the ideas that evolved in 1900 there were two more sites on the square: at the northernmost part of the square, and across from the *Kossuth* statue at the southern part of the main area of the square, immediately adjacent to the fountain.

A SIDESTEP—THE *ISTVÁN NAGYATÁDI SZABÓ* STATUE

The statue of István Nagyatádi Szabó, Smallholder Party politician and several times minister of agriculture, was not placed in a major area of the square but at the right wing of the Ministry of Agriculture, at the façade facing the Kossuth Square. The statue is adapted primarily to the ministry and has no particular meaning for the square. From the spiritualistic perspective it has to be viewed as a sidestep.

Furthermore, and probably contrary to the thinking of the sponsors of this statue, it does not represent a statesman, such as Hungarian Kossuth or Andrássy. Nagyatádi Szabó was important only for the conceptual/historical legitimization of the Horthy system. He was a politician who actively participated in 1922 in the establishment of the Egységes Párt (Unified Party), i.e. in the ruling party of the given system.

He died on November 1, 1924. His colleagues created a statue committee on November 13, 1924, and organized a plea for public contributions. In May 1931 submission of designs for the statue were invited.[26] Technically the sponsor was not the state or the city but Nagyatádi's friends. These friends, however, were all ministers or government party representatives. It is perhaps not an exaggeration to speak of a political sponsorship.

According to the criteria for the submissions the statue would be standing on a marble pedestal and would also be adorned with relief representing the handshake between Nagyatádi Szabó and Count István Bethlen, on February 22, 1922. Symbolically it was this handshake which initiated the Unified Party.

---

[26] Liber, *Budapest szobrai és emléktáblái*, pp. 421–423. I used the contemporary press reports about the dedication address.

The president of the statue committee was János Mayer, the minister of agriculture and at the time of the proposal Count István Bethlen was the prime minister.

The deadline for the submissions was September 15, 1931, and forty-nine proposals were received. The committee reached its decision on September 24 and István Szentgyörgyi was the winner.

The statue was rapidly completed and by April 19, 1932, was standing in its assigned location. There was no argument about the site because the area of the square between the façade of the building and the sidewalk, was under the control of the ministry.

It was decided to modify the unveiling ceremony and combine the usual protocol with the representative appearance of the Hungarian nation. It took some time to organize this and therefore the date for the unveiling was moved up to November 20, 1932.

At that time, everybody who mattered was present, from Horthy to Archduke József, from the entire government to the parliamentary representatives. Groups from 2,714 villages were invited to pay their respects.

The statue is three meters tall and represents Nagyatádi Szabó wearing Wellingtons and peasant garb. The relief was present on the pedestal. Underneath it a quotation from Nagyatádi from 1910, "We came to the Parliament to heal wounds and not to make them."

There were several speakers at the unveiling. Prime Minister Gyula Gömbös said, among other things: "In Erdőcsokonya István Nagyatádi Szabó remained a smallholder, but here in the Parliament he became a statesman. As the head of the Hungarian government I repeat the pledge which I gave in his house in Erdőcsokonya, when he said to me, 'Son, after I die take care of the Hungarian peasant and look after him.' Now here, in front of the Parliament I renew the answer I gave him at that time, 'I will watch over the Hungarian peasant, I will watch over everyone for whom the Hungarians are sacred.'"

István Bethlen, standing before the relief depicting him referred to the Land Reform Act of 1920 (Act XXXVI of 1920) linked to the name of Nagyatádi Szabó, and said: "István Nagyatádi Szabó came to the Parliament as a true-born son of the Hungarian village. He was a novel, but totally Hungarian soul. His is the lion's share for reestablishing the peace of the countryside after the postwar revolutions. It was his doing that provided land and homes to hundreds of thousand landless Hungarians."

The *Nagyatádi Szabó* statue is formally on the square but did not affect the spiritual content of the square. It represents an ongoing, given political course rather than an elevated political essence.

Another Sidestep—The Martyrs of the Nation Memorial

Another memorial had a politically legitimating function similar to the Nagyatádi Szabó one. It was not on the square but still became part of the visual spectrum of the southern part of the square. While the Nagyatádi Szabó one served only to justify policies, the Martyrs of the Nation 1918–1919 Memorial added sanctity to politics. I will not spend much time discussing it because topographically it is not part of the square. Yet, from a particular angle it is one of the sights of the square.

The memorial was unveiled on March 18, 1934. The area where three streets, Báthory Street, Vecsey Street, and Nádor Street come together was named Vértanúk tere (Martyrs' Square) in 1936 because of the site of the memorial. The area was briefly known as Ságvári Square but is now again known as Martyrs' Square.

According to a contemporary description the memorial, designed by sculptor Richárd Füredi and engineer Jenő Lechner, was carved of Haraszt limestone. It consisted of:

> A stepped pedestal from which a mighty stone pillar emerges, capped by a stone coffin decorated with Hungarian motifs dating back to the original conquest of the land. On both sides there was a sacrificial cup, resting on the head of a bull, copied from the so-called Attila treasure. On festive occasions these cups would hold either a candle or were used to burn incense. On one side of the column there is a huge statue of the Hungaria with an inscription below it: "To the martyrs of 1918–1919." On the other side of the column a strong muscular man fights a victorious battle with a monster writhing under his feet. Below it the inscription: "Erected with piety by the Hungarian nation on the initiative of the White House."[27]

---

[27] Liber, *Budapest szobrai és emléktáblái*, pp. 388–389.

Hungaria looks toward the Parliament. The monster, being defeated by the man, represents communism. "White House" refers to a social organization under the leadership of Archduke József, the White House Fraternal Organization, which in fact initiated the memorial plans in 1929. They collected the funds, received a major donation from the capital city, hired the sculptor and the architect, but the city fathers determined the site of the memorial.

The names of people murdered during the Soviet Republic were engraved on the memorial, but the first name on the list is that of Count István Tisza who was murdered at the start of the liberal democratic revolution in 1918.

The Third Step—The Count István Tisza Memorial

Tisza was murdered in his home in Budapest on October 31, 1918, the same day when Count Mihály Károlyi was appointed prime minister. In this sense he was the first victim of the liberal democratic revolution. This was the revolution in antithesis to which the Horthy regime defined itself.

It was an obvious step for the system to erect a statue in honor of Tisza. He was a victim of 1918 who always endorsed the concepts of Hungarian supremacy and of the inviolable nature of historic Hungary. Even though a liberal politician, he followed a generally conservative path and, if necessary, used non-parliamentary methods to control parliament.

He had strong relations to the Parliament as prime minister, as representative and as president of the assembly. Thus he could be viewed by the system as a precursor to be followed. As a counterpart to Andrássy, the obvious site for him was at the northernmost part of the square in front of the entrance to the Upper House.

In 1927 the István Tisza Memorial Committee was established. An appeal was made to all who respected the Parliament and the memory of István Tisza, to make contributions toward the Tisza monument. The appeal was written by Ferenc Herczeg, one of the best known writers of the day and a friend and colleague of Tisza. It declared:

> Rising from the mist of worldly existence, the noble figure of István Tisza stands in a bright light. He was an enlightening leader of the nation, filled with courage and unselfishness: an eternal image of the true man and the true Hungarian. His life was filled with superhuman struggle which he engaged in to save the falling nation. The fate of the country was weighing on his shoulders, every pain suffered by the Hungarians echoed in his heart. When the death bell tolled over the country, his blood was the first one that stained his country's soil red. The thousand year-old country had no son who was more unselfish than he, and there was no one who was more misunderstood. The nation does justice to itself when it elevates the memory of István Tisza. His bronze statue shall stand in the capital city and it will be the symbol of Hungarian unanimity and of the manly courage surviving all blows of fate.[28]

According to an established pattern, namely the *Nagyatádi Szabó* statue and the Martyrs' Memorial, this appeared to be a social endeavor. In fact it was a political process. Among the donors, and with generous contributions, we find the Lower and Upper Houses of Parliament, Budapest, and Tisza's native area, Bihar County.

The application package went out in 1919 and, within the same year, the award was given to the aged György Zala and to his associate Antal Orbán. The crafting of the pedestal was entrusted to Ernő Foerk.[29]

The memorial was unveiled with great festivity on April 22, 1934, in the park-like area in front of the northern entrance to the Parliament. At this time there was no building yet between this area and the Margit Bridge.

The statue group rests on a pedestal of Haraszt limestone. A historian of statues wrote:

---

[28] *Budapesti Hirlap*, November 1, 1927.

[29] For the applications see Ervin Ybl, "A Tisza-szobor pályamunkái" [The design submissions for the *Tisza* statue], *Budapesti Hirlap*, June 16, 1929; and Márius Rabinovszky, "Tisza emlékműve. Pályázati kiállítás a Műcsarnokban" [The Tisza Memorial. Exhibit of the submissions in the Art Galery], *Nyugat* 2, no. 13 (1929): 61–62.

In the foreground, the twice life-size *Tisza* statue shows the prime minister in a dignified stance with the arms folded. It was not the politician who was looking down but the proud figure of a man who looked at the murderous gun with cold indifference.

The memorial was adorned on each side with a group of bronze statues. On the right a group of farmers representing the former bounty of the country. On the other side the statue of a soldier saying goodbye to his family represented Sacrifice, a man with an anvil represented Work, and a woman with a paper and a compass represented Science. The large-scale subsidiary figures had thematically little relationship to Tisza. It can be said with some exaggeration that they could have appeared on the memorial of any important politician. On top of a huge stone column, behind Tisza, approximately ten meters from the ground, there is a mortally wounded lion fighting with a serpent, carved from a block of limestone. According to official explanation it represented Intrigue.[30]

The memorial was seveteen meters high, Tisza's statue, facing south, was five meters, the subsidiary forms were 4.6–4.8 meters. The lion was carved from a stone of thirty-six cubic meters.

At the unveiling of the statue, Prime Minister Gyula Gömbös and Albert Berzeviczy, the chairman of the statue committee spoke. Berzeviczy explained the statue and introduced Tisza as a symbol of self-sacrifice. He said:

> Much of his fight was against those impediments, which were rooted in the parliamentary system and which obstructed or delayed the evolution and effectiveness of our national defenses. He saw clearly that our dealing with our enemies, who were trying to destroy us, could be delayed but could not be avoided and that we would have to be prepared and strong when it came. Among his former opponents there are unbiased gentlemen who admit today that it had been a mistake to endorse the fight for advances in civil law in preference to developing the requirements of our national security.

---

30 Prohászka, *Szoborhistoriák*, pp. 114–115.

> In this parliamentary fight he twice resorted to violence. The first one resulted in sweeping him and his party from the sphere of active politics. The experiences of the next few years, however, convinced the nation that even though the method he chose was a dangerous one, there could be no doubt about his goals and about the validity of his motives. Consequently, when he reached for dangerous weapons for the second time, the nation acquiesced and the other components of the legislature and public opinion quasi sanctified the decisions of the House of Representatives, regardless how irregularly achieved.
>
> Whatever we have from István Tisza today is memorialized by this statue, erected by the piety of the nation and which we hand over to the capital city for preservation. It is the beating heart of our nation.[31]

There was only one available space left on the square, across from Kossuth, on the southern side of the central part of the square.

The Fourth Step— The Ferenc II Rákóczi Memorial

Prince Ferenc II Rákóczi died in 1735, in exile in Rodosto (Tekirdağ) in Turkey. He went into exile after his fight for freedom with the Habsburgs, trying to protect the rights of the Hungarian nobility. His followers made peace with the court; having achieved most of their goals, but Rákóczi did not wish to become a party to and a beneficiary of the compromise. Around his movement and his person a whole Hungarian mythology developed. The nineteenth century Hungarian

---

[31] Albert Berzeviczy, "Berzeviczy Albert ig. And t.t. elnök beszéde gróf Tisza István emlékszobrának leleplezésekor" [Address of director and president of the advisory council, Albert Berzeviczy, at the unveiling of the memorial statue of Count István Tisza in Budapest on April 22, 1934], *Akadémiai Értesítő* 19 (April–September 1934): 94–98. For the deeply critical reaction to the statue, see Artúr Elek, "Tisza István szobra" [The statue of István Tisza], *Magyar Művészet* (1934): 169–174; Zoltán Farkas, "Tisza István szobra," [The statue of István Tisza], *Nyugat* 27, no. 9 (1934): 515; and Rusztem Vámbéry, "A szobor" [The statue], *Századunk* (1934): 135–137.

independence endeavors viewed him and his followers, the Kurucok (Crusaders), as precursors. In 1906 his ashes were brought back and were solemnly deposited in the Kassa (Košice) Dome.[32] There was only one person who managed to become more of a part of Hungarian mythology: Kossuth.

After Trianon Hungary became independent but was permeated with a feeling of injury, knowing that one third of the former country was now under foreign rule. For this reason there was an increased need for a national mythology. It was in 1926 that the National Rákóczi Association was formed to "Permeate the lax Hungarian society with a strong national consciousness."[33] It was evident that the Rákóczi cult could serve the interests of the revisionist Hungarian nationalism. There being no *Rákóczi* statue in Budapest, the Rákóczi Association assiduously strove for a *Rákóczi* statue to be erected.

With the two hundreth anniversary of his death approaching and because the Rákóczi cult seemed eminently useful politically, Prime Minister Gyula Gömbös embraced the idea and convinced the regent to endorse the matter of the *Rákóczi* statue. In August 1934 Horthy ordered that a *Rákóczi* statue be erected on the Kossuth Square.[34]

The anniversary was in 1935 but the decision-makers were late as usual and therefore State Secretary István Bárczy, the official responsible for the issue, omitted the formalities of applications and entrusted János Pásztor to produce the statue.[35] The erection of the pedestal was entrusted to Dénes Györgyi.[36] The statue was unveiled on May 2, 1937, two years after the anniversary.

---

32 Hajnal Halász, Csaba Katona, and Zoltán Ólmosi, eds., *Dokumentumok II. Rákoczi Ferenc és társai újratemetéséhez (1883–1906)* [Documents to the Reburial of Ferenc II Rákóczi and His Associates, 1883–1906] (Budapest: MOL, 2004).

33 Ákos Kovács, "A ló kérdez. A Rákóczi-szobor mint kultuszhely" [The horse asks. The *Rákóczi* statue as a cult site], *Magyar Narancs*, no. 44 (November 2, 2006).

34 "Ahogyan a szobor készült" [How the statue was made], *Budapesti Hirlap*, May 2, 1937.

35 "Pásztor Jánosné emlékezései" [Recollections of Mrs. János Pásztor], manuscript, archives, Magyar Nemzeti Galéria (Hungarian National Galery). Bárczy told Pásztor that he (i.e. Pásztor) would make a new *Kossuth* statue.

36 The Györgyi plans for the Rákóczi Memorial can be found in the architectural collection of the urban history section of the Kiscelli Museum of the Budapest Historical Museum (inventory no. 66120 i–34).

The memorial is baroque in style and faces north. If it would look toward the south the other mythological personality across from it, the bronze Kossuth would look at the rear end of the horse. Rákóczi, on a prancing horse, faces the Parliament. On both sides of the pedestal there are inscriptions. On the one side the sentence which comes from the proclamation that Rákóczi addressed to the nation and that signaled the beginnings of the fight for freedom. On the other side the prince's motto: "With God for country and freedom." Both inscriptions are in Latin. On the back it is stated: "Erected by the Hungarian nation on the occasion of the two-hundredth anniversary of Rákóczi's death." The year is given as 1935–1937.

The unveiling was performed with the usual ceremonies in the presence of the regent.[37] The principal address was delivered by Bálint Hóman, the minister of culture. He spoke at length and, at the end he summarized his remarks as follows:

> Today we salute in Ferenc Rákóczi one of the greatest representatives of purposeful Hungarian politics, the representative of the concept of national independence and the first proponent of the Hungarian national idea which transgresses social barriers and which expresses the racial, cultural, and national identity of the Hungarians living both within and beyond the borders. We see in him the symbolic personification of the living national conscience, of the national self-confidence, of the national willingness to make sacrifices, of the active strength of the nation, and of the constructive national determination. Without this there is no national life, with it resurrection will come![38]

---

37 "A Rákóczi szobor leleplezésének ünnepi rendje" [The program for the unveiling of the *Rákóczi* statue], *Budapesti Hirlap*, April 25, 1937.

38 "Történelmi fény és pompa a Rákóczi-szobor leleplezésén" [Historical glow and pomp at the unveiling of the *Rákóczi* statue], *Budapesti Hirlap*, May 4, 1937. For the critical echo: Zoltán Farkas, "Rákóczi szobra" [The statue of Rákóczi], *Nyugat* 27, no. 16 (1934): 233; Aurél Kárpáti, "Két új lovas szobor" [Two new equestrian statues], *Pesti Napló*, May 6, 1937; Ervin Ybl, "Pásztor János újabb szobrai" [The new statues of János Pásztor], *Magyar Művészet*, (1938): 129–137.

The square, at least in a spiritual sense, was complete. Those in a position of power who thought about it must have agreed with this. There were no more spaces, every space had an occupant.

A New Situation—Damage, Destruction, Purging

By 1945 Hungary's situation and political structure had changed. The country emerged from the World War II, which it fought as an ally of Germany, as a loser. The Germans were expelled from Hungary by the Soviet army which then occupied the country for a long time. The loss of the war also meant the end of the Horthy system.

Starting in 1945 a new constellation came into existence, in which after a democratic start the Stalinist-Communist influence increased in strength. By 1948 the Soviet system was in complete control.

The square also suffered during the war. The *Andrássy* statue was damaged, and so was the principal figure of the Tisza monument. In addition the Germans destroyed the bridges in Budapest and the idea of a temporary bridge became a matter of emergency.

It was evident that something had to be done with the damaged statues. The Andrássy case seemed to be the simpler one because the Pest bridgehead of the temporary bridge was constructed precisely over the area where the statue stood. Thus it was removed from Kossuth Square. On May 16, 1945, a start was made on the piers of the new bridge. It opened for pedestrian traffic on January 15, 1946. Three days later it was opened for vehicular traffic. The removal of this bridge was completed by January 1, 1963. In 1971 a memorial stone was placed at the former Kossuth Square end of the bridge with an inscription: "This is where the Kossuth Bridge used to be."[39] The *Andrássy* statue, which was taken down during the summer of 1945, never again regained its place.

During the siege of Budapest the *Tisza* statue was also damaged. The injured principal figure was knocked down during the spring of

---

[39] László Berza, ed., *Budapest Lexikon, A–K* (Budapest: Akadémiai Kiadó, 1993), p. 708.

1945. It is not known who did it. The fragments were removed during the summer of 1945 and the remainder of the memorial was removed in 1948.[40]

The Public Works Council decided on April 16, 1945, that the National Martyrs' Memorial on Martyr's Square had to be removed just like the *Tisza* statue. Both of them were considered to be counterrevolutionary memorials. In September 1945, some young people, presumably leftists, not waiting for the official action, knocked down the memorial.[41]

Demolition was the fate of the *Nagyatádi Szabó* statue as well. In 1948 the relief showing the handshake with Bethlen was removed and in 1949 the entire structure was put in storage.[42]

It seems that the new system, just like the Horthy one, considered the spirituality of the square to be of importance. The Horthy system populated the square with expropriated ancestors, the new system did away with these spiritual sites. One system reacted in a positive fashion the other in a negative one to the demands of spirituality which they both sensed keenly.

Of the four statues that had been removed this was the case for three of them. The counterrevolutionary system erected them, the new regime disposed of them.

It was only the disappearance of the *Andrássy* statue that was not due simply to the enthusiasm to change the spiritual content of the square. The damaged statue had to be removed because of the bridge but it could have been set up somewhere else, if....If, according to the storage report, the statue was not in an irreparable condition.[43] The Communist system obviously disliked the reliefs, but had no problem with Andrássy himself. They condemned the Compromise as inconsis-

---

[40] Prohászka, *Szoborhistóriák*, pp. 113–116; Potó, *Az emlékeztetés helyei*, pp. 43–46. These works inform us about the sometimes adventurous fate of the removed statues. See also János Potó, "A Tisza szobor építése, lerombolása" [The Erection and destruction of the *Tisza* statue], *História* 29, no. 4 (2007): 28–29.

[41] Potó, *Az emlékeztetés helyei*, pp. 50–52.

[42] Ibid., pp. 84–86.

[43] Mihály Pál, inspector of monuments, visited the workshop of Vignali Gusmann and reported: "Andrássy's equestrian statue, bronze. The work of Zala. It is in several pieces and cannot be repaired." In "Mihály Pál emlékműkiadó jelentése" [Report of Mihály Pál, inspector of monuments], July 9, 1949, XXIII, 114, fol. 10, a 3855–4/1950, (5834), BFL. The archival material also reveals that much of the bronze, very valuable after the war, was systematically stolen.

tent with their own historically legitimized worldview, but they did not touch the *Deák* statue. The most representative avenue in Budapest was called the Andrássy Avenue until 1950. It was then changed to Stalin Avenue. In 1950 Josip Vissarionovich Stalin was greater and more important than anybody or anything. Since 1990, following some renaming detours, the avenue again bears Andrássy's name.

It is a fact that after the war there were empty places on the Kossuth Square and the possibility of spiritualizing it again came to the fore.

Kossuth to Replace Kossuth

In the Communist interpretation of history a high position was given to revolutions and to the idea of "social progress." The entire independence tradition could be viewed in this way because the struggle for freedom could be shown as a form of class struggle. The oppressed Hungarians were fighting against the oppressor Habsburgs and against the lackeys serving them.

The spotty political legitimization added value to the justification of power through history. Neither the Horthyites nor the Communists could say that they were the trustees of the freely expressed popular will. They thus had to have historic justification. It was unique for each system but the elements of justification were the same.

For the Communist justification of power national independence traditions, re-interpreted as concepts of social progress and class struggle, had always been important. The Hungarian language broadcasting station they set up during their exile in the Soviet Union was called the Kossuth Station. This all became even more important when they came to power. On the 1848 centennial in 1948 the Communists claimed that they are the true heirs of 1848–49 and of the Hungarian independence and freedom movements.[44] They said this in a country that was under Soviet occupation and had no autonomy, which was the reason for their being in power.

It became evident that the Communist system would not remove Kossuth or Rákóczi from the square. It was not evident whether they needed a depressed, sad Kossuth.

---

44 Gerő, *Imagined History*, pp. 144–149.

The *Kossuth* statue had also been damaged during the war. In 1948 the authorities believed that it was worthwhile to repair it. It was not completed for the centenary but was almost finished by 1949. At this time they still thought that the Horvay *Kossuth* statue would remain.[45]

The year of 1952 was approaching, the hundred-fiftieth anniversary of Kossuth's birth. In spite of the fact that the Kossuth on Kossuth Square was repaired and patched up it was decided that, instead of the figure filled with gloom, a precommunist, people's tribune figure would be desirable.

In 1951 a government committee was set up. Its task was the "monumental construction of...Lajos Kossuth's heroic figure." The contest was announced and at its meeting on October 30–31, 1951, the committee rendered its final decision.

Forty-three artists had submitted designs for the statue to be erected on the Kossuth Square replacing the old one. According to the decision the award was given to Zsigmond Kisfaludi Strobl, András Kocsis, and Lajos Ungvári with the stipulation that the figure of Kossuth had to be carved by Kisfaludi.[46] As described in *Szabad Művészet*,

> The memorial was erected in an expressive compositional form. The principal figure of the harmonically composed group of statues is the bronze statue of Lajos Kossuth. The fiery leader of the 1848 War of Liberation stands on a tall, dark red stone pedestal. The structure of the memorial has wings on both sides at a level lower than the principal statue. It is here that the other figures of the memorial are located with three mighty bronze statues on each side.
>
> Lajos Kossuth points forward with his right hand. With this motion he encourages the people to rebel and to arm itself. The statue represents him at the culminating moment of his great oration. The Kossuth who stands before us is the one who, in Comrade

[45] According to the text on the Lord Mayor's stationary, the city accepted the bid of sculptor and stone carver Ágoston Fischer for the repair of the Kossuth statue group. The description reveals that some of the statues were damaged by shrapnel, breaking off certain parts. The pedestal was also damaged. See XXIII, 114 3835–135/1950, BFL.

[46] *Szabad Művészet*, (1951): 508. The models were shown at an exhibition. Gábor O. Pogány, "A Tavaszi Tárlat anyaga" [Material of the Spring Exhibition], *Szabad Művészet*, (1951): 201–207.

Révai's characterization, "Called the people to arm with revolutionary fervor, did not shrink from a critical situation but faced the storm, and dared to stand up against it bravely and courageously." And who, "In 1848–49 dared to entrust the defense of the country to the strong arms of the masses, did not shrink from mobilizing the people, and who dared to rely on the multitudes." The intrepid fighter in the struggle against the oppressors, the true patriot speaks to the people with his strength increasing many times in the hours of peril.

The sculptural display of the secondary figures is particularly striking. The designers and sculptors were not satisfied with only the principal figure displaying his revolutionary character but also put considerable emphasis on the figures surrounding Kossuth. It was only thus that the Kossuth concepts could be made fully comprehensible. The simple sons of the country appear here, to offer their life to Kossuth and to their country, if necessary. On Kossuth's left the armed worker grasping a rifle, the young law student and the peasant representing the people of the land, all express great strength and a fighting determination. On the other side, on Kossuth's right, a dynamically moving '48-er Hungarian soldier is saying good bye to his wife and child, leaving for a glorious fight against the invaders. It is this composition to which, tightly linked, we see an elderly peasant worn out by villeinage, one of the former serfs having regained his human dignity. He looks toward Kossuth with gratitude and determination shining from his face."[47]

The statue was unveiled on Kossuth's one hundred-fiftieth birthday, on September 19, 1952. The formal address was delivered by József Révai. The speech shows, in many respects, why the newly refashioned, precommunist Kossuth was important for the regime. Among other things, Révai said,

We know that Lajos Kossuth was a man of the still-evolving bourgeois society. He was not a socialist and never became one. He

[47] László Halápi, "Az új budapesti Kossuth-szobor" [The new *Kossuth* statue in Budapest], *Szabad Művészet*, (1951): 496–498. For the fate of the *Horvay* statue, see Prohászka, *Szoborhistóriák*, p.80.

> was a patriot and he fought for social progress. It is this which entitles us Communists and representatives of the workers and of the working people to view ourselves as the heirs of his progressive ideas and the continuers of his work. We are the only ones who have the right to do this, no one else does.
>
> Today's government of the People's Republic can proudly say of itself that it is the heir to Lajos Kossuth's revolutionary, national government. Our people's democracy accepts a relationship with that national-revolutionary state power which Kossuth labored so hard to create among the fires of the War of Liberation.

Révai finished his speech by saying,

> The Hungarian people builds a new country for itself, it wants peace and does not bother anyone. But while building peacefully and working to realize our great five-year plan the Hungarian people have not forgotten Lajos Kossuth's message! For the country, for Hungarian independence, and for the accomplishments of our socialist building programs it is willing to work and fight under Mátyás Rákosi's leadership, just as well as it did a century earlier under the leadership of Lajos Kossuth.[48]

The equation is simple: the Communists are the sole heirs of Lajos Kossuth. Mátyás Rákosi is the leader of the Communists. Rákosi is therefore Kossuth's only legitimate heir and successor.

The representatives of the working classes, formed into statues and appearing at the rear of the Kossuth statue were also placed, as decorative elements, in front of the Ministry of Agriculture. In 1954 it was the *Agronomist Woman* and in 1956 the *Man with a Scythe*, both the work of Árpád Somogy.[49]

---

[48] For József Révai's dedication address, see Zoltán I. Tóth , ed., *Emlékkönyv Kossuth Lajos születésének 150, évfordulójára* [Memorial Volume on the Occasion of the 150th Anniversary of Lajos Kossuth's Birth] (Budapest: Akadémiai Kiadó, 1952), vol. 1, pp. vi and viii.

[49] It was designed as a decorative element and hence there was no inscription on the statues. This was mentioned immediately. See *Béke és Szabadság*, no. 24 (1954): 15. According to the statement nobody knew what or whom it depicted. This is true even today.

A New Element—The National Banner

The process of Communist spiritualization was broken by what happened in the square on October 25, 1956. From this day on, spilling of blood, mass murder, and the concept of the Kossuth Square were linked. The ones who carried on the system would have had a hard time trying to make people forget what happened. All they could do is to keep quiet about it.

After 1956 nothing happened in the square for nine years. In 1965 a flagpole for the National Banner was erected on the main part of the square, between the *Kossuth* statue and the main entrance to the Parliament, close to the Alkotmány Street corner of the Curia. This served the purpose of displaying the National Banner on certain state holidays and thus creating a certain ritual around the event, including honor guards, etc. On the designated days the square thus became the site of state self-representation. I could say that the state created a spiritual and symbolic spot on the square. The National Banner did not have any specific conceptual content associated with it. The structure was functional and meant nothing more than what it was designed to do. It was not built as a memorial and its content was furnished by the combination of the banner, the designated holiday, and the celebration.[50] The pedestal of the National Banner was rebuilt in 2006 but it remained purely functional.

I have no proof for it but I do believe that it was the bloody event of 1956 which took place in the square that was the reason behind the National Banner's functional Puritanism. It seemed that the direct political power-based spiritualization of the square could not continue, at least not through the existing regime. More accurately, there could be spiritualization but not in the same way as before.

---

[50] It can not be compared to the profoundly ideological irredentist memorial, the "National Banner with Relics," which was erected on Szabadság (Freedom) Square. It was unveiled on August 20, 1928. This monument was dismantled in 1945 and in its place there is the Soviet Heroes' Memorial. The National Banner with Relics, in all its elements was related to the ruling regime and to the revisionist ideas. See Miklós Zeidler, *Ideas on Territorial Revision in Hungary, 1920–1945* (Boulder, CO: East European Monographs, 2007), pp. 191–193; and Rajna, *Budapest köztéri szobrainak katalógusa*, pp. 207–208.

There were still two unfilled sites on the square, Tisza's in the south and Andrássy's in the north.

Tisza Replaced by Károlyi

An anniversary furnished an opportunity to fill Tisza' place. Count Mihály Károlyi, Tisza's great adversary and the leading statesman of the 1918 revolution, was born on March 4, 1875. He was the prime minister of the revolution and the president of the new republic. After the Soviet Republic was proclaimed, he emigrated at the beginning of July 1919. The victorious counterrevolution condemned him in absentia and confiscated his property. He returned after World War II and became the second republic's ambassador in Paris. In 1949, fleeing the Stalinism in Hungary he again sought exile and died in France in 1955. The one-hundreth anniversary of his birth was in 1975.

Károlyi was not a communist although his ideas were occasionally very close to this concept. He was emotionally tied to 1918 and was just as opposed to the Horthy system as to the Rákosi rule. His persona, however, was not antitethic to the so-called "People's Front" politics of the 70s. The leader of the post-1956 Communist system, János Kádár, who could utilize what he had learned in 1956, shaped that era with the un-Leninist slogan, "whoever is not against us is with us."

The "People's Front" approach was extended to the dead as well precisely in order to buttress with history that which they proclaimed as being their path. They believed that the dead could legitimize the regime.

It did take some political perversity to place Károlyi on Tisza's site, when they could have put him on Andrássy's. Delicate sensitivity is not usually a feature of politically oriented thinking, particularly not in the case of authoritarian regimes.

As it was customary in the Communist system, the erection of the Károlyi statue came as a suggestion from the Central Committee of the Party. The Agitation and Propaganda Department of the Central Committee took a position, the Science and Public Instruction Department recommended, and the group holding the real power in the Party, the Political Committee, decided to dedicate and crown with a wreath the bronze statue of Mihály Károlyi, cast by Imre Varga.[51] It was also decided at the April 9, 1974, meeting of the Political Committee that at the dedication the address would be given by János Péter, the vice president of the National Assembly. At the February 25, 1975, meeting they also decided who would place the wreaths.[52]

The statue was dedicated on March 3, 1975. It closely reflects the Parliament: the approximately 220 centimeter Károlyi, stands on a gray granite pedestal. Behind him, in imitation of the Parliament's Gothic style, two visually joined arches. The sculptor shows Károlyi with a cane. He wears glasses and seems to emerge from the Parliament in a suit decorated with a fancy handkerchief.[53] On the left-side arch there is an inscription: "Mihály Károlyi, the president of the first republic."[54]

The erection of the statue is testimony to the weight of the People's Front politics and the place of the speaker in the political hierarchy indicates that we were dealing with a relatively minor matter.

There was only one place left.

---

51 "Jegyzőkönyv a Politikai Bizottság 1974. április 9-én megtartott üléséről" [Minutes of the April 9, 1974 meeting of the Political Committee], M-KS 288 f. 5/634, ö.e. R/69, MOL.

52 "Jegyzőkönyv a Politikai Bizottság 1975. február 25-én megtartott üléséről" [Minutes of the February 25, 1975 meeting of the Political Committee], M-KS 288 f. 5/658, o.e. R/69, MOL.

53 It was not an accident that Imre Varga was entrusted with the preparation of the statue. He was a gifted artist who maintained close relationships with the prominent members of the regime. (Christa Nickel, *Beszélgetések Varga Imrével* [Conversations with Imre Varga] *Imre Varga im Gespräch* (Budapest: Nickel Ch., 1995), p. 59; Zoltán Árpási, *Varga Imre: A gondolat mestere* [Imre Varga: the Master of Thought] (Budapest: Kossuth Kiadó, 2002), pp. 105–107. Árpási reports that Katinka Andrássy, Károlyi's widow took exception to the fancy handkerchief and to the monocle that was part of the original design. György Aczél, the omnipotent cultural politician of the system offered Varga a compromise. Let the monocle disappear and he may keep the handkerchief. Varga naturally agreed to what Aczél asked and this is why Károlyi is shown with glasses. In this he, Katinka, and Aczél all followed the traditions. The Andrássy family also interfered in the matter of the *Andrássy* statue. They asked that he be shown on horseback. Prime Minister István Tisza interfered and claimed that on the relief of the Berlin Congress, Alajos Károlyi's dress was not Hungarian enough. Zala complied with all requests. As it can be seen, contrary to all appearances, in Hungarian history the method of dealing with problems had not changed.

54 For criticism of the statue, see Zoltán Nagy, "Varga Imre Károlyi szobra" [The statue of Imre Varga], *Kritika*, no. 5 (1975); András Székely, "'Száz év szobrászata,' Varga Imre: Károlyi Mihály" ["The plastic arts of one hundred years," Imre Varga: Mihály Károlyi], *Népszabadság*, April 3, 1978; Márta Harangozó, *Varga Imre* (Budapest: Rézkarcoló Művészek Alkotóközössége, 1989); and Nóra Aradi, "A szobrász és a történelmi tudat" [The sculptor and historic awareness], *Művészet*, no. 5 (1979).

Andrássy replaced by Attila József

Another anniversary offered an opportunity to fill the empty space. It was Attila József's seventy-fifth birthday on April 11, 1980. The poet, who had committed suicide in 1937, was canonized, appropriately, as one of the most outstanding lyricists in Hungarian literature. The Communist system liked him particularly well not only because at one time he was a member of the illegal Communist Party but also because he was most deserving of affection. A number of his poems and lines could be appropriated directly in political slogans and his unquestionable talents and human credibility could serve as justification for the system. He was a man who could be understood politically but who had no political accomplishments. He fit well with the Kádár system which represented the People's Front but which preferred to depoliticize it.

It was on March 30, 1979, that Dezső Tóth, the deputy minister of culture, went to the Agitation and Propaganda Committee of the Party in the matter of celebrating the seventy-fifth anniversary of the poet's birth. At the end of 1979, the Central Committee recommended György Aczél, the deputy prime minister to chair the memorial committee to be established. At this time the plans did not yet include the erection of a statue.[55]

This was only considered officially, during the autumn, after the poet's birthday. The minister of culture wrote,

Proposal

To the Agitation and Propaganda Committee of the CC of the HSWP on erecting an *Attila József* statue.

---

[55] "Tóth Dezső előterjeszése az MSZMP KB Agitációs és Propaganda Bizottság április 10–I ülésére, továbbá az MSZMP KB Tudományos és Közoktatási és Kulturális Osztály javaslata a Politikai Bizottságnak (1979. december 3., Kornidesz Mihály)" [Dezső Tóth's proposal to the CC of the HSWP (Central Committee of the Hungarian Socialist Workers' Party) Agitation and Propaganda Committee meeting on April 10 and the recommendation of the Scientific, Public Education and Cultural Division of the MSZMP KB to the Political Committee (December 3, 1979, Mihály Kornidesz)], MOL.

> The Council of the Budapest Capital City, in agreement with the Propaganda and Education Committee of the Budapest Committee of the HSWP would like to erect László Marton's statue "At the Danube" in honor of the seventy-fifth anniversary of Attila József's birth. The statue shows the poet sitting on three steps looking at the Danube.
>
> Concerning the place for the statue the capital city, in agreement with the Arts and Crafts Expert Committee, makes the following recommendation:
>
> Sixty meters from the Parliament, at the southern façade of the Parliament, at the confluence of the Akadémia Street and Garibaldi Street, and at the intersection of the axis of the southern main entrance to the Parliament with the extension of the northern façade of the Chamber of Commerce building.
>
> The Ministry of Education is in agreement with the above recommendation and we are requesting the approval, in principle, of the Agitation and Propaganda Committee. Budapest, September 26, 1980.
>
> Imre Pozsgay[56]

The wording suggests that progress had been made in this matter but, so far as the birthday was concerned, they were quite late. The wording also suggests that it was the capital city that recommended the site, although, knowing the way the system worked, we cannot be certain about this. It is very possible that the site was suggested by somebody on the Central Committee.

Henceforth there was no question about the statue and the site. The only matter of suspense remaining was whether they could still make it within the year 1980, now that they had already missed the birthday.

They managed, albeit barely. The statue, the pedestal of which was designed by György Vadász, was unveiled on December 21, 1980. Attila József is a bronze figure, 3.5 meter tall, sitting on a three 60 cen-

---

[56] "Pozsgay Imre előterjesztése az MSZMP KB Agitációs és Propaganda Bizottsághoz József Attila szobor felállításáról" [Imre Pozsgay's proposal to the CC of the HSWP's Agitation and Propaganda Committee on erecting a statue of Attila József], September 26, 1980, XIX, pp. 1–7, MOL.

timeter high steps. He holds his hat in his hand, his shoes are already unlaced and his coat lies on the ground beside him. Next to him, on an oval stone there is an inscription: "As though it flowed from my heart, the turbulent, wise and grand Danube" (Attila József, "By the Danube").

The statue was unveiled by Zoltán Szépvölgyi, the president of the Capital City Council during a relatively modest celebration. He spoke of the poet's Marxist-Leninist views and also mentioned that, "He had understood the life of the workers and the peasants, having shared it. His poetry was to serve them."[57]

With Attila József the square was once again filled. It had gained a different kind of spirituality from the time when it was first filled in 1937.

The spiritualization of the square was begun during the Dualist Era but it was not completed then. The system came to an end before it could accomplish it. The Horthy system completed the square according to its own spiritual needs but a few years later this system also disappeared. Then came the Communist world and in the aura of the temple of the constitution created what it wanted. It also completed and filled up the square. Of course, Communism also came to an end.

Spiritual Explosion—Spiritual Fragments

From 1989–1990 to essentially 2001 a real spiritual explosion took place on the Kossuth Square.

Nobody wanted to disturb the memorials already there. Who would have wanted to bother with Rákóczi at the time when Hungary gained its independence? Who would have wanted to make Kossuth disappear just when the constitutional form of a people's desires and parliamentary representation returned to life from suspended animation? Who would have wanted to make Károlyi disappear when Hungary became a republic from having been a people's republic? Who would have

---

[57] For the dedication, see *Magyar Hirlap*, December 23, 1980. For critical echoes, see Gyula Rózsa, "A dunaparti József Attila szobor" [The *Attila József* statue on the bank of the Danube], *Kritika*, no. 7 (1981): 23–24; and László Heitler, *Marton László* (Budapest: Képzőművészeti Kiadó, 1985), pp. 37–38.

wanted to raise his hand against one of Hungary's greatest lyricists? As soon as the Communist system disappeared these spiritual points lost the contextualization which until that time was attributed to them by the regime.

In Budapest many statues, which were directly related in principle to the Communist era, disappeared, or went into storage. The statues of Kossuth Square did not and could not suffer the same fate. The essence of the spiritualization was not the disappearance of the former spiritualization.

It was difference in concept. It was part of the square's history, covered by silence since 1956. We are speaking of the victims of the mass murder by the machine gun volleys of October 25, 1956. They did not fit, could not fit, into the worldview of the Communist system, but they were part of the history of 1956 and of the square.[58]

The Magyar Demokrata Forum (Hungarian Democratic Forum) placed the first memorial tablet on the wall of the Ministry of Agriculture, at its corner with Alkotmány Street, and facing the square. It reads, "To the memory of our compatriots who marched into this square on October 25, 1956, many of whom became victims of violence. Erected by the Fifth District Organization of the Hungarian Democratic Forum, October 25, 1989." Because administratively Kossuth Square is part of the fifth district the tablet was signed by the recently organized party's district organization.

One of the first laws enacted by the National Assembly, elected in 1990, was to declare the first day of the uprising, October 23, 1956, a national holiday. This gave further incentive to the societal demand that a sanctified representation of the victims of the salvo and of '56 appear in the spiritualization of the square.

In 1991, without any official permission, the Magyar Politikai Foglyok Szövetsége (POFOSZ) (The Association of Hungarian Political Prisoners), erected, or more accurately laid down, a tombstone on the square just in front of the *Rákóczi* statue. The stone sarcophagus was designed by Imre Makovecz. As a supplement to this memorial for the victims of the salvo of 1956, the POFOSZ placed a headstone at the

---

58 For the Kossuth Square '56 memorials I relied mainly on the work of Géza Boros, *Emlékművek '56-nak* [Memorials to '56] (Budapest: 56-os Intézet, 1997).

end of the tombstone in 1996. This headstone was the work of László Gömbös. The relief on the headstone shows a woman waving a national flag with a hole in the middle, the symbol of '56, while treading on the Communist emblems of the five-pointed star and of the hammer and sickle. Behind the headstone they placed the national flag with the hole in the middle and in front of it they placed a tablet in two languages (Hungarian and English) which read, "Protest: Guard Duty of the World Council of '56-er Hungarians on the Kossuth Square—Protest! The English text reads:

> The Hungarian flag has a hole in it because on October 23, 1956, the revolutionists, those Hungarians who revolted against the Soviet Union, tore out the foreign coat of arms that symbolized the power of the Soviet Union and Communism. Since the flag has symbolized the freedom of the Hungarian nation.
>
> This memorial is a symbolic grave. Here, on this square, several hundred people fell dead onto the ground due to the killer blow of a firing squad on October 25, 1956. Honor and remembrance to the victims!

The caveat appeared only in Hungarian: "The murderers and their successors are still among us!"

The symbolic grave is a forceful creation of a sanctified nature. Even though it was set up without permission, nobody had the courage to remove it or disturb it in any way.

In 1996 the square was again enriched with a '56-er spiritual point of a sacred nature, the creation of the *Flame of the Revolution.* This memorial was created for the fortieth anniversary of the revolution. It was initiated by Árpád Göncz, the president of the republic, one of the condemned participants of '56 and by Imre Mécs, another condemned participant of '56, a parliamentary deputy of the Free Democratic Party and president of the "'56 Memorial Committee." The funds necessary for the project were provided by voluntary public contributions but, in view of the initiators' position, there was some government pressure as well. Mária Lugossy was chosen from the applicants solicited by the Budapest Galery. At that time the revolution did not yet have a central memorial in Budapest.

The memorial was erected on the Kossuth statue side of the square, in line with the National Banner, and closer to the Parliament. The black granite block is in the shape of a stylized torch. On the granite block the date: 1956 and the Kossuth coat of arms. An inscription states, "Erected in 1996, from voluntary contributions—a cooperative effort."

According to the original idea, the torch would be lit only on October 23, the first day of the revolution, of each year and burn until November 4, when the revolt was put down. At the flame-extinguishing ceremony on November 4, 1996, the flame was not extinguished and it was decided that it should continue to burn all the time.

The *Flame of the Revolution* is not limited to the victims of the fusillade but is to recall the entire revolution. Yet, the entire context of the square and the symbolic grave just across from the memorial make it largely in honor of the victims murdered at this site. The flame and the torch motif are also culturally more adapted to the dead.

In 1996 another statue, referring to 1956, was erected near the square. The statue of Imre Nagy, the executed prime minister of the revolution, was erected on the Martyrs' Square, not too far from the National Martyrs' Memorial. Because this memorial is not part of the square, and does not visually emphasize it, I only mention it and will not discuss it in any detail.[59]

The spiritual explosion of the square, at least to date, was closed in 2001. At this time, and again in memory of the victims, spheres representing bullets are embedded in the pavement in front of the entrance of the Ministry of Agriculture facing the square on the right. The ministry bore the costs even though a memorial tablet on the wall states, "Remembering the victims of the bloody Thursday of October 25, 1956—the survivors." The memorial was the creation of József Kampfl and Ferenc Callmeyer.

Adding it all up and, in view of its potential context including the *Flame of the Revolution*, we have maximally five and minimally four points reminding us of the mass murders which were under a cloak of silence for a long time. This is what I mean by spiritual explosion. Yet

---

[59] The Imre Nagy Memorial was made by Tamás Varga.

it is equally appropriate to talk about "fragments of spirituality" because the above tends to dilute the memories of the massacre. On the basis of the initial societal spiritualizing experiments the political powers also came into the act. Instead of considering a single approach it chose a number of parallel sites. Thus the most appropriate spiritualizing explosion, only resulted in dissociated memorial fragments. A single approach would have been much better because the square was already structurally replete. Here, one or two would have been more than four or five. It did not happen in this way.

Furthermore, the Ministry of Agriculture, in addition to memorials to the victims of the 1956 salvos nearby, was further encumbered. Starting in the 1970s the arcades of the building facing the Kossuth Square were filled with reliefs and busts. This is not evident from the square and even though the arcades are open to pedestrian traffic it does belong to the ministry rather than to the square. Everything here reflects the greats of the agricultural sphere. On the right eight busts and three reliefs, at the entrance one relief, and in the left arcades ten busts and three reliefs can be seen. None of this is a burden on the square and does not affect its spiritual content.

In 1990 the statue of István Nagyatádi Szabó was reerected without the ominous relief showing the handshake with Bethlen. In 1998 a memorial plaque was affixed to the building, close to its corner by the Báthory Street, which commemorates the freeing of the serfs in 1848.[60]

All this made the Ministry of Agriculture the most crowded and burdened spiritual element on the square. The building is loaded with spiritual fragments.

---

[60] The text of the memorial tablet reads:
IN MEMORY OF THE 1848 LIBERATION OF THE SERFS, AS A RESULT OF WHICH 2,203,307 FAMILIES WERE FREED OF COMPULSORY LABOR WHICH HAD FORCED THEM TO GIVE 20 PERCENT OF THEIR ANNUAL HARVEST TO SOMEBODY ELSE FOR NO COMPENSATION; 1,429,779 FAMILIES RECEIVED LAND; 656,251 FAMILIES CAME TO OWN A TOTAL OF 10,254,100 ACRES OF LAND; 328,102 HEADS OF PEASANT HOUSEHOLDS WERE GIVEN THE VOTE; 328,102 PEASANT FAMILIES HAD ONE MALE MEMBER AUTHORIZED TO SERVE IN THE MILITIA; 1,538,096 PEASANT FAMILIES BECAME EQUAL BEFORE THE LAW WITH THE NOBILITY.

A Grimace of Spirituality

The already overly filled square was given no rest. In 2002 another memorial was implanted there.

The Hungarian legislature decided in June 2000 that in Hungary a "Memorial Day for the Victims of the Communist Dictatorship" would be established. The designated day was February 25 of each year. This was the day when, in 1947, the Soviet forces occupying Hungary arrested the secretary general of the Smallholder Party, Béla Kovács. The politician was taken to Moscow, sentenced to twenty-five years in prison in 1951 and returned home only in 1955. In Imre Nagy's government he was first minister of agriculture and then minister of state. After the defeat of the revolution, he became a parliamentary representative in the Kádár regime in 1958. He died in June 1959.

Thus the day Béla Kovács was arrested became the Memorial Day.

In 2001 the Ezerkilencszáznegyvenöt Alapítvány Emlékbizottsága (Memorial Committee of the Nineteen Hundred Forty-Five Foundation) initiated the plans for erecting a statue of Béla Kovács.[61] The idea was embraced by the Ministry of National Cultural Heritage and, with the assistance of the Budapest Gallery it invited applications. As the site for the statue the ministry selected a place that had never been considered for a memorial. The place is the northern end of the Kossuth Square, where there is a parking area in front of the Prime Minister's Office bordering on the other side on a public street. The statue was to be erected in the narrow space between the parking area and the street.

The submission process was not successful. The jury recommended a second round of applications. In spite of this the ministry, with the approval of the capital city, charged the Szeged sculptor, Sándor Kligl to produce the *Kovács* statue. Kligl had not previously cast a statue for public display.

---

61 For the Béla Kovács statue I used, Lajos Csordás, "Emlékmű egy régi kisgazdának" [Memorial to an old smallholder], *Népszabadság*, February 23, 2002; Gyula Rózsa, "Törpe galleria" [Mini Gallery], *Népszabadság*, March 20, 2002, p. 32; and Géza Boros, "Három radikális köztéri project—Bevezetés az utca művészetébe" [Three radical project of public space—ntroduction to the art of the street], *Beszélő* 9, no 5 (July-August 2004): 152, on the web, http://beszélo.c3.hu/04/0708/boros.htm.

The statue was completed and was unveiled on February 25, 2002. The statue is adorned by the following inscriptions, "Béla Kovács, 1908–1959, a statesman carried off by the Soviet authorities; February 25, 2002, the memorial day for victims of the Communist dictatorship." There is also the name of the sculptor and another inscription stating that the memorial was created by the Memorial Committee with the assistance of the Ministry of National Cultural Heritage.

Béla Kovács stands on a marble pedestal. The pedestal represents a cloth-covered rostrum. Kovács is leaning against the protective balustrade of the rostrum.

Just as earlier, I am not anxious to discuss the esthetic merits of the statue. Yet it is not an accident that between 1906 and 2001, nobody considered this site as suitable for a statue. By placing the statue in this location the spiritual overcrowding of the square was increased. Also, it is practically impossible to inspect the memorial from close up. The statue facing the Parliament can be seen only from the back when viewed from the parking lot. In front of it there is no sidewalk but only a busy street so that it is very difficult to look at it from the front. I will not even mention that Béla Kovács was not a politician who played a role in Hungarian history deserving to be in the company of Andrássy, Kossuth, Tisza, Rákóczi, or Károlyi. The way these statesmen are viewed might change from time to time but their outstanding role can never be denied. Béla Kovács cannot even be compared to Nagyatádi Szabó who is strictly in the second rank behind the above.

Béla Kovács does nothing for the spiritual and symbolic role of the Kossuth Square and the site picked for his statue reflects this fact. In many ways, this statue is a grimace of the spirituality of the Kossuth Square.

* * *

It seems that the Parliament building, the temple of the constitution, acquired an aura over time. It managed to convince the decision makers of the day, frequently in a lame and halting fashion, to fill (overfill) the Kossuth Square with a spiritual content.

Thus then the square, in general, reflected the spiritualizing fantasy of the particular political system and political power of the day. There was only a single case when there was a true societal initiative:

during the broadly interpreted period of the change in regimes and concerning the remembrance of the 1956 massacre.

All the other apparently societal initiatives were more or less openly due to actions by the authorities. For this reason the history of the square and of its spirituality can be seen as the political essence of individual political power structures and can be so interpreted.

On the Kossuth Square everything speaks of power. Either by a political power placing itself into as spiritual dimension or if someone or some others question this.

In this way this square differs from any other square. In this way the Kossuth Square is unique. Precisely because here, directly or indirectly, pro or con, everything always is about power or about the power being questioned. Even the spirituality.

POSTSCRIPT

Kossuth Square was complete by 1972. Except for the streets opening into it, it was surrounded by buildings. New buildings could be added only if an old building was torn down or if the streets were reoriented. There does not seem to be any intention of making such changes at the present time. According to the plans, the Ministry of Agriculture building will serve as an office for the prime minister and the Museum of Ethnography may again become the Palace of Justice. None of this will change the architectural nature of the square. It was in 2002 that the square was changed for the last time in a spiritual sense. The Kossuth Square had become an area saturated with memorials and memorial sites. It might remain like this or it might change. It is striking that there are several items reminding us of the October 1956 volleys and it is also peculiar that the 2002 statues could be placed only at the edge of a street. It is possible, however, that it will occur to some politician, in a position of power, to replace some statue with another one.

From a symbolic perspective the square has functioned familiarly since 1896. The more familiar it is, the more unlikely that any changes would be made. The only element seeking a change would be a renewal from a point of view of refinement.

As I have indicated the square is ready for several such changes, such as the issues of parking and security. We also see that since the beginnings of the 2000s this need for fine tuning improvements has appeared at the level of political decision-making but, in fact, the square had not changed and nothing has been done.

Uncivilized behavior was reflected in a 2006 innovation in the symbolic use of the square, the encampment of the demonstrations that the legislators and law enforcement were unable to handle properly.

Finally, prior to the October 23 festivity, in order to improve the safety of the visiting statesmen and stateswomen, the square was emptied of the squatters and then barricades were installed. Due to the politically formal protests of the opposition representatives, the barricades were removed in February 2007.

The lack of practical, civilizing innovations and the innovative demonstrations, defying all traditions, signified that something had to be done so that the individual civil rights were protected while the square was revived.

On February 5, 2007, at a morning television show and, on the same day, at an evening commercial station radio broadcast program[1] I had the opportunity to explain that I viewed the domestic renewal of the square as a combination of a large underground parking structure and public park. It would be closed at night thus putting a time limit to new types of demonstrations. It would detract nothing from the spiritual nature of the square and would even add some esthetic features. None of this would interfere with the fixed symbolic use of any part of the square or of the end of the Constitution Street. The basic idea was that the civilizing and political anthropology problems could be reconsidered and unified by civilized means.

By coincidence, the Lord Mayor listened to the broadcast. He called me and arranged a meeting with the president of the National Assembly and others for February 8. I had to explain my ideas which were augmented by legal and safety considerations by some of the attendees. It appeared that the National Assembly would be able to generate the financing required for the renewal.

The story henceforth followed its own path. On April 13, 2006, the city, the owner of the square, had signed an agreement according to which the National Assembly of the Hungarian Republic was entitled to use the square for fifty years. According to the agreement the new structures had to be kept open from 8:00 A.M. to 8:00 P.M. every day, except for events controlled by a protocol.

---

[1] February 5, 2007. TV2, *Mokka*. Director: Henrik Havas; Klubrádió, *Kontra*. Director: József Orosz.

The Office of the National Assembly requested applications for plans to redesign the surface of the square:

> The proposed reconstruction of the Kossuth Square should make it possible to create a public park-public parking combination that will be modern and will give a character to that district of the city. It will be a meeting and recreational area which also serves the pedestrian traffic of the surrounding streets as a link while satisfying the demands of safety and security. The applicant shall work out a solution which will preserve and utilize the existing assets of the Kossuth Square and contains a proposal for redesigning the surface of the square in order to accommodate the placement of the future underground parking and meeting facilities and of their surface access facilities.
>
> The public park-public square area above the underground garage has to be designed so that the reconstruction of the surface above the future underground garage is possible without disproportionate costs.
>
> The proposal need not include plans for the underground garage.
>
> The purpose of this invitation is to select a proposal which most closely accomplishes the detailed instructions of the above planning program.[2]

The winner was announced on August 14. It was Studio 73, Ltd. According to the announcement,

> On the Studio 73 plan the National Banner was placed in the middle of the square with a trapezoid-shape pool on either side. The historic statues presently on the square will remain in their place even though the application package gave permission for their being moved. The area of the square between the two pools will be paved with a pleasing light-colored stone. Lighter stone stripes will be embedded in the pavement. The axis of the Alkot-

2 http://epiteszforum.hu/print/5642.

> mány Street will point at this zone. The total area of green surface has been enlarged and its components, square islands, will be framed by the Metro entrance and by the pedestrian paths located in the axis of the Alkotmány Street. This frame will be strengthened by newly planted rows of trees providing walls for the area. On the southern side of the square, near the Attila József statue, there is a possibility to gain access to the Danube rampart. The square has also received careful consideration from a security perspective and the furnishings on the public square are restrained and modern in design and are covered with wood.[3]

As seen from the above, the matter of the underground parking garage and the attached visitors' center was left open. Lack of the latter shows the obsoleteness of the square from the view of public needs.

Since regime change, the building can be approached more freely and with fewer restrictions. In 2000 the Holy Crown and the coronation regalia were deposited there. Viewing by the public is regulated by a Hungarian-American agreement. This was a condition for the return of the crown and of the regalia to Hungary by the United States which had come into their possession at the end of World War II. The Parliament and the Holy Crown are visited annually by several hundred thousand

---

3 http://www.hg.hu/3kg3. The team members of the winning proposal were: Péter István Balogh, Borbála Gyüre, János Homann, Zalán Kuti, Sándor Mohácsi, Máte Pécsi, Klára Katalin Pintér, Mónika Radices, Antal Gergely, Gyula Barkács, Alajos Sadeczky, Gábor Csabi, and János Volkay. An important part of the winning submission states that the square "must make a participation in the most important Hungarian historic events possible." They wish to accomplish this with inscribed tablets inserted into the pavement. The symbolic grave, in a renewed form will be placed by the *Flame of the Revolution*.

For the analytical review of the competition, complete with architectural-historic material, see Luca Csepely-Knorr, "Budapest, V. Kossuth tér térépítészeti pályázat" [Budapest, V. Kossuth Square architectural design competition], *4D Tájépítészeti és Kertművészeti Folyóirat*, no. 8 (2007): 3–25. The study lists all the spatial and architectural concepts related to the square.

Based on Steindl's original ideas, there is a tripartite arrangement. On the eastern side of the square, as viewed from the Parliament, at the level of the *Kossuth* and *Rákóczi* statues there are two fountains. The placement of these two statues was based on Antal Palóczy's idea. Jenő Lechner further developed Palóczy's ideas. It was on the basis of his ideas that in 1926 the area before the main entrance was paved. Károly Räde, the gardening director of the city, was concerned about the effects of the architectural changes on the traffic requirements and vetoed the idea of an "arithmetic garden." Thus, in reality, it was always a compromise which determined whether the square was a forum or a park.

people but the square has no covered reception area to accommodate these visitors.

It seems that perhaps there will be some forward movement in these matters as well. According to the plans, the surface rearrangement will be completed by the end of 2008. There is much, however, that may delay this, such as the matter of the underground parking garage and the visitors' center.

One thing is certain, for many reasons Kossuth Square expects a renewal of high quality. It is badly needed.

Perhaps it will materialize.

* * *

We have come to the end of the history of the Kossuth Square. Actually we have not reached the end.

Because the square, as a human creation, with its own particular and peculiar character, and multigenerational span is not really a historic manifestation but a political-cultural one. The events attached to the square disappear but the linkage becomes a cultural continuity. It had become permanent and therefore its symbolic history will definitely continue and its spiritual history will hopefully do likewise.

These are the dimensions which give the square its strength. So long as the country's central political magnet will reside here, so will its political heart. This is what, in the final analysis, gives the square its strength. We cannot see the strength of the square, but we know that it exists and that it is there. The more invisible it is the more it exists.

PRESS REPORTS

Political Position of the Selected Dailies

Az Est (The Evening)
Apolitical, stressed the importance of objective news reports.

Budapesti Hirlap (Budapest News)
Conservative nationalist paper, major supporter of revisionism.

Friss Ujság (Recent News)
Politically independent, sought its readership from the lower middle class and the peasantry.

Függetlenség (Independence)
Right wing with racialist overtones, supported the Gömbös government.

Kis Ujság (Little Journal)
The newspaper of the agrarian Independent Smallholder Party.

Magyarország (Hungary)
Independence Party supporter, identified with the politics of Count Mihály Károlyi.

Magyar Nemzet (Hungarian Nation)
Right of center, during World War II took an anti-German stance. In 1954 it became the paper of the Patriotic People's Front. After 1998, following the 1989 regime change, it came to support the right-wing Fidesz Party position.

Nemzeti Ujság (National Journal)
Conservative, Christian-nationalist paper.

Népszabadság (People's Freedom)
The daily of the communist Hungarian Socialist Workers' Party.

Following regime change became an independent paper with a left-of-center position.

Népszava (People's Voice)

The paper of the Social Democratic Party. After the Communist takeover in 1948, it became the organ of the labor unions. Following regime change it became the Hungarian Socialist Party daily.

Pesti Hirlap (Pest News)

Moderate, supported the government party.

Pesti Napló (Pest Journal)

National liberal daily which after 1901 tried to deemphasize its political commitments.

Vörös Ujság (Red News)

Newspaper of the Communist Party in 1918–19. Became the official organ of the government of the Hungarian Soviet Republic.

The Day of Piety

— The Great Parade —

In Front of the Parliament

The fact that we have a discreet, good public was demonstrated in the square in front of the Parliament, Budapest's only truly metropolitan square. It knew that the square had to be left empty for the paraders and even in the early morning hours the people gathered on the edges of the square. The large square was left empty. Thus the police had little to do when, at about 8:30 A.M. they asked the few curious people in front of the Parliament to move on.

The policemen were courteous and friendly and there were none of the now regrettably frequent angry confrontations. The representatives and the members of the Upper House had begun to arrive about 8:00 A.M. One of the first ones to arrive was Károly Eötvös who wore a formal black ceremonial dress and was a fine figure of a justice. Gyula Horváth also looked fine in his fancy uniform. Then a few prelates arrived and all the gentlemen hastened to enter the Dome Chamber.

In the meantime the military formed a cordon. The 52nd Infantry Regiment, named for Archduke Frederic, performed this task with no difficulty. The Akadémia, Nádor and Báthory Streets were closed off and thus only the people having a ticket were admitted to the Parliament Square. Béla Rudnay, the chief of police (in ceremonial dress) and Dezső Boda, the captain of police for the fifth district, could be well pleased because nothing disturbed the order they were responsible for. They had nothing to do and could limit their activities to observing the magnificent spectacle developing in front of the steps of the Parliament.

Facing the Parliament was the Palace of Justice and the Ministries of Justice and of Agriculture. The buildings were beautifully decorated but the loveliest decorations were the ladies looking out from the windows.

How many lovely women everywhere! In every window, on every grandstand. There were a number of grandstands lined up along the edges of the square. Smaller ones were erected in front of the two palaces. On the south side there were huge stands filled with rows of people in colorful dresses and on the north side there was a stand for foreign dignitaries. This grandstand intended for the diplomatic corps, for the Austrian government and delegation remained empty, but this did not create any dissonance in the overall success.

The gentlemen and their ladies looked for and found seats within the Parliament and from all the windows and balconies of the new Parliament a large number of spectators were waiting for the parade.

The Parade Arrives

The steps of the Parliament also became a grandstand where the most illustrious company took part in the events. Many were standing at the foot of the steps, including Mór Jókai who tolerated the heat like an athlete. The photographers were adjusting their equipment. There never have been this many photographers!

They are coming! They are coming!

After 10:15 A.M. Bornemissza, the Police Commissioner appeared on horseback at the end of the Nádor Street, at the head of a group of mounted police. Shortly thereafter the trumpeters arrived in the square. Then, for the next hour and a half, the parade marched in front of the Parliament.

The parade was welcomed here just as enthusiastically as anywhere else but the enthusiasm could not manifest itself with the same amount of noise as it did when there were thousands upon thousands of spectators. It was only after the parade had made a circle and arrived at the end of Alkotmány Street that there was a veritable storm of hurrahs which was echoed from Nádor Street and from Markó Street.

In front of the Parliament the marchers were received in a more friendly fashion, but there was still plenty of admiring and cordial hurrahing, which greeted Dezső Perczel who led the parade. István Tisza was noisily welcomed by those from Bihar County and Algernon Beöthy was greeted by people yelling:

"Hi (servus) Algy!"

Others were greeted similarly:

"Hi Lord Lieutenant!"

This was the way the youngest and most splendidly dressed Lord Lieutenant, Vilmos Pálffy-Daun was greeted.

Gyula Lits marched at the head of the most decorative Fehér County group proving that he was not a "counterfeit hussar."

An opposition representative commented that this made Fehérvári a liar.

"Where is Lulu?"

Everybody was yelling, "Where is Lulu?"

"Here is Lulu," yelled Lajos Meszlény from the end of the line.

The group from Heves County was very attractive although one malicious Member of Parliament commented that the medieval knightly garb did not go well with pince-nez. The group from Jásznagykúnszolnok raised comments,

"They sent a whole army!" One of the drivers of a cart from Komárom proudly exclaimed

"We are citizens!"

The ones from Lipót County also did very well. Their wolf skins were much admired. Lord Lieutenant Kürthy was one of the most elegant men and was loudly cheered.

The banner from Nyitra, made in 1660, was noted. The most enthusiastic welcome was given to the group from Pest County. Lord Lieutenant Berniczky had difficulties acknowledging all of the hurrahs.

The marchers from Ugocsa were received with:

"Does he really put on the crown?! Long live Ugocsa!"

In general the groups which were best liked before the Parliament were the same ones which received the most enthusiastic welcome along the entire route. The group from Fiume was receiveded most frenetically. In the parade group of the legislators the warmest welcome was awarded to Ödön Miklós, Baron Dezső Prónay, Baron Elek Nopcsa, Aurél Münnich, Count Aurél Dessewffy, Count Géza Zichy, and Count Kálmán Nákó. Yet all of them were received with pleasure and, when they dismounted in order to participate in the formal meeting, they were asked what they had seen on the way? It was then that the rumor was spread about the breaking of the staff of the Serb banner.

Then came the festive carriages. The emerging prelates were hurrahed. They had to take their time to leave the carriages and in the carriage of the capital city Károly Ráth became impatient.

"Wait a bit, Your Honor," yelled the crowd.

"But I want to go to the meeting."

"By the door."

"I thought you would not let me go."

Then came the magnates carrying banners and their appearance before the Parliament made a lasting impression. When Count István Keglevics appeared with the Serb banner, they asked,

"Is this it?"

The Holy Crown

Following a detachment of crown guards the festive carriage, carrying the crown and the coronation regalia, appeared.

Off with the hats!

The honorable assembly stood there with uncovered heads. The playfulness disappeared and was replaced with deep piety and a religious sensation. It was a gripping sight.

The crown and the coronation regalia were placed on three cushions and were carried into the Parliament by Marquess Sándor Pallavicini, Count Albin Csáky, János Klobusitzky, István Szluha, and Count Jenő Zichy.

On the broad steps a large group of people, consisting exclusively of excellencies, lordships, and honorables, followed the crown. How much light, how much radiance! The crown guard with their halberds formed an impressive wall....

Pesti Hirlap, June 9, 1896.

September 15.

On September 15 the workers of Budapest marched to the Parliament to demonstrate in favor of a universal, equal, and secret franchise.

The demonstration must be quiet and dignified.

If the opponents of universal franchise want to make trouble, let no one allow themselves to become angry. If somebody penetrates our ranks and there shouts abuse, let not 500 of you descend on him. The hands of the two comrades nearest to him suffice to shut up such a hireling. The others should show no interest.

The shouters should not be expelled from the group because this would make trouble. They have to be kept in the group so that they can not shout.

It will be the most shining proof of our political maturity if the demonstration is performed without any trouble,

We must not shout hurrahs or abuse. We shall sing our Credo, *La Marseillaise*, so that our representatives will march to the Parliament to the sound of this revolutionary tune.

Our enormous mass of people shall prove, by having an orderly demonstration, that we are a formidable, determined opponent and that we will not let up until the universal, secret franchise is enacted into law.

We call on all comrades to follow the above instructions.

* * *

On September 15 the workers will gather in the following locations:

II. Pálffy Square
VI. Lehel Square
VI. Ferdinánd Square
VII. Hunyadi Square
VIII. Tisza Kálmán Square
IX. Ferenc Square

The workers from the surrounding area will march directly to the Parliament.

The assembly is at 6:30 A.M. Departure at 7:00 A.M. Those groups which march to the assembly points must be there by 7:00 A.M.

Népszava, September 13, 1905.

Red Friday

The Workers of Budapest before the Parliament

(From Our Own Correspondent)

...In the history of the Hungarian social democracy today, September 15, is a red-letter holiday. The workers deprived of their rights introduced themselves to the Parliament. What a majestic introduction! The honorable Members of Parliament gazed at the hundred thousand men mutely, pale and blinking. The street did not bow down before them; facing them without blinking. The honorable gentlemen dropped their eyes. Their conscience was stirred by this introduction.

How it must hurt the enemies of social democracy that they could not disrupt this majestic demonstration with police attacks, sabers, volleys and that thereafter they cannot deny us the issuance of a certificate of political maturity. The workers made sure that this would not happen. Just a few scenes to show the magnificence of the workers' Red Friday.

The masses marched to the Parliament in a tight group four abreast. They were ordered to be quiet. It was forbidden to hurrah or abuse. Whoever does that is probably an *agent provocateur* who had infiltrated our ranks. One of our comrades could not control his enthusiasm and involuntarily exclaims:

"Long live the universal and secret franchise!"

He is immediately shushed. If he could not have identified himself immediately, he would have been in trouble.

The house painters march by. Somebody yells at them in the street:

"Layabouts!"

Nobody answers him. Two workers leave the ranks, grab him and march him into the group. Now he has to march among the "layabouts." They take him along to Szabadság Square and there he has to stand among the workers. After a few hours he is crying, asks for pardon and to be allowed to leave. Other provocations were managed similarly.

In front of the Parliament the battle cry of the hundreds of thousands deprived of their rights, *La Marseillaise*, rings out in majestic unity.

The March

In the morning at 7:30 A.M. the masses of workers started from the assembly areas almost all at the same time. It was an unforgettably beautiful sight to see the tens of thousands of workers, in their Sunday best, marching through town to the music of *La Marseillaise*. On their way the march grew enormously and turned into a huge uncountable mass of people by the time it reached its destination, Szabadság Square.

Only the banners and inscribed placards rose above the mass of a hundred thousand. Some of the inscriptions read:

The country is only where the rights are.
The magnates defrauding the people deprive the people of their country in the name of the country.
Political rights lead to the end of economic exploitation.
Long live universal suffrage.
Down with the magnates who defraud the people.

On Váci Boulevard the marchers, coming from all directions, created a bottleneck. From the Andrássy Avenue to the Western Terminal the slowly moving masses could be likened to an enormous snake. There was no singing and there was no yelling, only dull stamping, and the sound of the marching feet of a hundred thousand proletarians. Then came the music. The comrades from Budafok, Soroksár, Kispest, and Újpest each came with a band which played stimulating songs along the way. On the Váci Boulevard they had to go very slowly because there was such a congestion.

In Front of the Parliament

The police had made preparations as though they expected a revolution. One thousand five hundred policemen on foot and a hundred and fifty on horseback marched out. They closed off all the adjoining streets and set up a cordon. In the Radetzky Barracks, on the Outer Nádor Street, two squadrons of the 16th Hussar Regiment and two companies of the 18th Honvéd Infantry Regiment were held in readiness. The latter were brought to the capital for this purpose only.

The cordon left a large part of the square empty. And therefore comrades Kúdos and Bokányi talked to Police Councilor Gyalokai and asked him to let the marchers use the square, according to a prior agreement and because tens of thousands of workers were filling up all the neighboring streets. Gyalokai said that he could do nothing until Béla Rudnay, the chief of police arrived and that he would give the orders. In the meantime masses of workers arrived from every direction. The Alkotmány Street was packed all the way to the Váci Boulevard. The people from Újpest were stuck at the Western Terminal and could go no further. On the other side the masses were pushed back into the Szabadság Square, Rudnay arrived soon thereafter and gave the order that except for the main entrance [to the Parliament], the workers could occupy the square. Even this way at least half of the mass was compressed into the Alkotmány Street, the Szabadság Square, and adjoining streets.

Thousands of people on the Parliament Square, black masses of people are swirling on Kiss Ernő Street, Aulich Street and Alkotmány Street. Báthory Street is jammed as far as Hold Street and Vécsey Street, Nádor Street, and Szabadság Square are fearfully packed with people. It is impossible to estimate the numbers accurately but there must have been 120–150,000 people. It was the group that gathered on the Hunyadi Square which was the first to march to the Parliament, at about 8:00 A.M. The printers, with their chorus and banners in the lead, were followed by all the others. One and a half hour after the first groups arrived, people were still streaming into the square.

The steps to the Parliament and the area before the entrance were occupied by their representatives and by a number of foreign journalists. Interest from abroad about the events of the day was remarkable. Almost every major European newspaper had sent a correspondent and a graphic artist. There were the foreign representatives of the Temperance Congress who could not withhold the expression of their admiration for the imposing and disciplined demonstration. The foreign correspondents who came to Budapest to be present on this day are amazed in seeing the beautiful sight and one of them exclaimed: "Nowhere in the world would a hundred thousand men be so disciplined. Off with our hats, Gentlemen...."

Dispersal

While the deputation was inside the Parliament the people waited patiently. The bands played workers' songs and even though three or four played at the same time, they did not interfere with each other on the huge square occupied by the people. While the masses waited peacefully and calmly for the deputation to return, a number of them collapsed in the heat. They were led out along the path, opened cheerfully by the people, to the edge of the square where several ambulances were waiting and where the sick were attended to....

There was no grandstand and therefore the comrades raised the speakers onto their shoulders from where, by prior agreement they said the following:

> What we had promised we have kept. We have shown that in Budapest there is only one common opinion which demands the universal franchise. Gyula Justh, the president of the Lower House had stated that the universal franchise issue would be resolved to everybody's satisfaction. We are people of peace and culture. We understand that the matter of the universal franchise will be resolved peacefully by parliamentary means. We will stand watch and if the promise is not fulfilled we will do what we have decided to do and will call for a general strike. Today is just the beginning of the fight and there will be no peace and quietude until we have gained universal franchise. Now let our disbanding be as peaceful as our gathering has been. Let everyone beware so that our enemies cause us no trouble. Disperse calmly and peacefully. Long live universal franchise.

It was a gripping spectacle when 100,000 workers raised their arm and waived their hat toward the speakers. The huge mass began to move and it started to disperse in every direction.

It took over half an hour for the mass to depart. Organizers watched from all the street corners to avert any trouble and there was none. The discipline of our comrades was unprecedented. One hour later the streets had regained their normal appearance.

The Discredited Patriots

The defrauders of the people coalition wanted to disturb the dignity of our demonstration and wanted to make trouble by hiring people to do so, but they failed miserably.

Yesterday and the day before thousands of leaflets were distributed in the streets of Budapest by some "Patriotic Committee" asking that the citizens stop the Socialist demonstration and march. The area of the square next to the *Andrássy* statue was designated as the gathering point but only the issuers of the fliers, a few well-known rascals, willing to do anything for money appeared, nobody else. The planned "counterdemonstration" went up in smoke.

The leadership of the party was aware that disturbances were planned. They knew that it was impossible to mobilize sufficient forces against the masses of our comrades but were concerned that if 2–3,000 people started to make a noise, the mass of Socialists would respond. Those further away, and not knowing what was happening, would try to get closer and thus unforeseeable problems might arise. This was the reason why the party leadership asked the comrades by printed instructions that should the above mentioned trouble occur, the ones closest to it should make the troublemakers shut up, while the others should remain calm as though nothing had happened. The counterdemonstration never took place and only on Alkotmány Street was there a well-dressed man who, to make trouble, started to yell against the coalition, Ferenc Kossuth and Apponyi. An organizer, with the assistance of three comrades who hastened to his assistance from the crowd, grabbed the troublemaker by his arm, dragged him into the midst of the workers and forced him to go with them to the Parliament Square, where the three comrades watched him and did not let him go until the entire group disbanded.

Népszava, September 16, 1905.

Arrangements in Front of the Parliament

The individual groups lined up side by side in an orderly fashion. By 9:00 A.M. the entire square between the Curia and the northern wing of the Parliament, the area in front of the Ministry of Justice and further toward Nádor Street were filled with people carrying red leaflets, banners, and placards. They stood in a solid semicircle around the House of Representatives. The area in front of the main entrance, the driveway toward the side entrance on the southern wing where the representatives entered, and the area around the *Andrássy* statue were left empty.

The police was out in force. 360 policemen on foot and 80 on horseback were assigned to the Parliament. In addition the groups approaching from various directions were all accompanied by police escorts consisting of twelve higher officers, sixty mounted and 440 regular policemen. The police set up an iron cordon from the Upper House side of Parliament, i.e. from the Margit Embankment all the way around the giant square. The iron cordon closed off the square from the Margit Embankment, across Nádor Street, Szalay Street, Alkotmány Street, Báthory Street, the other half of Nádor Street, Zoltán Street, and Géza Street.

Description of the Square in Front of the Parliament

The huge square around the Parliament and the enormous crowds assembled there presented an incomparable picture. In front of the main façade, within the iron cordon there was a sizable open area in which the army of journalists ran around in a forlorn manner. Among them, the leadership of the Socialist Party and police officers.

By 10:00 the heat was oppressive. There were no enterprising food vendors or boys hawking water and so the workers jammed together visibly suffered from the heat. Sweat was dripping from their forehead but they were still enthusiastically singing this verse of the "workers' *La Marseillaise*":

The wealthy have a country
The dales and hills are theirs
We build their palaces
That look down on us proudly
Not a yard of this land
Is ours anywhere,
Only when it covers us,

When the bell has tolled for us
The right to vote…
Our patience is gone!
We are not asking we are demanding
We must have the right to vote.

The four brass bands were making noises from time to time but they were not playing the workers' march but some bad Viennese waltzes.

In the middle of the empty space there is a very tall, three-legged ladder with a photographer climbing to the top. Ten feet from him there is another photographer with a camera on a small tripod looking as though it was trying to beat its larger brother in a race to the steps of the Parliament. The large porter of the Parliament, with a large blonde moustache, stands guard there with the huge crown prepared for the millennium in his hand. He also holds the decorated silver staff which carries the inscription:

896–1896 MILLENNIUM

Those standing on the steps admire the scene before them as provided by the large crowd. Many lean against the lions which decorate the steps. The windows and balconies of the Curia are filled with people and some people, endangering their life, even climbed up onto the sloping top of the Ministry of Justice's risalith. On the right, from the roof of buildings backing Parliament Square women and children gawk at the square across the empty lots. A reporter crosses the square with long strides, stopping every so often to click his Kodak, mercilessly capturing even those who are protesting.

All the windows on the Lower House side of the Parliament are closed and are opened only around 10:00 A.M. by the representatives. The windows on the Upper House side are wide open. The workers, demanding their rights do not even glance at the golden reflection of the corridor. One man can be seen at the window, Baron István Sennyey, in a blue Hungarian suit and a white hat.

The Upper House side of the square to the Curia and to the Danube is crowded with people while the emptiness of the square before the lateral façade of the Parliament is occupied only with policemen on horseback. In front of the principal façade there are twenty-two policemen on horseback. A journalist, wearing yellow leggings and reminding people of a war correspondent, causes people to smile. He probably expected a revolution.

They wonder in the square: what is going on in the house? The government is presumably under attack. Yet most people are interested primarily in finding out how many people had gathered in the square. Chief of Detectives Krecsányi puts it at no more than thirty-five to forty thousand. Yet comrade Weltner and comrade Bokányi claim that they had distributed one hundred thousand red leaflets saying:

> Long live the Universal,
> Equal and Secret
> Franchise.
> This emblem is to be
> Attached to the hat.
> The Party Leadership.

But Weltner becomes concerned that he has exaggerated and states that he had given emblems to the children as well. Yet he insists on no less than eighty thousand. Then they try to figure it out. There are fifty-five organizations present, including, Soroksár, Török-Bálint and other regional villages. He only mentions the major trades as justification, such as 12,000 iron workers, 5,000 metal workers, 3,000 tailors, 8,000 construction workers, and 1,200 carpenters, all in marching groups, four abreast.

Shortly, nobody is interested in anything else, The Zeysig affair overshadows everything.

The ambulance people were also working hard. They did not have very many cases, only nine, but working in the huge crowd was very difficult. Emil Schönberger and Dr. Lajos Erkel had to carry an unconscious woman in their arms who then had to be revived for about an hour at Gate Ten.

There were a number of women among the Socialists, and many students as well. Even the women caused no trouble and that was truly amazing.

There policemen stationed even under the Danube Embankment arcades. This had a valid reason. It was here that the Orsova steamer, named *Albrecht*, was cruising up and down, bringing voters from Kobolkút whom Miklós Szemere ordered up to celebrate the coalition. Exactly at 10:00 A.M. a delegation was sent to the house with one boat and the ship floated down the Danube.

It could not have been later than 8:30 A.M. when a delegation of the newly organized Social Democratic Party marched up from the banks of the Danube. There were about fifty of them under the leadership of Vilmos Mezőfi and András Achim. They marched into the Parliament and now the time had arrived for which the whole "Red Friday" was organized, namely to send a Social Democratic delegation to the president of the house, to present him with a memorandum in which they demanded a universal, equal, and secret franchise....

The Dispersal

On the request of the eight Socialist leaders the entire giant assembly left with the greatest dignity. One hour later the square in front of the Parliament was again quiet.

The imposing order was incomprehensible to the police. All the preparations had been in vain and it had been in vain to mobilize the military. The people behaved magnificently and gave absolutely no reason for any interference. The dispersal of the masses progressed with military discipline and precision. The workers followed the instructions to the letter and the instructions ordered that everybody should leave the square by the street closest to them. This became obvious. Looking down from the steps toward Alkotmány Street all one could see was a black ocean of people. There was not a square inch of free space here, or in the streets leading toward Szabadság Square. The same was true on the left, on Nádor Street, leading toward Lipót Boulevard. Naturally all traffic had to stop but half an hour later everything was open again. It was thus that the huge crowd could depart in perfect order and very rapidly. Barely five minutes after the decision of the president of the house was announced, the square was empty. There was nobody there except the many reporters and the police.

Pesti Hirlap, September 16, 1905.

Unveiling the Andrássy Statue

Budapest, December 3.

The unveiling of the statue of Count Gyula Andrássy was made into a major occasion by the presence of the king, the court, the government, the diplomatic corps, a multitude of elegance and nobility, and delegations gathering from all parts of the country. It was in their presence that the veils were dropped from Count Gyula Andrássy's monumental bronze statue.

The festive oration by Kálmán Széll and the king's response revealed the respect for the memory of the man who, with Ferenc Deák, had the lion's share in the drafting of the Compromise. Today both of them have a bronze statue proclaiming the piety and respect of the present generation for the memory of the creators of the new Hungary....

The Gathering

...The Hungarian gentlemen were without exception in the traditional Hungarian ceremonial attire, while the foreign diplomats were wearing either military or diplomatic uniforms. Noteworthy among the latter were the two very large Chinese ambassadors and the very small Japanese one. The German ambassador was in a military uniform.

Arrival of the King

Five minutes before 11:00 A.M. the arrival of the king was announced by a distant, approaching and swelling ovation.

Dr. Sándor Wekerle, the prime minister, welcomed the king at the entrance of the park surrounding the memorial and conducted him to a tent where the king, accompanied by Count Paar, general of cavalry and principal aide-de-camp to the king and by the aide-de-camp on duty, welcomed the members of the royal family.

Kálmán Széll's Speech

Now Kálmán Széll stepped forward, removed his fur cap and delivered the following effective address with ringing tones and growing emphasis,

> Imperial and Apostolic Royal Majesty!
> Most Gracious Lord, our King!
> Act III of 1890, mandated that for his meritorious services to the throne and to the country a memorial be erected at public expense in Budapest to Count Gyula Andrássy.
> This is the memorial we dedicate today....
> It was his grand political concept to establish intimate relationship with our great neighbor to the west and to assure the independence of the countries to the east with unfettered opportunities for their development. He reestablished the respect and standing of the two-country Austro-Hungarian Monarchy which was its due both by its past and by its weight.
> The fundamental principles of his policy are just as valid today....

The King's Speech

The king, the royal family and the public listened to this speech with great interest and profoundly affected attention.
Then the king said in a strong voice that could be heard over a long distance,

> It fills me with great satisfaction to be able to participate in the unveiling of a statue erected by Hungary for its great son in a place appropriate to do him honor.
>
> Remembering gratefully the eternal merits that the late Count Gyula Andrássy earned for his king, his country, and the Monarchy, I express my hopes that this outstanding man, who created the persistent base for Hungary's political life and for the Monarchy's foreign policy, will serve as a model for future generations.
> Let the veil be lowered!

The veil fell accompained by loud hurrahs. At this moment the clouds in the autumn sky parted and a ray of sunshine fell on the beautiful monument....

The King Inspects the Statue

The king viewed the statue with great interest and attention. Then he turned to the ladies of the Andrássy family who sat to the right of the tent, Countess Lajos Batthyány, née Ilona Andrássy, the widow of Count Tivadar Andrássy, Countess Géza Andrássy, Countess Sándor Andrássy, and Countess Jenő Karátsoni, exchanging pleasant words with them. He then descended from the platform and went to Kálmán Széll whom he thanked warmly for the excellent speech which was very much appreciated by the king.

Then His Majesty turned to Count Gyula Andrássy, minister of the interior and son of the man honored, and chatted with him amicably. Then he spoke to other members of the cabinet, including Ferenc Kossuth, minister of commerce, and then they all went to inspect the statue.

In front of the statue, dressed in a simple blue Hungarian ceremonial dress, the sculptor of the statue, György Zala was waiting for them. The king shook hand with the artist and said,

"The statue turned out very well. I am pleased to congratulate you."

The artist thanked the king for the compliment and stayed at his side to provide any information requested. The king commented on the principal figure:

"Andrássy is perfectly done" and then he said,

"The shape of the horse is excellent."

Looking at the first relief on the pedestal, depicting the coronation ceremony, the king asked,

"How come that the patina is already so dark?"

"The patina was produced artificially by the application of acids" said the artist.

"It was done very successfully" said the king.

At the relief of the Berlin Congress the king was interested in the individual participants and asked:

"Other than Andrássy is there another Hungarian in the relief?"

"Yes, Your Majesty," said Zala, "Count Alajos Károlyi, the ambassador to Germany."

Then when the king heard the name Bülow mentioned, he asked:

"Which Bülow is this?"

"The father of the present chancellor of Germany," answered the artist.

After having made the circuit the king thanked the artist for the information and added,

"The whole work turned out beautifully. I am very pleased with today's festivities".

He than said goodbye to the artist with a handshake.

The king walked around the statue again looking attentively at the various parts. Having said goodbye to Prime Minister Dr. Sándor Wekerle, and to the members of the cabinet, the king, accompanied by the members of the royal family, was driven back to the Royal Castle.

Magyarország, December 1, 1906.

A Workers' Deputation Visits Gyula Justh

The chief of police did not allow the Social Democratic Party to take their protest march to the Parliament. In order to make sure that his instructions were not circumvented the police took definite steps. The streets leading to the square were blocked off and only those were permitted to pass into the square who had valid tickets to the Parliament. The cars were stopped by the police and the passengers were asked to show their tickets. Yet, somehow about one hundred people managed to sneak into the Parliament building, who were afraid of making any noise and therefore expressed their feelings about the politicians arriving in the square, by waving their hats silently.

Naturally, the delegation of the Social Democrats was admitted readily and they presented a written request about the enactment of a general franchise to Gyula Justh, the president of the House....

Pesti Napló, October 11, 1907.

THE SUNDAY MASS MEETING OF THE NATIONAL COUNCIL

The Hungarian National Council called a rally to assemble on Sunday afternoon. It was both imposing and dignified. After two hours the march toward the Parliament Square began and the square rapidly filled up with the participants of the rally. From the outer areas the workers came, four persons abreast, in complete order, carrying placards in the first row with the inscription, "Long live the immediate peace! We demand peace in the whole world!" On the streets leading toward the Parliament there were gendarmes and policemen, while on the empty lots near the Parliament and in the basement of the Ministry of Agriculture and of the Curia armed forces were in readiness. By 3:00 P.M. the enormous crowd completely filled the Parliament Square and the streets leading toward it.

In the name of the sponsors, István Farkas welcomed the rally. On his recommendation Count Tivadar Batthyány, Vilmos Bőhm, and Pál Szende were elected as chairmen of the rally. In his opening remarks Count Tivadar Batthyány stated the reason why the rally was called, stated the program of the National Council which demanded that peace be made immediately, that universal franchise, including the vote for women be introduced, and that there should be a change toward democracy. He indicated that a government was wanted that immediately dissolved the alliance with Germany, granted freedom to the press and released the political prisoners.

Márton Lovászi asked that all present support the National Council. He was happy to see that Budapest accepted the credo of those who proclaim the coming of a more beautiful and happier Hungary.

Sándor Garbai was received with a storm of applause when he approached the rostrum. He declared that the Social Democratic Party joined the National Council with the greatest pleasure and complete confidence. The country must have peace immediately. There were great tasks before us and we must make every effort to sweep away those who have profited from the war. The returning warriors must be given land, they have to be assisted in going back to their workshops and they must be given bread. Today was for a general review and a sign of readiness for a fight. Tomorrow all workers shall be at their work, start to work and if the time for action arrived the leaders would give the signal.

Oszkár Jászi spoke after Sándor Garbai.

"Those who are afraid of revolution," he said, "and shudder when they think that the National Council will achieve what it wants, do not realize that the revolution had already arrived. The king is surrounded by malevolent evil counselors who do not allow the voice of the people to reach the throne."

László Fényes brought greetings from the villages to the workers of Budapest. The villages are happy to join the urban citizenry to engage in the fight together.

Pál Szende spoke on behalf of the Radical Party and told the assembled people that they should signal their acceptance of the program of the National Council. This invitation was followed by several minutes of applause and thousands of hands were raised high to indicate that the proposals were received with the greatest satisfaction.

This was the end of the agenda for the rally and only Lajos Böhm gave a short speech in which he asked those present to disband in complete order and give no opportunity to the authorities to interfere. The huge, enthusiastic crowd, cheering the name of Count Mihály Károlyi, departed in different directions without even the slightest trouble. The large square in front of the Parliament was emptied in a short time.

Pesti Hirlap, October 29, 1918.

RALLIES IN THE STREET

...Masses reaching thousands gathered in the forenoon in the square in front of the Parliament. Comrades Gyula Pálffy, József Buckler, Sándor Sugár, and Vera Singer made rousing speeches to the huge crowds which, after receiving the speeches with enthusiasm, applauded the republic. Led by the speakers the multitude then marched to the Alkotmány Street prison and there a group of soldiers, under the leadership of a sailor, József Erszinger, freed comrade János Lékai-Leitner, the assailant of István Tisza, from jail.

Népszava, November 1, 1918.

Victory Celebration

*

Gigantic Mass Meeting of Our Comrades in Front of the Parliament.
—The Military Band Played La Marseillaise—
—Victory Parade—

...A multitude in the square in front of the Parliament: a mass of people and thousands of workers. Order and dignity. The wind makes the red banners flutter. Our banner, red as our blood, the banner of our freedom is held by the rough hands of workers. They are the ones who took the banners to victory. The military band plays music. Our song, the march of the victorious revolution: *La Marseillaise*. The song is heard from thousands of mouths: "The future will be free!"

Holiday. After All Souls' Day came the holiday of the resurrection of freedom. It is a meeting of inebriated hearts and fighting souls: this was our Sunday mass rally.

Who could possibly forget it, having lived through it? How happily they will depart the world of the living with the memory of this day!

Already at 10:00 A.M. the Parliament Square was black with thousands lined up and more were streaming in from the streets. Workers' groups under red banners and slogans on placards. Revolutionary enthusiasm everywhere. There are no policemen around the rostrum or anywhere else without whom there could have been no gathering in the past. There was a troop of police in the square but they were welcomed with pleasure by the people because they helped in making the Hungarian revolution.

In their enthusiasm the masses were impatient. Until the rally was officially opened ad hoc speakers emphasize the significance of the revolution in brief, unrehearsed phrases. One speaker after another. One revolutionary cry after the other. Then the declamation of revolutionary poems, particularly the verses of Petőfi.

The coming together of extraordinarily important events makes it impossible to report the mass rally with the usual details. What follows is barely an outline of what happened Sunday morning at the rally.

Two rostra were erected, one in front of the main steps of the Parliament, the other in front of the Curia. The speakers addressed the crowd from three directions. From the rostrum in front of the main steps of the Parliament, Heltai, the city commander, gave a short speech followed by an address by comrade Dezső Bokányi:

> On July 14 the French people demolished the Bastille and this started the French Revolution. The day of our revolution is October 31, because on this day we demolished the old, outmoded system in order to erect on its ruins the new Hungary of popular rights and of freedom. Three weeks ago Wekerle smiled when the revolution was mentioned to him and said that the Hungarian people were not ready for a revolution. Yet, we accomplished it in three days. And this political earthquake swept away all those who were the enemies of the people's rights. I wonder where all those are who sat in Parliament as "trustees of the people?" They disappeared as though they were not interested in the fate and future of the new Hungary. Archduke József took an oath before the National Council, but where are the others? Where are those representatives who have not yet reported to the National Council, to seek pardon for their former sins and submit themselves to the National Council?
>
> Let us rejoice for having removed them from our path. The time has finally arrived when we can direct our own affairs. The government of the people will sweep away the last remnants of class privilege and its first task will be the enactment into law of a universal, secret franchise, extended to women, and the provision of rights to those who were without them. Parliament must be the will of every living person, regardless of language, race, or nationality. (A voice: how about the Upper House?) The people will decide through the universal franchise. Raise your hand if you do not want it!

"We don't need it! It must be abolished! Down with the magnates," yelled the crowd, which had raised their hands in unison.

"The question of the universal franchise," continued comrade Bokányi,

> is the most important one. The House must be called into session to enact it into law and, if it doesn't, the national Council will

declare it its mortal enemy, chase it away and impose the franchise by force. We will hold the elections not with the Lord Lieutenants but with the people's commissars and only after the elections will we decide on the form of government. The first constitutional assembly will extend a fraternal hand toward all the peoples of the world. We will devote all our strength and energy to liberate the presently oppressed nations. Today we have all become brothers. (Stormy clapping and cheering.)

Judge Kálmán Kiczkó spoke next: "The workers liberated the Hungarian nation and the oppressed intellectuals, who will now fight on their side against class rule. As a Hungarian judge he would not dare to sentence Tisza's murderers. The dynasty was the cause of all of Hungary's troubles. Royal power should be abolished. He would no longer pass sentence 'In the name of His Majesty the King.'" The state should confiscate the gains made by the people enriched by the war and devote them to the good of the nation. He demanded a progressive taxation, which, he believed, would decrease the burden of the war debts.

After this speech a worker smashed the marble tablet that he had brought from the statue of Hentzi, destroyed the day before. In the meantime the military band continued to play the national anthem, the Kossuth song and, most often and to the greatest enthusiasm, *La Marseillaise*.

On the rostrum, erected in front of the Curia, comrade Sándor Garbai delivered a powerful, enthusiastic speech to the masses, whom he urged to ensure the advances of the revolution. In the same sense comrades Ferenc Klárik, Lajos Kitajka, and Mór Preusz spoke from a third location about the enormous importance of maintaining order. After the speech of comrade Garbai, comrade Andor Péterdi recited his poem entitled: "You are free, my people" which caused a tumultuous enthusiasm. Then the Richárd Fricsay band again played *La Marseillaise* and the masses, following the military band, marched along the Podmaniczky Street to the Grand Boulevard, in perfect discipline and perfect order enthusiastically cheering the revolution.

Népszava, November 2, 1918.

The New Hungary

The Hymn of Brotherhood—Awaiting the Returning Soldiers—Toward a Cheaper Life

Mass Meeting of the Workers

On Sunday forenoon the working population of Budapest held its first monster rally since the mass meeting of the National Council and the victory of the revolution. There has never been such a workers' meeting in Budapest. The police of the former reactionaries were not in attendance and no rifles with bayonets were aimed in the direction of the workers' multitude. A military band, sent by the Hungarian people's government, played for the workers. The military band played *La Marseillaise*. And Hungarian songs. Who would have believed it ten days earlier? Since then everything had changed greatly and the meeting of the workers was held under the auspices of the glorious changes.

The City Commander Heltai admonished the workers to remain calm and called on everybody to protect the achievements of the revolution. Then Dezső Bokányi stepped to the rostrum.

> The French people demolished the Bastille on July 14 and this was the start of the French Revolution. Our day of revolution is October 31, because it was on this day that we demolished all the institutions of the old superannuated Parliament, in order to build the new Hungary of popular rights and of freedom. The political earthquake swept away all those who were the enemies of the people's rights. I wonder where are all those who sat in Parliament as "trustees of the people?" They disappeared as though they were not interested in the fate and future of the new Hungary. Let us rejoice that they have been moved out of our path. The government of the people will sweep away the last remnants of class privilege and its first task will be the enactment into law of a universal, secret franchise, extended to women, and the provision of rights to those who were without them. The fate of the Upper House will be decided on the basis of the universal franchise. The matter of the universal

franchise is even more important than the form of government. The House must be called into session to enact it into law. The first constitutional assembly will extend a fraternal hand toward all the peoples of the world. We will devote all our strength and energy to liberate the presently oppressed nations. Today we have all become brothers. There is no longer a polite "you" and a "your honor" but only a familiar "thou" and a "brother."

After Bokányi Judge Kálmán Kiczkó spoke. He outlined the gigantic fight of the workers and their lion's share of the victory. They are the ones who liberated the Hungarian nation. As a Hungarian judge he would not dare to sentence Tisza's murderers. The dynasty was the cause of all of Hungary's troubles. Royal power should be abolished. He would no longer pass sentence "In the name of His Majesty the King." The state should confiscate the gains made by the people enriched by the war and devote them to the good of the nation. He demanded a progressive tax which, he believed, would decrease the burden of the war debts.

After this speech a worker smashed the marble tablet that he had brought from the statue of Hentzi, destroyed the day before. Speeches were also delivered from an improvised rostrum in front of the Curia. The rally responded with loud cheers to the words of Sándor Garbai, Mór Preusz, and Lajos Kitajka.

Pesti Napló, November 5, 1918.

Hungary—A People's Republic

The House of Representatives Declared That It Was in Recess—The Upper House Halted Its Deliberations—A Decision of the People Introduced the Universal, Equal and Secret Franchise, Extended to Women—Telegrams to All Nations of the World about Hungary's Rebirth.

(Correspondents of the *Pesti Napló)*

..."The Hungarian people have won," said Mihály Károlyi, the prime minister, this forenoon before an assembly of several hundreds of thousands of people. The mass was undulating around the Parliament, an immense ocean without beginning or end. An unforgettable sight.

"The revolution has won," continued Károlyi, "and we have established the Hungarian People's Republic." In one sentence, this is the history of November 16, 1918. It is Hungary's red letter holiday. In barely two weeks, under great difficulties, in dark times, but with so little upheaval and blood as has never before been seen the first days of a revolution: The Hungarian revolution progressed with immense force, laid down the basis for the fortress of the new people's state, put an end to the history of the imperial-royal era, and opened the pages of the chronicle of the people's republic.

National colors and red banners fluttered in the wind everywhere at the birthplace of the People's Republic of Hungary. Finding itself, the middle class shaking off its privileged masters and the ever growing workers' army of Social Democracy shook hands under the national colors and under the red banners. The huge square surrounding the Parliament has never seen such a mass of people not even during the rally preceding Károlyi's appointment. Shoulder to shoulder, side by side, hundreds of thousands, with blushing, enthusiastic countenances, men and women, citizens and soldiers, who for four hours stood and waited in imposing order, with occasional outbursts of happiness and enthusiasm, to be witnesses to the new foundation of the country and so that they could tell their children and grandchildren: "I was present on the great day, at the birth of the Hungarian Republic...."

On Parliament Square

What is perhaps the most beautiful and monumental square in Budapest, the one in front of the Parliament was perhaps more monumental than ever, on this, the morning of Hungarian freedom. The Gothic lacy walls of the Parliament gazed with historic solemnity on the wintry gray sky, the mighty dome carried layers of snow along its ribs with solemn sublimity with the festive and beautifully lively, snow-covered Buda hills fluttering above and behind all this.

At 9:00 A.M. the square was deluged by myriads of people, deputations, associations, or trade unions with large, silken, and gold embroidered banners, or small red flags, or placards. Alkotmány Street, opening directly onto the square, was busy pouring in additional hundreds of thousands.

The first glance of the arrivals falls upon the projecting frontal façade of the Parliament which is decorated on its five little turrets with previously never seen flags. On both sides enormous national banners fluttered above them and above and between these flags, in the middle of the tympanum, the blood-red flag of the republic.

In front of the main entrance there are draperied stands from which, as everybody knew, the republic would be proclaimed. Above the stand three enormous signs announcing with huge letters the events to follow later today. The balconies of the palaces surrounding the square are billowing with draperies, most of them red ones.

Everybody remembers the coronation of last December. Compared to the colorful, medieval, pomp with glass carriages, white stallions and ceremonial dresses, the Parliament Square presents a simpler, colder but bold and sublime image with the strongest impression created by the multitude of people. The square with its enormous size and the uncountable multitude represents the true greatness of the people. Károly Kernstock, who designed the artistic pomp of the square made a large-scale and mighty concept come to life, which is reminiscent of Zola in its monumental conception.

While in the House of Representatives, in the Upper House and then, in the Dome Chamber the events follow a pattern and signal the end of the kingdom and the creation of the republic, the multitude in the square in front of the Parliament is increasing minute by minute. It is a heartwrenching feeling to be in the crowd as a tiny particle of the people's will, and worry about being swept by a wave of humanity toward an unknown destiny. The ones looking down from the balconies gets dizzy watching the infinite multitude of heads, which appear to be fitted to each other and it is only the flags and placards which indicate that the masses are not confluent but are separated into distinct groups by rope cordons.

Here and there speakers addressed the crowd and some spoke from balconies pouring forth their Hungarian rhetoric about the republic. The words of some can be heard only by the people nearby but the majority of the speakers are public orators whose bell-like tones can be heard from one end of the square to the other. In the meantime military bands, gipsy bands, and choirs send the sounds heavenward to soften and elate the somber firmament.

It is not only every step of the crushed lawns which is filled with people but so are the lampposts, every balcony, every window, and every roof. People perch on the roofs like some peculiar congregation of cats.

All at once the air is rent by a scream of victory, louder than anything heard before. The force of the scream suggests that the republic had just been proclaimed.

The ones with keen vision and further away those who brought binoculars can see that, on the rostrum clobbered together between the two Fadrusz lions in front of the main entrance to Parliament, Márton Lovászi and Dezső Bokányi had appeared to announce the decision of the Great National Council, It is twelve noon.

The speeches of Jászi and of the other orators are ended with resounding cheers. The military brass band blares out the national anthem and *La Marseillaise,* the workers march. It seems as though some monster orchestra was blaring forth the song of the revolutionaries and of the proletariat with the clamor multiplied by the song coming from thousands and thousands of throats.

A series of speeches comes not only from the festive rostrum but an oration comes also from the balcony of the Curia. With ringing, far-reaching voice Ernő Garami announces that the People's Republic of Hungary is born. Below him busy hands are already affixing the red and white posters to the wall of the Curia, which will proclaim the republic throughout the city.

The Republic is Proclaimed

At 11:15 A.M. Dezső Bíró, deathly pale from the exhausting excitement of the activities, steps forward to the topmost step of the Parliament's entranceway's landing and in a hoarse voice announces to the people that the last session of the House of Representatives had come to an end. His words do not penetrate very far but the ones in the front rows hear them and pass them on. There is an indescribable excitement and all present are thinking of the moment when Count Mihály Károlyi will appear to proclaim the desperately desired people's republic.

What Do the People Say

At the corner of the Honvéd Street I am stopped by an old policeman who came in civilian clothes, on his own.

"There will be an awful turmoil here!" he complained, "Please talk to somebody that there should be a troop of policemen at the end of the Alkotmány Street."

"For what reason?" asks a people's guard, who happens to be a printer of the *Esztendő*.

"Cause the ambulances can come in there only from the Markó Street and in this crowd there will dozens of people who will get sick."

The guard answers quietly,

"We do not need mounted police or gendarmes. We will show that there will be order even without police."

The old bastion of the former powers shakes his head sadly but the guard proved to be right. In the afternoon I called the ambulance service and they reported that, "There were only four minor swoons around the Parliament during the entire celebration. There was no other problem."

These numbers are a rarity and represent a record. Most of the people were standing there in the open for three and a half hours with incredible patience,

"Look", said one of the chief guards, "there is a sailor on the "lion steps," but down here the people themselves are holding the ropes."

And they held it for four and a half hours.

In front of the Palace of Justice they entertained themselves for a while with funeral orations under a black coffin which they raised high in the air so that all could see the name of the deceased: "The Kingdom."

Further on, beyond the Báthory Street, students and young workers sing and recite. The young man with waving hair yells loudly, "'Song of the Hungarian Jacobins,' written by Endre Ady." They liked it very much. But they preferred the last verse of an Ady poem called "A Hadak Útja" (The Path of the Armies):

> Here is the people. They will sit on the throne.
> For a thousand years worms in the dirt.
> The people judge, the people will judge.
> Woe a thousand times to the guilty.

When the news comes out that the Upper House no longer existed somebody yells out:

"Now they can put these mummies in mothballs for the winter!"

Then two airplanes flew by. One came very low and threw out the flowers of the revolution, white roses. Thousands of white faces looked up and waved their hats and caps. The motion picture photographer of the *Pesti Napló* was making a movie from the balcony of the Ministry of Agriculture. Later I took him and conducted him through the multitude to the great steps of Parliament without any trouble. The people, and particularly the union workers, readily opened a path for us through the densest crowd. Somebody called out:

"Give way, give way, they are recording history for eternity."

An old soldier, Szirmai, came to the main entrance. Within a moment they made room for him:

"Go up, to the highest position. Notice that you had not fought in vain in forty-eight."

When Bokányi finally arrived and proclaimed the people's decision about the republic, most of the people yelled,

"Long live the republic!"

"Long live Prime Minister Károlyi!"

"Announce the prime minister too!"

After Károlyi's speech the sailors picked him up and carried him through the crowd.

It seemed that Károlyi took a long glance and looked longingly at the streetcar.

Pesti Napló, November 17, 1918.

News

Rally of the jobless on the Parliament Square. At the rally, scheduled for Tuesday, the jobless met and accepted three, completely communist-colored resolutions. The first resolution demanded that the government take the strongest steps against the counterrevolutionaries and arm the proletariat. The second resolution demanded that the government immediately take over the enterprises of the do-nothing capitalists so that the trained workers get employment. This demand also asked that the army and the security forces be opened to the jobless, particularly because an armed multitude of the proletariat was the only protection against the counterrevolution. The third resolution condemned the campaign against the *Vörös Ujság* (Red News). Our comment on all of this is that we have also asked and ask now that the government proceed with the utmost severity and most forcefully against the counterrevolution. We also agree that there is a need for forceful action against the do-nothing capitalists and we also condemn the government excesses committed at the time to the search of the premises of *Vörös Ujság*. We wish to emphasize again, however, that we considered it to be wrong when organized workers take actions outside of the trade unions, when they ought to know that such movements must be made within the trade unions and in agreement with them. Only the united action by the trade unions can assure the success of the workers' actions.

Népszava, February 5, 1919.

The Nations's Social Democrats against the Bolsheviks

The Huge Demonstration of the Workers in the Capital City
General Strike in Budapest and in the Country—
March of Hundreds of Thousands—
The Soldiers Participate in the Demonstration—
Huge Rally in Front of the Parliament—

Action of the Government and of the Police—
The Bolshevik Leaders Arrested—
More Dead

To the Parliament

From the early morning hours on large masses hastened from every direction towards the Parliament. It was exciting to see the two thousand butchers parading, coming directly from the slaughter house, in work clothes, with cleavers and axes, cattle horns and cudgels, in disciplined ranks to take part in the demonstration. Multitudes kept swarming towards the Parliament, the workers of the various trades. Huge numbers of women factory workers came and with the same enthusiasm as the men pledged their faith in Social Democracy. Public employees also marched toward the square in enormous numbers. They included men from all of the ministries, government offices, university, mail service, telegraph offices, courts of justice, fiscal services, all the employees of the postal savings bank, the workers health services workers, the officials of insurance companies and banks, and city employees. The employees and workers of the military industries were there and all the waiters of the restaurants and the casinos, including the National Casino, demonstrated against the left and right wing counterrevolution.

The Great Mass Meeting

The enormous square in front of the Parliament was full to overflowing by 10:30 A.M. but still gigantic crowds tried to worm their way into it. It emptied out three times within the hour and filled up again each time. There have not been this many people on Parliament Square since the day when the republic was proclaimed. In every corner of the square speakers addressed the crowds, telling them about the events and about the position of the party.

Comrade Mór Preusz gave a convincing talk from the steps of the Parliament. Among other things, he said,

Thursday was a sad day because people perished but it is joyful too because it gives us the opportunity to proceed most ruthlessly against both the right-wing and the left-wing counterrevolutions. Socialism is humanism. Socialism is communism as well but this does not mean that it allows us to destroy ourselves. We love the fight for principles and we have never evaded it. There cannot be any fight for principles where the spirit is fueled by money. Is there a single one among the Communists who is not a hired man of the so-called Bolshevik ideals? Furthermore, they never fought the bourgeoisie in any way whatever and where they did appear, like in Salgotarján and other places, they accomplished their glorious work with robberies. In the eyes of the Social Democrat proletarian the counterrevolution of the counts and of the phony Communists is equally dangerous for maintaining the gains of the revolution. It is our duty to be watchful in every direction and let the proletarian fist strike if the people's republic is threatened again. It is our duty to work so that Social Democracy is enlarged with new armies. In this dual task nobody should relax and then we will not only muzzle the counterrevolution but create an opportunity to reach the final goals of social democracy.

The assembed received comrade Preusz's speech with great enthusiasm and very loud expressions of pleasure. It then accepted the proposed recommendation which states that the popular assembly demands that the government start a merciless war against the Communist leaders who abase the true communist principles and who abandon the true workers' movement for Russian rubles. It assures the government that in this activity it had the complete support of the Social Democratic Party.

The assembed empowered comrade Preusz to convey the will of the people to the government.

On the huge Parliament Square speeches were made to the comrades in a number of locations. At the end of the Alkotmány Street, where masses of people were rolling in and out of the square, comrades Rudolf Potlák, János Vanczák, Mrs. Ernő Müller, József Miagray, Sándor Propper, and Antal Dovcsák alternated in making speeches explaining the obligation of the organized, self-conscious revolutionary Social

Democrats against both the right- and left-wing counterrevolutionaries. Comrades József Büchler and Sári Goldschmiedt also spoke in the square. Artúr Fehér, an actor at the Vígszínház, declaimed impressive revolutionary poems from the steps to the Parliament. The march of the 1st and 32nd Honvéd detachments was impressive. At the corners of the square military bands played *La Marseillaise* which the masses listened to with bare heads.

The Demonstration of the Communists

The so-called Communists also marched onto the Parliament Square. There were about two hundred of them in front of the Ministry of Agriculture and they shouted their familiar slogans. The commander of the security force reported to the chief of police that the Communists had arrived. Chief of Police Schreiber gave orders that if they had came armed, the weapons had to be taken away. This is what happened. Several of the Communists were taken to a room in the Palace of Justice where they were searched. The ones carrying arms were detained. This action might have had more serious consequences but the organized Social Democrat workers of the state printing and publishing organization requested the police to refrain from any further such activities. The misguided people tried in several places to provoke the comrades. When they saw that there were no Social Democrats nearby they attacked the *Népszava* (People's Voice) and the party leaders with nasty insults. When they saw that the audience included Social Democrats they slunk away in a cowardly fashion. We must note that a "communist" military officer tried to disturb comrade Preusz's speech in Parliament Square but the comrades gave him a few slaps to the face, made him shut up and removed him from the mass meeting.

Népszava, February 2, 1919.

THE PEOPLE OF BUDAPEST HAD A BURIAL SERVICE

Funeral of the Heroes Fallen in the Defense of the Népszava
—Funeral Parade of Hundreds of Thousands—
The Sympathy Expressed by the Masses of Workers
—The Grieving Street

...On Thursday of last week men having lost their mental balance and dazzled by heated slogans, with souls contaminated with the poison of hatred, wanted to attack the *Népszava,* wanted to wrench the flag from the hands of the fighting proletariat, in order to debase the flag, trample it into the mud, to make trouble among the ranks of the mighty proletarian army marching under the banner, and place the rule of force into the chair of power, replacing the rule of democracy.

The intention did not succeed. The will of the blinded crowds was stopped by the brave and determined defense by the policemen, people's guards and sailors defending the *Népszava* building. The evening was a soul-wrenching, shocking tragedy for the Hungarian workers' movement. Proletarians attacked proletarians, proletarians soiled their hands with blood for a cause which should never be supported by proletarians because there is nothing more sacred than the unity of the workers' movement. The attack against the *Népszava* by these misguided people shed blood and dead men remained on the gray pavement. Wounded men were hoarsely seeking assistance and the feeling of trouble and fear raced through the soul of the city, but the attack did not succeed, the attack collapsed and fell apart on the brave persistence of the forces defending the *Népszava* building and who were willing to shed blood in so doing.

The weapons of the rebellious and destructive crowd murdered six men.

March to the Funeral

On the news that the funeral would begin at 2:20 P.M. unusually large groups began to move from every direction. The streetcars, already full, disgorged whole regiments of people. Along the major avenues compact groups marched to Parliament Square, the various trades, representatives of military councils, postal workers, policemen on foot and on horseback, gendarmes, firefighters and mounted police, the gendarmes, the firefighters and the fiscal agents. Parliament Square was almost full when an army of several hundred construction workers, the serried ranks of iron and metal workers, the railway men, armies of postal workers, the employees of financial institutions, cable and wire workers, the employees of funeral homes, photographers, the sleeping and restaurant car attendants, the glazers, the employees of Auer-lights, the workers of the fourth state railroad works, the organized tile and slate roofers, the merchants from the markets, the workers in the Ludovika Military Academy, the workers of the Hungarian-Belgian Metal Works, the workers of the Victoria Flower Mills, etc. When the funeral began the streets opening onto Parliament Square were also packed with endless masses of people.

In Front of the Parliament

In front of the ornately rising palace of former servitude and gentlemanly rowdiness, consecrated as the temple of the people's legislature, the proletariat of Budapest gathered to perform a funeral. Like multi-delta rivers pouring into the ocean the multitudes poured into the huge square in front of the Parliament. Above the black masses the wind was snapping the red banners and there was a forest of wreaths of red flowers. The proletariat of the factories, the workers of the workshops, the officials of administrative offices, the soldiers from the barracks, working women, young girls at the edge of life, the brave and busy workers of the railroads and postal services all swarmed in masses towards the six coffins. Everywhere people and more people. On top of the trees, on top of the streetcars, on the balconies of the houses, like a black drapery, again people whom their heart had pulled toward the coffins of the heroes. Looking at the multitudes, covering every space, one no longer felt the crushing weight of sorrow: the soul of man is captured by something uplifting and progressive. How much force, how many hands that can build, how many heads that can think.

One felt that these many, many lives, these hands, and these thoughts must be protected from destruction. Then rises the memory of a forenoon in May when this area, the square in front of the Parliament, the gray pavement of the Szabadság Square were painted red by the blood of the proletariat fighting for their rights....Yes, police bullets penetrated proletarian hearts...and now the proletariat has come forth to bury policemen who had joined them to further the Socialist ideals and to fight the good fight together....

On the large square the orderliness and the discipline were amazing. There were cordons going in this direction and in that one. Behind the cordons the multitude stands calmly and in dignity. The red banner with black ribbons fluttered victoriously and not just sadly. The placards show: here stood the ones from Csepel, there the ones from the arms factory, over there the construction workers, then the woodworkers and all the others. The square in front of the Parliament was full but still people were pouring in. A deputation of officers arrived and then a regiment of rifles, the 32nd and the 1st Honvéd formations, the latter with military bands, and finally the workers from distant factories. There was no disturbance anywhere, no restlessness, the faces were serious and the eyes watch the flames of the candelabra. The pilots have arrived for the funeral, they circle above the multitudes and dropped two wreaths from the planes as symbols of their respect. There were still more and more groups marching toward Parliament when

in the Dome Chamber

the funeral ceremony began. Sadness covered the Dome Chamber with black cloth, the color of the struggle is also represented, the banners waving above the coffins were red, indicating that outside of the coffins the flames and the fires have not stopped....The coffins were surrounded by innumerable wreaths. Next to the huge wreath of the Social Democratic Party, decorated with red ribbons, there was the laurel wreath of the government of the Hungarian People's Republic, and all the labor unions have placed their wreaths on the catafalques. A forest of flowers and a forest of laurel grew below the mighty dome. In the Dome Chamber there was only sadness and gravity. Suppressed, but occasionally audible, sobs ruled the air.

Those left behind are standing in front of the coffins. Sad and pale women and children, torn by life. In front of one of the coffins stood a bride, she would never again be held by the bridegroom locked in the metal coffin. We inspected the coffins and the names on the coffins to see how long they had lived. The letters seemed to grasp our heart: József Kresner, lived for twenty-three years, Károly Bilik, lived for twenty-four years, Imre Víg, lived for twenty-nine years, Zsigmond III Nagy, lived for thirty years, Ferenc II Kovács, lived for thirty-four years, and Sándor Kolonics, lived for thirty-nine years. All young lives that had barely entered the portals of life gone to waste. János Hock performed the funeral rites over the Catholic dead and Pastor Benő Haypál bid good bye to the two Calvinist ones. After the religious ceremony was completed the band of the Budapest rifle regiment played Wagner's "Siegfried March."

Then the coffins were carried down among the draperies and palms of the huge staircase. Three-hundred members of the Budapest Ethnic Gipsy Music Union were placed on the balcony of the staircase and they played the tune beginning with the words: "The poplars have shed their leaves...." The sobbing of the violins had a heart-wrenching effect. The coffins were placed on top of a catafalque covered with black cloth, with candelabra at the four corners, decorated with red ribbons. On the steps of the Parliament there was also a stand, covered with black....It was from here that the

funeral orations

were delivered....

Népszava, February 26, 1919.

The Inaugural Festivities of the Rule of the Hungarian Proletariat on Parliament Square

More than a Hundred Thousand People Participated in the Mass Meeting of the Hungarian Socialist Party on Sunday

The Parade

The major mass meeting of the Hungarian Socialist Party was scheduled for Sunday afternoon at 3:00 P.M. Shortly after noon masses began to stream toward Parliament Square. From the streets leading to the square streams of people rolled along with red placards, red flags, singing socialist revolutionary songs, cheering the proletarian revolution, the dictatorship, and the rule of the proletariat.

By 3:00 P.M. more than a hundred thousand people were on the square and masses were still arriving. The spring breeze made a whole forest of red banners flutter over the heads of the multitude. On the façade of the Parliament there was only one red banner which was received by a thunderous ovation when placed there by the comrades. The black color of the ancient fortress of the robber barons had been changed to red.

While waiting for the members appointed to attend the meeting of the Revolutionary Governing Council to arrive, more and more people assembled in the square. It became evident that it would be insufficient to address the huge crowd from one site only, the steps of the Parliament. There were speakers who made speeches in a number of places in the square, within the multitude and from the balcony of the Palace of Justice and from the balcony of the Ministry of Agriculture.

On the Steps of the Parliament

Comrade Bokányi arrived a few minutes before 3:00 P.M. and was followed shortly by comrades Garbai, Béla Kun, Béla Szántó, and Tibor Szamuely. The *Internationale* was played, then *La Marseillaise* and then the grand rally, imposing in its dimensions and importance, began.

Comrade Sándor Garbai

opened the historically important meeting after tens of thousands of comrades completely filled the huge square and the groups still arriving kept the multitude in continuous motion.

> I bring greetings, comrades, from the Revolutionary Governing Council at the moment when we have assumed power in this country in the name of the proletariat. This Governing Council gets its right to power from the united proletariat fighting in unison and not from the former ruling classes or kings.

> In this country, today, the proletariat has assumed the ruling powers and will conduct the affairs of the country on the basis of a proletarian dictatorship. The dictatorship of the proletariat can be safeguarded only if the proletariat is one in thought and unity and endeavors to create a proletarian state in Hungary with enthusiasm.
>
> I call upon you in this sense of sacred unity to support the Revolutionary Governing Council persistently and be ready to make sacrifices for it. I greet you again and most cordially in the name of the council.

The multitude responded to the greetings of the president of the Governing Council with enthusiastic cheers. Great enthusiasm welcomed

Comrade Béla Kun

who gave a powerful oration to the masses standing bareheaded around him.

"Comrades," he said,

> today the proletariat of Hungary came together into sacred unity. In the international struggle of the world's proletarians for such unity, the Hungarian proletariat is the advance guard of world revolution. We have fought for and claimed this most sacred role with pride and happy jubilation. In the footsteps of the Russian revolutionary proletariat it will make the eternal and unshakable rule of the world's proletariat. On this festive day of the united Hungarian proletariat we have received the greetings of the Eighth Russian Communist Congress, currently sitting in Moscow. The Russian brethren send their fervent greetings to you, comrades, in the sacred struggle which we have started to create the proletarian state. This struggle will be a hard one, comrades, we are at the beginning of the fight and those who have assumed the power will forward the cause of the proletariat with the most rigorous rules of the dictatorship.
>
> It is to the eternal glory of the Hungarian proletariat that it united into a single organization at a critical moment. Two proletarian parties have fused together. Now the city and the village must fuse into an unbreakable fraternal association! There will be major battles and hard fighting against the imperialistic robbers. The dictatorship of the proletariat is not an Eldorado. We have not promised

to give bread to everybody but we have promised that we will create the system where all those who work will have bread. This cannot be accomplished in one or two days but we promise, in the name of the Hungarian Soviet Republic, that we will create this system. In the meantime we will know that if we are starving, we are starving for a free and happy future. Long live the Hungarian Soviet Republic! Long live the international dictatorship of the proletariat!

There was loud cheering lasting for several minutes while three hundred musicians, under the baton of Laci Rácz, played *La Marseillaise*. The next speaker,

Comrade Dezső Bokányi

went into the crowd and, sitting on the shoulders of the comrades, delivered a mighty oration on the tasks of the proletariat. "The proletariat has come to glory! We wish to create a council of workers, soldiers and peasants, a red army and build our proletarian state struggling against foreign imperialists and domestic counterrevolutionaries. Our most important and immediate task is the creation of a red army. Comrades! This will be your army, it will fight for your rights and for your country and only you can be its soldiers."

"We will be it! We will enlist!"

"Long live the Red Army!"

"What we did, we did it on your behalf. Now we need all the strength, enthusiasm, and self sacrifice of the established sacred proletarian unity, to create the Communist state along the Danube and the Tisza. Just give us a year and you will see what the proletarian state can do for you...."

The huge crowd started to disperse about 5:00 P.M. while the sixty members of the organized musicians played the socialist revolutionary march and the crowd sang it.

Népszava, March 25, 1919.

May Day Festival of the Proletarian Revolution

Six Hundred Thousand Proletarians Marched on the Streets of Budapest

The Red Budapest

Never, in the memory of man, was Budapest so beautifully decorated. Among the festivities of the last decades there is not one single one that can be compared with the glow, pomp, and warmth of the May festival of the proletarian state. Every small house in every small side street just like every major boulevard was decorated with the outward manifestations of the mood of the festivity. All of Budapest participated in the celebration of May Day and it was touching to recall the May Day festivities of Hungarian Socialists that the capitalist, and the authorities they controlled, tried hard to impede. What a long way between the ban on work stoppages on May Day and the present May Day when a government decree mandated a holiday and there is an official celebration of the day of the proletariat.

The decorations of the city showed that an "official" organization of a holiday could indeed be appropriate to the monumentality of the day's significance. The entire city took on red garb and everywhere artistic red banner displays, triumphal arches, artistic stands, artistic creations, allegorical pictures and the statues of the great men and women of socialism showed the respect and awe with which the proletarian leadership and the people of the city prepared for the festival of freedom. For days these preparations were the center of attention. Slowly the entire image of the streets turned red and yesterday streetcars, newly painted red, traveled along the rails with a large sign on their sides proclaiming: "Proletarians of the World Unite!"

On Parliament Square globes are placed on two red columns. The *Andrássy* statue is encased by planks and it was surrounded by a pavilion in Greek style, designed by architects Bálint and Jámbor while its artistic decorations were painted by Géza Faragó and Andor Székely. The slogan on the pavilion read, "Glory to the Workers!" The entrance to the Parliament facing Alkotmány Street is also decorated with draperies and statues....

Vörös Ujság, May 3, 1919.

Day of Joy for the Proletariat of Budapest

Celebration of Victory in the Streets—Large Demonstrations and Mass Meetings on Parliament Square

The happy news about the occupation of Kassa, Selmecbánya, Korpona, and Nagysurány arrived in Budapest late last night and the workers learned about them from the morning papers. In the factories and in the offices word about the great news was passed from person to person and produced joy among the proletarians. Sparkling eyes and red cheeks indicated the self-conscious pride and the even stronger faith permeating the mind of the proletarians when they heard about the new great victories of the soldiers of the communist state.

At 8:00 A.M. all the military bands in Budapest marched along the streets making music and the notes of the *Internationale* and of *La Marseillaise* filled the streets under the sunny canopy of the heavens. The military bands were welcomed everywhere with good humor and gayety. Shortly after 8:00 A.M. the first red banner appeared on the balconies of the houses and very soon the entire city was decorated with red flags....

At 2:00 P.M. the workers in all the factories and workshops laid down their tools and, gathering under red flags, started out toward the assembly points. The assembly points were on the Vérmező, Korona Square, Múzeum Boulevard, Lehel, Hunyadi, Almássy, and Tisza Kálmán Streets, and on Martinovics Square in Kőbánya. Shortly after 2:00 P.M. the military bands appeared at the places and welcomed the marching groups and the masses of workers with fiery, revolutionary music. The workers of the factories and certain organizations arrived in tightly organized columns and took over the square with laughter and good humor. Perfect order was maintained everywhere and the proletarians expressed their enthusiasm with rousing cheers and songs. They cheered the proletarian army, the Soviet Republic, world revolution, the Russian allies, and Lenin. Ecstasy bubbled hotly from the proletarian hearts.

The marches from the assembly points started shortly after 3:00 P.M. From various points of the great city a huge multitude of people rolled and snaked its way along the streets toward the single goal, the Parliament Square. Everywhere enthusiastic cheers and shouts of pleasure received the marchers. In front of the theaters the theater orchestras were playing.

The first of the crowds arrived to Parliament Square around 4:00 P.M.. From then on the city floods the Parliament Square with multitudes of people, with new groups pouring in from all sides as though the square was a collecting basin. On the square a two-hundred member gipsy band played revolutionary marches. The place slowly became organized and in various locations on the square commissars and the leading members of the Party welcomed enthusiastically by the crowd, addressed the people. Béla Kun, Sándor Garbai, Dezső Bokányi, László Rudas, Béla Szántó, Sándor Vincze, Jenő Landler, Mátyás Rákosi, Jenő Hamburger, József Haubrich, and other comrades spoke of the great importance of the Red Army's victory and their speeches were frequently interrupted by the outbreaks of popular enthusiasm....

Vörös Ujság, June 8, 1919.

Funeral of The Proletarian Victims of the Counterrevolution

An impressive display of grief and piety will accompany the proletarian heroes who have lost their life while doing their self-sacrificing duty against the counterrevolutionary coup on Tuesday to their eternal rest. József Szokoli, Ferenc Korbély, Géza Gyenis, István I. Szabó, Gyula Pető, Mór Grósz, István Pigécz, and Ferenc Szentgáli, comrades from the 32nd Red Infantry Regiment, János Meleg, János Deutsch, Gusztáv Budai, and Mihály Hemin, comrades from 1st Red Infantry Regiment, comrade István **Szory** from the Red Artillery, and comrade Béla Lőwy a political commissar were those who, as victims of the counterrevolutionary coup and with their heroic death, forever inscribed their names into the history of world revolution.

The funeral of the proletarian heroes was entrusted to the Presidium of the Budapest Revolutionary Central Workers' and Soldiers' Council with the support of the Presidium of the Revolutionary Governing Council. The lying in state will take place Sunday afternoon on Parliament Square. The funeral of the proletarian heroes will mobilize all the workers in Budapest and the Presidium of the Budapest Central Workers' and Soldiers' Council calls on all the Budapest workers' organizations, the workers' and soldiers' councils, the unions and the Party organizations and all the workers in Budapest to make the funeral as grandiose as possible with an imposing march of the working masses.

On Parliament Square Sándor Garbai, president of the Revolutionary Governing Council, will speak for the council and István Biermann, a member of the Presidium of the Budapest Revolutionary Central Workers' and Soldiers' Council, will say farewell to the martyrs of world revolution. Funeral orations will also be delivered by representatives of the Labor Union Council, the leadership the Hungarian Socialist-Communist Workers' Party, the Red Guard, and the regiments. The memorial service will be opened and closed by music from the combined band of all Budapest military bands and songs from the workers' choruses.

Vörös Ujság, June 29, 1919.

THE FUNERAL OF THE MARTYRS OF THE PROLETARIAN STATE

On Parliament Square

We have never seen a more beautiful and moving sight than the one on Parliament Square on Sunday afternoon. The eighteen metal coffins, surrounded by hundreds of tropical plants and wreaths, were placed on the steps of Parliament. Huge black draperies and a black banner, waving from above, presented the background for this huge catafalque when the proletarian state buried its eighteen heroes. On the square those regiments stood in military order in which the heroes had served. The huge square was completely silent and people watched the progress of the funerary festivities with bated breath. The coffins of the heroes were placed along two lines:

István Csőr, twenty-year-old Red Soldier
Lajos Blasek, twenty-year-old Red Soldier
János Deutsch, nineteen-year-old Red Soldier
Mihály Hennig, twenty-year-old Red Soldier
János B. Melegh, eighteen-year-old Red Soldier
Gusztáv Gulási, eighteen-year-old Red Soldier
István I. Szabó, nineten-year-old Red Soldier
Ferenc Korbély twenty-three-year-old Red Soldier
Miklós Kósa, twenty-three-year-old Red Soldier
Ferenc Szentgáli, twenty-one-year-old Red Guard
Gyula Pető, twenty-three-year-old Red Guard
Géza Gyenis, eighteen-year-old Red Guard
Gyula Gosztonyi, twenty-three-year-old Red Guard
József Szokoli, eighteen-year-old Red Soldier
Ferenc Lajkó, sixteen-year-old Red Guard
István Pigécz, twenty-one-year-old Red Soldier
Mór Gross, thirty-two-year-old Red Soldier and
Béla Lőwy thirty-two-year-old political commissar

The bands, the military delegations and the emissaries of the Party and of the labor unions began to gather in front of the House of the Soviet Republic building at one o'clock. Honor guards from the 32nd and the 1st Red Infantry Regiments and from the 1st Red Artillery battalion formed a cordon around the catafalque. The soldiers placed oak leaves or red flowers in their caps. Some detachments carried arms and other carried full military equipment when they marched to the funeral service....

Népszava, July 1, 1919.

Funeral of the Proletarian Martyrs of the Counterrevolution

Memorial Service of the Workers of Budapest

The Victims on the Catafalque

The catafalque of the eighteen heroic proletarian victims was erected on the steps of the House of the Soviet Republic building facing the Alkotmány Street. The huge black catafalque glorying in the revolutionary colors of red flowers and red ribbons presented an incomparably moving picture on the mighty Parliament Square. The major gateway and the columns were covered with black drapes and a large platform was erected over the stairs also completely covered with black drapes. Tropical plants were placed between the coffins. The coffins of the martyrs were arranged in two lines with the first one on the right being István Csőr, twenty-year-old-old Red Soldier, then Lajos Blasek, twenty-year-old Red Soldier, János Deutsch, nineteen-year-old Red Soldier, Mihály Hennig, twenty-year-old Red Soldier, János B. Melegh, eighteen-year-old Red Soldier, Gusztáv Gulási, eighteen-year-old Red Soldier, István I. Szabó, nineteen-year-old Red Soldier, Ferenc Korbély, twenty-three-year-old Red Soldier, Miklós Kósa, twenty-three-year-old Red Soldier, Ferenc Szentgáli, twenty-one-year-old Red Guard, Gyula Pető, twenty-three-year-old Red Guard, Géza Gyenis, eighteen-year-old Red Guard, József Szokoli, eighteen-year-old Red Soldier, Ferenc Lajkó, sixteen-year-old Red Guard, István Pigécz, twenty-one-year-old Red Soldier, Mór Gross, thirty-two-year-old Red Soldier, and Béla Lőwy, thirty-two-year-old political commissar.

Wreaths with red ribbons on every coffin, wreaths from the Governing Council, from the Socialist-Communist Party, from the military, from relatives, and from the *Vörös Ujság*, masses of red ribbons and red flowers glowing in the somber blackness of grief under the sunny, blue infinity of the firmament.

The Start of the Memorial Service

Bands, military delegations and groups from the Party and from the labor unions marched in at 1:00 P.M. in the afternoon.

Silently, with the festive piety of historic seriousness, lines of comrades came to say goodbye to the fallen heroes of the Soviet Republic. The soldiers placed oak leaves or a red flower in their cap and wore black armbands. They came armed to the funeral and some detachments were in full battle gear. They were followed by more and more tides of people flooding the square.

Honor guards of the 32nd and the 1st Red Infantry Regiments and of the 1st Red Artillery Battalion marched in and made a cordon around the catafalque. The other units of the Budapest garrison and of the other military organizations were all represented by delegations of five members each. The huge wreath of the Red Army, sent from the front, was brought in by comrade Béla Vágó, at the head of a special delegation.

At about 2:00 P.M. all the members of the Revolutionary Governing Council arrived, who under the leadership of comrades Sándor Garbai and Béla Kun participated in the memorial service, and comforted the relatives of the proletarian victims with soothing solace....

The service was started with the Red Army Band playing the *Internationale*. Then the big band of the capital city's folk musicians played a folk song beginning with: "They placed the body in the yard." Then the Acélhang Chorus sang the funerary song beginning with: "Why so gloomy..." and other funerary songs. Many thousands of people stood around with their hats in their hands, listening with emotion to the funerary songs, after which comrade Sándor Garbai, the president of the Revolutionary Governing Council stepped to the black, wreath-decorated rostrum set up between the coffins.

The Funerary Procession

Then the musicians played the folk song beginning with: "The leaves have fallen from the shaking aspen" and, accompanied by these notes, the coffins were removed from the catafalque and taken to the hearses. The first, large carriage was for the wreaths and a good number of these, decorated with purple ribbons and red flowers were piled on it. Then came a long line of hearses to accommodate the martyred victims of the counterrevolution on their last journey.

The huge funeral cortege left Parliament Square at 4:00 P.M.

Vörös Ujság, July 1, 1919.

Rally of the Unemployed on Parliament Square

They Demand a Government in Which the Workers Are Represented

With the permission of the Romanian military command the council of the Hungarian Council of Trade Unions called on all unemployed in Budapest to gather for a meeting on Friday morning. The police was present in large numbers and the Romanian military command also did everything in order to assure the undisturbed conduct of the meeting. At 9:00 A.M. people started to gather slowly. First the organizers of the meeting arrived and performed the necessary preparations.

They distributed leaflets to the arrivals on which the Social Democratic Party called on the workers to stick together and protest against the present form of government. Another leaflet called upon the workers to refrain from all disruptions.

The jobless gathered slowly so that it was 11:00 A.M. before the meeting could be started. Prior to that Károly Peyer the president of the Ironworkers' Union and construction worker Gyula Battiz spoke.

Suddenly, at about 10:30 A.M. huge numbers of people swarmed toward Parliament Square from every direction. By 11:00 A.M. the multitude became restless and demanded that the meeting be started. Then Samu Jászai, the president of the Hungarian Council of Trade Unions, rose to speak and asked the assembly to elect Géza Smarilla, ironworker, as chairman of the meeting, iron worker Károly Peyer as speaker, and Albert Király as recorder. The participants accepted the recommendation and then Chairman Géza Smarilla stated the sole purpose of the meeting. He asked the assembled large crowd to behave with the seriousness demanded by the occasion.

Then rapporteur Károly Peyer started to speak. He emphasized that the workers had behaved in recent times with immovable calm. In fact, public life in general was characterized by peace and quiet. "You know, however," he said,

> that this peace and quiet was the deathly peace of quiet of misery and desperation because this is what has taken hold of the Hungarian workers. We are confronted by the murderous attack of a new enemy, the inescapable destruction of hunger and misery are waiting for us. There is no bread, no chance to find work, no firewood and those whose duty it would be to help us in the dreadful want, are doing nothing. The holders of power are fomenting racial strife instead of doing serious work. They sow the seed of recession instead of that of understanding. They rile up the villages against the towns and urge the villages to withhold all food and all assistance from the towns not knowing that this might sow the seeds of a new revolution.
>
> If we look around Europe we will be struck if we look at Germany which was also among the vanquished. The German workers enthusiastically and lovingly work for an extra hour each day, for no pay, to promote the prosperity of Germany. Why do they not learn such policies here? What need is there to continue to kick the Hungarian workers?

During Peyer's speech, about 11:30 A.M., leaflets were thrown from the windows of the Parliament. These leaflets were distributed to cause trouble because they contained lists of the leaders of the party in such a way as to show them all have Jacob as their first name, that they were all Jews and that the Social Democratic Party was a party of Jews. The leaflets caused agitation among the multitude and it became very irate but Peyer calmed down the masses.

Then Chairman Smarilla again read the recommendation of the meeting which the multitude accepted unanimously.

During the meeting a Romanian regiment marched to the sound of trumpets in front of the Ministry of Agriculture. They positioned themselves along the street car tracks on Parliament Square in such a fashion that the street car traffic remained possible. The meeting came to an end at noon. And on the request of the chairman the multitude dispersed quietly.

* * *

The secretariat of the Social Democratic Party estimated that the meeting was attended by ten to twelve thousand people. The fact that relatively few out-of-work people showed up was attributed to the fact that the meeting was not properly prepared in advance. Before the meeting was held a number of problems and difficulties arose and it was not decided until Thursday afternoon to hold the meeting. There was no time to put up posters. A large number of the unemployed learned about the meeting too late....

Friss Ujság, October 11, 1919.

The National Army Is in Budapest

Commander in Chief Horthy was received on Parliament Square by the prime minister. After greetings had been exchanged the prelates, under the leadership of the prince primate celebrated mass. After the festive mass the delegation of women presented the Banner with the Virgin to Horthy.

The rest of the meeting was devoted to receiving the various delegations. It was at this time that most of the armed force detachments arrived in the square and marched through it. Wherever the soldiers marched representatives of the associations with banners in their hands and children with small tricolor flags lined the streets. Along the line of the march, the Social Missions Association distributed small loaves baked from flour handed out by the minister of public supplies. Similar loaves were also distributed at the hospitals and to the inmates of the poorhouses.

Népszava, November 18, 1919

Festivity of the National Army on Parliament Square

Every street and avenue of the capital city poured its flood of people into Parliament Square.

The square was again decorated with banners like so many times before! But what a difference between the May Day of last year and today.

After so many humiliations, pain and suffering, on Sunday forenoon Parliament Square became the birthplace of the Hungarian colors and Hungarian national defense. After centuries the Hungarian colors and the Hungarian words have regained their proper leading position.

The wind was whistling and rain was falling but the sun broke through the clouds on the Hungarian sky and the clouds were covered with the rainbow of national colors.

On top of the steps there was a tent for celebrating the mass. It was made of white boards and covered by green cloth, surrounded by palms and laurels and with a crucifix in the rear. On the broad, dignified front of the building there were red-white-and-green banners without coats of arms, the balconies on the right and left were decorated with red velvet and there was a line between the Parliament, the Curia and the Ministry of Agriculture with alternating flags of the capital city and of the country. On the balconies of the Curia and of the ministries there were tapestries and banners—banners with coats of arms and crowns. The Alkotmány Street looked like a flower garden. Deputations and schoolchildren lined the street with pine branches decorated with white autumn roses and large bouquets of chrysanthemums. Everything and everybody was waiting for Horthy.

The Preparations

The square was lined by detachments of officers, a police cordon blocked off Falk Miksa Street to prevent congestion, the streetcar traffic was stopped and bright young newspaper boys were peddling papers and Horthy memorial postcards. The card had the commander in chief's picture and the following lines in facsimile:

"Villagers, strong stem of our race, depository of our hopes, my thanks go out to you today and my warmest greetings from this large city that had gone astray. If the ancient strength radiating from your small white houses fills the hearts of the residents of the stone palaces and of the workers' homes, Hungary will be greater and mightier than ever before! Horthy."

Officers with feathers in their caps hasten across the square to arrange matters, smaller detachments arrive and march by, every invited guest goes to his assigned place by a prearranged route. On the left side of the steps the white-red-gold line of the Crown Guards, on the right side the Royal Guards in red trousers, white mantle, green jacket, with golden clasp and white egret plumes on their hats. The lines extend all the way to the tent.

The official world gathers slowly. Some members of the government appear by the tent, the prelates of the Christian denominations arrive with the prince primate in the lead. Wlassics with a smile on his face, Count Gyula Andrássy and, much to everybody's notice, Count Albert Apponyi....

Down below, organizers issue instructions:

"If possible, cheer only for Horthy and for the National Army and refrain from any other exclamation."

The delegation with the banner of the Hungarian Women arrives, planning to present the banner to Horthy and to the National Army. The beautiful silken banner is taken out of its black container. The tricolor silk is covered with beautiful embroideries and there are three ribbons with the inscriptions:

"The Hungarian Women—National Alliance—Augusta, Royal Princess."

Voices are raised from several areas:

"Long live Christian Hungary!"

"Long live Horthy. Long live the National Army!"

"Long live Friedrich...."

Apparently Friedrich has arrived. In a black overcoat and a top hat. He looks up to the balcony where his little daughter is clutching a bouquet of chrysanthemums waiting for the moment to present it to Horthy. Next to her, her mother and ladies in Hungarian ceremonial dress. On another balcony a lady with two little boys in sailor suits, the Horthy family.

Horthy Arrives

Alkotmány Street is lined by people holding flowers. In the distance a troop of mounted police appears. Two carriages advance in gallop, the chief of police is in one and the Lord Mayor in the other. Both in Hungarian ceremonial dress. These were the only two at the festivity.

Cheering is heard, the street is buzzing, flowers are thrown from the windows along the Alkotmány Street, the cheering is getting louder and louder and, like a fairytale hero, Horthy appears on a white stallion.

"Look! That one! On the white stallion! That's Horthy!"

Slender, tall, his face sharp like an eagle's, his eyes clear and hard naval officer's eyes, in naval uniform with all his medals and ribbons, and with a red-white-green button on his cap....

At long last the Hungarian colors are worn by the commander in chief of the Hungarian army.

How much had to happen until the Hungarian colors and the Hungarian commander in chief had come together!

The whole square rejoices and enthuses. Kerchiefs are waved and there is a deluge of flowers. Just before Horthy enters the square the trumpeter blows the commander in chief's trumpet call from the highest balcony....

Horthy is surrounded by his staff. He is accompanied by the commander in chief's banner, the national banner, affixed to a lance, bordered by red- white- and green triangles, with large initials in the middle : F. V. (Fő-Vezér) [commander in chief].

He descends from his horse...

Horthy stops in the middle. He is hard, disciplined, strong—a soldier in every way. At the steps Prime Minister István Freidrich hastens toward him, greets him and welcomes him in a voice audible from afar....

The Commander in Chief's Response

Horthy responds. His words are calm and careful. He starts quietly but as he becomes hardened by emotions and ideas, his voice becomes louder and carries further. The women press forward, stand on tiptoes, everybody wants to see him.

"Silence...Silence...Let us hear him...Let us hear him..." comes from every side and Horthy says:

Mister Prime Minister!

In the name of the Hungarian National Army I thank you for the warm and welcoming words. Our path to this square was difficult and scattered with boulders. It was here, exactly one year ago, that the fate of the country was entrusted to a man who took our nation to the edge of its grave. I will not seek to find out what his motives were but there is no doubt world history knows of no other person who has brought on his country such painful humiliation, so much absolute deterioration, so much bitterness, and so much shame.

The revolution did not only fail in bringing freedom or rights to the people but it did not bring the so intensely hoped-for peace. Its only achievement was to make us familiar with the entire range of the destructive forces, to give us a glimpse into the witches' kitchen and see how demagogy can take a strong, blooming country, corrupt it and trample it into the mud.

We learned the lesson and drained the cup to the last drop!

From the prolonged process of corruption reconstruction will also take some time. If we want to accelerate the process, we must extirpate all poisons from the soul of the nation and every Hungarian patriot must unite for a sacred goal which has two pillars: the national ideal and Christian morality. First of all, all dissension must stop, so that the population agitated unto death with a thousand slogans, might come to a resting point. It is now more important than ever before that the political parties refrain from dividing the country into opposing camps. The National Army stands as one body and one soul, solidly and unselfishly for service to the country and will bring the Christian view of the world and the rule of decency, honor, and truth to victory.

Under the protection of its arms every section of the nation can again begin the critically essential productive work with which we want to build a more beautiful, happier, and blooming Hungary.

When we now beseech the God of Hungary, before the altar, to assist us in this arduous task we are united by one sacred thought only:

Long live the Country!

The Mass

"Long live the country! Long live Horthy! Long live the National Army!" shouted the multitude in response.

The commander in chief got started, accompanied by his banner and by the members of the government, and proceeds up the steps where under the tent he is received by the prince primate.

Now Horthy is above the entire square and everybody can see him. He takes off his cap, his hair is still dark with just a tinge of gray. The sailor hat has left an indentation in his hair. He stands at attention, a real soldier, while he receives the welcome from the prince primate. Down below the band starts to play church music and the mass begins. The *Kyrie Eleison* sings out with majestic strength and its interrupted melody has a quasi tragic force. When the host is raised, the small bells ring and everybody bows their head, pondering the fate of man and the changes in the history of the nation.

From afar the sound of trumpets mingles with the sacred melodies of the mass. The beautiful purity of the "Maria" hymn is invaded by the trumpets of the infantry arriving into the square. Horthy turns around. Like a father when his children are coming. He looks out over the square and his eyes used to the vast distances of the sea scan the square to see his soldiers arriving. It is apparent that all his pleasures, concerns, and thoughts are focused on this. The army which the day before yesterday did not yet exist, exists today, will exist tomorrow and into eternity. It is the hope and faith of the Hungarians.

The Prelates Bless the Banners

The singing has come to an end and the square resounds with brief, snappy commands.

"Attention! Eyes right!" is heard and the banners are beginning to move.

They start and then stop in front of the commander in chief and in front of the tent.

From the front rows of the public another banner starts out. It is the banner of the Hungarian women. It is handed to Horthy by Cecil Tormay.

"Take the banner and do not rest until it has been reflected by the four rivers and has been raised over the three hills. Take it, the hand of women have blessed it. The hands of you men will hallow it in glory."

Horthy Responds:

> Honored Ladies! Please accept my thanks replete with respect and gratitude for the beautiful banner you have presented to the Hungarian National Army. When the ladies appeared here and presented to me their noble gift, my soul recalls the memory of the sadly beautiful days and memory returned to the banks of the Tisza in Szeged where it was also a group of Hungarian ladies who presented the very first banner to the National Army full of confidence and with hesitant hopes.
>
> There were only a few soldiers at the time but all of them were proud and determined Hungarians who refused to consider any compromise. With the banner in my hand I swore with the soldiers, with enthusiasm, and not with fears and concerns, that we would end up with it or on it. We either regain our country with it or it will be our shroud. This is how we entered. Holding it high, we entered Budapest, the capital of the country, and since that time the few hundred soldiers marching under the banner have grown to many thousands. Yet we have not yet reached our goal. We must proceed from Pest. We must hold this banner high. The new banner with the old one, with our stubborn determination and the ancient slogan: "With it or on it."

The commander in chief holds the banner in his right hand and hands it over to his flag bearer so that it will be next to him throughout the entire event.

Now all banners were lowered to the ground to receive the blessing of the Church.

The National Anthem

A sacred moment ensued. The military band struck the first notes of the national anthem. The many thousands of people stood with bare heads and the song burst forth from the very depth of their hearts, more intense than a religious prayer it was the prayer of the martyred country returning to its rights. Everybody sang. The soldiers stood at attention with the right hand at their cap, saluting the country's prayer, with tears rolling from their hard eyes. The huge square, where the last multitude sang the deadly tune of the *Internationale*, was filled with the sublime song and with the wind making the national tricolor flutter above their heads.

The Flowers Wrapped in Mourning Veils

Now sixty-three women in black dresses and mourning veils marched up to the commander in chief and placed small bouquets tied with mourning veils at his feet, the sad autumnal flowers of the lost Hungarian counties.

The last one of the ladies was Cecil Tormay who said, "Let these mournful flowers lead the banner to its heroic master. We, the daughters of the torn away and occupied Hungarian counties, have come so that here the dismembered, suffering country becomes united in the flowers and the women, the country which among its tears expects a better future from you."

The national anthem was played again and then a charming scene took place. Beautiful girls in Hungarian dresses marched in with István Friedrich's daughter in the lead who presented a bouquet of white chrysanthemums to Horthy.

The Troops March Off

There was a sudden movement. The police and the gendarmes move the masses away from the road. Horthy descends the steps, the commander in chief banner on his side and the members of the government behind him. They stop at the foot of the steps.

A standing rider points toward the Személynök Street indicating the direction in which the troops have to march.

The drum beat sounds, the kettle drum is struck and the enthusiastic sounds of the "Rákóczi March" fill the square. The infantry begins its march.

The festivity reaches its peak.

In Horthy's person, in all enthusiasm, and in all the cheering we salute the soldiers, the Hungarian soldiers. The loyal sons of Hungary, who fought like lions for five years on all the battlefields of world, and even though they had lost the war against the world, they gained honor for Hungarian loyalty with their heroism until the red horror cast a shadow on this term.

Now they stand again before us!

Poor, ragged, with inadequate equipment, they stand proudly, with self-esteem, national self-consciousness, strength, and filled with the coming justice. In front an assault troop! Steel helmet on their head, a breast shield over their mantle to protect them from barbed wire. One of them has only one eye, but he is with them and stands in their line!

They march and the wet pavement resounds under their boots. They march firmly and proudly. Then come the sons of Transdanubia in closed and resounding rows. Regular soldiers! Courageous determination in their eyes and as they march by Horthy, they look into his manly eyes and understand each other. They are Hungarians!

Their coats differ, some of them have no coat. No matter!

We exist, we live, these hard young men, these determined looks no longer signify the past, they are the future. The terribly ill country is back on its feet, it lives, give it time and it will perform miracles.

The officers cleave the air with their sabers, every one of them feels what today means, and they stand straighter!

"The Szeged troops are coming."

A troop of lads from Szeged march by, followed by brigades of officers, the pavement resounds, the marching song rings out and brigade after brigade marches proudly by the commander in chief.

Then come the cadets from the Ludovika Academy!

The heroic sons of June 24 are greeted with thunderous cheers.

Troubridge, the British Admiral, stands on the steps surrounded by his staff and so do a number of foreign journalists. They are obviously enthralled by the splendid young men.

More cheering. The gendarmes are coming and then an even louder cheer. This is for the hussars. They sit martially on their horse, their sabers appear to be a part of their arm. They are only waiting for the command: ride, ride!

Then, in the end, come the canons decorated with pine branches and white flowers.

How the multitude shivers, murmurs, and cheers….

"Canons!...The canons of the Hungarian National Army!...

Do we really have any canons left?..."

The multitude disperses with such thoughts, while the music of the military bands echoes from the distance and a British gunboat, which had been anchored by the Parliament, slowly steams down the Danube….

Az Est, November 18, 1919.

Horthy Was Elected Regent

The Election Was by Secret Ballot. A Deputation Went to Fetch Horthy—The Regent Takes His Oath of Office in the Chamber—The Government Has Resigned—It Continues to Govern in the Interim.

The regent of the country was elected on Monday forenoon in the chamber of the National Assembly.

There was much activity around the Parliament well before 10:00 A.M. A large number of curious people assembled by the *Andrássy* statue, by the main entrance to the Parliament. Police in festive uniform and soldiers maintained order. The houses facing Parliament Square were decorated with flags….

Friss Ujság, March 2, 1920.

LIFE AND TRUTH

On Parliament Square a carved piece of white marble proclaims the truth of a former great life with artistic triumph. It also proclaims, at the same time, the eternal validity of ideals. The power which enslaved the conceptual truths of the '48 revolution has been crushed into fragments and no longer exists. Yet the ideals of March are alive today and Kossuth's name still has a magic force. Hearing the name of Kossuth the failed Hungarian War of Liberation comes to everybody's mind everywhere in the world. The heroic effort of a shackled people with which it endeavored to free itself from the yoke of the Habsburg dynasty and of the feudal Hungarian magnates.

Of the endeavors of the '48 Hungarian Revolution only one, "Independent Hungary," has become reality even now, seventy years later. The victory of the Habsburg dynasty in the War of Liberation meant not only that the Habsburgs continued to rule over Hungary but it also meant that the Hungarian land owners, the feudal oligarchy, and the clerical reaction, assisted by the victorious power, could continue to hold the Hungarian workers in a state of servitude. The Habsburg dynasty and the Hungarian magnates came to understand each other very well, rapidly made peace with each other but did not make peace with the Hungarian people, with the destitute peasantry and with the exploited workers. In 1867 the Compromise was established. The Hungarian ruling classes made peace with the ruling house in a lawful manner but made no attempt whatever in their own country to reach a compromise or to make peace with the oppressed, legally deprived and exploited masses. The completely subordinate role of the racial ties became manifest and the financial ties proved to be a far stronger factor.

For seven decades 1848 played the role of sleeping beauty in Hungarian public life. The entire might of the state confronted the 1848 ideals and endeavors. Even seven decades, however, were insufficient to eliminate these ideals but even seven decades were also insufficient to bring the items dealing with public liberties of the twelve points of March to realization. Yet developments could not be sidetracked and 1848 did not want to become the past before it could become the present. And it came in 1918 because it had to come. 1918 collapsed just as 1848 did and the victorious counterrevolution persecuted its ideals just as 1848 had been persecuted.

While at that time they confronted the ideals of freedom with brutal directness, the white counter revolution added lying to hate and brutality. It expropriated the slogans, expropriated the great figures of the 1848 revolution but did what Bach did and what the holders of power did during the counterrevolutionary era after 1848.

The Bethlen group drafted a legislative proposal about March 15 and about the memorial to Kossuth but trampled the public freedoms and every one of their government activities opposed the ideals which ruled the 1848 revolution. They are getting ready for the festive unveiling of the Kossuth statue when the Kossuth ideals were never more suppressed and shackled than they are today. Never have politics been conducted more hypocritically and with more lies than they are today.

The Kossuth statue will be unveiled on November 6 and the House of Representatives will debate the enactment of the March 15 law and of the Kossuth Memorial law on November 7.

Népszava, November 3, 1927.

WE SAY IT AGAIN : HYPOCRISY

A statue will be erected in Budapest for Lajos Kossuth, the fighter for civic democracy, equality before the law, the liberation of the serfs, and an implacable foe of the Habsburgs. Very late! Seventy-eight years after he fled and thirty-three years after he died. During the period of the Habsburg rule the most that could be done was some planning and Kossuth's merits could only be whispered about. Enactment of his virtues was ignored as much as the casting of his figure in bronze or carving it in marble. Even now they would have preferred to forego the recognition of the great rebel but the enormous pressure of the historic forces driving from below forced them to take action.

Them. This is how we put it. By this definition we mean the representatives of the political system who ninety-five years after Kossuth first stepped onto the scene installed a system which Kossuth had fought against, for the destruction of which he took the nation into a revolution and war of liberation, after the failure of which he fled the country and emptied the bitter goblet of exile to the last drop.

We have to state this as a preface because later on the seemingly unimportant formal question of who are the real organizers of the unveiling ceremonies of the Kossuth Memorial will become a critical matter. We must therefore conclude in advance that the commanding lords of today's regime, even though they know that they have no business to be present at the statue of the revolutionary Kossuth, and they make every effort to dissociate themselves from the appearance of having an active role, yet they are inseparable from the preparations. This is because in a dictatorial system everything always happens, and happens in a way the dictators demand it and by what is required by their controlling interests. We cannot accept the argument as decisive that the ceremony is organized by the capital city and not by the government.

We cannot accept it because Ripka would never do anything that would be displeasing to Bethlen. The unveiling ceremony of the *Kossuth* statue is an undeniable action of a government which tramples Kossuth's ideals into the mud and is just as inimical to Kossuth's spirit and endeavors as the quondam Habsburg rulers and their advisors, Metternich, Windischgraetz and their cohorts....

The Workers Are Forbidden to Celebrate Kossuth

Even before the Unveiling of the Kossuth Statue the Reaction Unveiled—Itself

We have stated in our Thursday issue that the organized Hungarian workers and their leaders will nor participate in the official festivities arranged by the vanguard of Hungarian reaction for next Sunday. The workers did not want to celebrate the memory of Lajos Kossuth in the company of the reactionaries and decided that on Sunday afternoon, after the separate festivities of the official gentlemen were over, they would make a pilgrimage to the *Kossuth* statue, unveiled that forenoon, and there and then organize the Kossuth celebration of working Hungary.

The secretariat has reported to the police that the Hungarian Social Democratic Party has called a meeting, to be held in front of the *Kossuth* statue on Sunday afternoon, with the single agenda item of praising Lajos

Kossuth and his times. We were well aware of the fact that the government is not chary of forbidding assemblies and likes to put padlocks on people's mouths whenever it is faced by the depositories of the Kossuthian endeavors and the fighters for human rights, freedom, and equality.

Knowing the nature of the reaction, we did not want to assume that after they ceremoniously unveiled the *Kossuth* statue on Sunday forenoon, they would forbid the Kossuth memorial meeting of the Hungarian workers to be held a few hours later.

We did not assume that the government would hasten to prove our indictment that the powers are acting with total hypocrisy when, day after day it demolishes the most fundamental right of the Hungarian workers, their right of assembly, at the same time when it goes to—celebrate Kossuth.

We were wrong! The reaction has shown that it no longer cares even for appearances and the powers are not afraid of showing that the accusations made against them are, in fact, true.

The police do not permit the Kossuth memorial meeting scheduled for Sunday afternoon by the Social Democratic workers!

Our Party Secretariat has been advised of this after the police earlier endeavored to talk it into withdrawing its application to hold a memorial Kossuth meeting.

Claiming some "technical problems," the police "was concerned" that because of the official forenoon celebration, the workers' afternoon meeting might not be possible without some problems. Evidently the so-called responsible gentlemen felt that a frank denial of a permit for the workers to hold a Kossuth memorial celebration and an open statement that

today the workers in Hungary are not allowed to celebrate Kossuth,

would place them into a somewhat awkward position. The Party Secretariat responded to the telephone message of the police by stating that it was not willing to withdraw the announcement of the meeting and was unwilling to relinquish the rights of the workers to participate in the Kossuth memorial celebration. The police responded by simply forbidding the announced meeting of the Social Democratic workers....

Népszava, November 4, 1927.

UNVEILING OF THE KOSSUTH STATUE

The Feast of Official Hungary—Habsburg Archdukes and the Upwardly Mobile around the Kossuth Statue—The Opposition Middle-Class Parties Are Excluded from the Celebration—The Roman Catholic Church Demonstrated by Staying Away

The Parade

In the early morning hours the military, boy scouts, and deputations marched to the Parliament Square. They marched to the tune of music or to the rattle of drums, in military order, and took their place on the large square. On the northern edge of the huge square, along the streetcar tracks, a mighty, gray canvas tent was erected. In the tent the completed *Kossuth* statue waited for the unveiling. To the right of the base of the statue the members of the Statue Committee took their place while the area to the left of the base was reserved for the members of the press. The honor guard took their position to the left of the statue and on the right side stood a ceremonial tent. The public buildings facing the square were decorated with flags and the apartment house, being constructed behind the statue, owned by a coalmining corporation, had its entire front covered with canvas and decorated with flags.

By 10:30 A.M. all the invited guests had arrived, delegations from the House of Representatives and from the Upper House under the leadership of Albert Apponyi, and the delegation from the capital city with the mayors. In the ceremonial tent the members of the government took their place and were joined by the other notables. A chorus, accompanied by a military band, sang the national anthem and then the "Appeal" and then

Dr. János Buzáth, deputy mayor,

the chairman of the Statue Committee stepped to the podium and related the story of the statue. He said: "Every stone in this statue was created by the pennies from the people of the country and every penny meant the beating of the people's heart. Here stands the statue, the figure of Lajos Kossuth and the statues of the members of the first responsible government, erected by the eternal gratitude and pious recollection of the united nation and by the genius of the artist inspired by the people's gratitude and piety."

Lord Mayor Jenő Sipőcz

then stepped to the podium and accepted the statue on behalf of the capital city. He said:

> Kossuth was not only the interpreter of unique national thinking but he was also the manifestation of the most secret desires, hopes, and dreams of the nation. This dream of his life was the achievement of freedom as a historical necessity, the introduction of the nation to the rank of the modern constitutional countries, and the assurance of national independence and self-government. Much of his desires and hopes became reality, others remained a dream.

At the end of his speech he declared that he accepted to statue for safe keeping. Then

the huge veil dropped from the statue

and the large statue in glistening whiteness rose before the eyes of those present, illuminated by the sun breaking through the clouds. There was some clapping and a few, faint cheers when on Deputy Mayor Buzáth's invitation

Count Albert Apponyi appeared on the podium

The spectators clapped enthusiastically and Apponyi started his festive oration:

> Every statue immortalizing an individual represents whatever was truly immortal in that individual, whatever survives the short-lived debates and confrontations of short-lived life, that which is imperishable force, value, and glory, valuable force and glory not only of the individual but of the entire community of which he was a part and which he served: his country and all of humanity. Two great concepts and a great energy are associated with the name of Lajos Kossuth in the mind of the public. Two concepts which live with elemental necessity in the soul of every nation. Two concepts, two principles which state that
>
> **national security rests on a firm base only if it includes the entire nation within the confines of its legal practices and within its benefits**
>
> and can be truly happy only if it regulates its own fate indepen-

dently, not dependent on any foreign power, according to its own interests and purpose and not according to the directives of foreign goals. Stating it briefly: the two concepts, freedom of the Hungarian people and Hungarian national independence are twin concepts.

He then discussed why Lajos Kossuth was particularly outstanding. He was the representative of the concepts of the nation's liberation and of the country's independence. In propagating these great ideas his genius soared the highest and in implementing them he demonstrated the most inflexible determination. This exceptional, quasi demonic determination was necessary to free the irresistible spiritual thrust from the decayed conditions and to

liberate the independent, responsible Hungarian government from the suffocating grasp of the Viennese court counselors who were not recognized by common law but who, in fact, exercised all powers.

He then discussed the effects of Kossuth's greatness and talents abroad. He indicated that there was a greater need than ever before to have the foreign countries recognize that national strength and its transmission as manifested in the Kossuthian symbolism. He finished his speech by saying:

"Shaken we stand before the statue of our compatriot whose greatness arched over fragmented parts and periods of the world, over ideas and intellectual waves, debates and confrontations, upheavals and new developments in a daring curve with the strength of a single, indestructible idea incorporated in his soul: the independence of Hungary."

Then followed

the placement of wreaths.

Prime Minister Bethlen laid down the wreath of the Hungarian government, Deputy President Puky the wreath of the House of Representatives, and Baron Gyula Wlassics the wreath of the Upper House. Of all the political parties only the Unified Party could place a wreath according to the preset protocol. It was not allowed to the opposition middle-class parties. Ambassador Buttler Wright put down the wreath of the United States of America and read a short speech in Hungarian. The wreaths of the Italian government and of Torino were placed by

State Secretary Bodrero who also made a short speech. The Dutch Captain Hinden, a member of the jury of the European wrestling championship currently being held in Budapest, placed a wreath in the name of the participating athletes and gave a speech in the Dutch language. The wreath of the Polish government was placed by Lieutenant Colonel Durski-Trzaska, the one from the Turkish government by Ambassador Noureddin Ferouh Bey. This was followed by the wreath of the Hungarian army and then came the wreaths of the various denominations with

the wreath of the Roman Catholic Church being absent.

Masses of wreaths came from a large number of deputations but by this time all order was disrupted and everything proceeded contrary to previous arrangements. The wreaths were deposited in a chaotic manner caused primarily by the large number of people departing from the square. The square soon became empty except for some groups of uninvited people who came to see the newest statue in Budapest, the statue of Lajos Kossuth.

Three Airplanes over the Kossuth *Statue*

The *Magyar Légiforgalmi Részvénytársaság* [Hungarian Airlines Company] placed three Fokker planes at the disposal of the reporters of the Budapest newspapers so that they could see the festivity of the unveiling of the Kossuth statue from a bird's-eye view. The reporter of the *Népszava* flew in one of the planes, piloted by Captain József Maier. All three planes departed from the Mátyásföld airport at 11:15 A.M. and followed each other at an altitude of six hundred meters and then circled over the *Kossuth* statue and the Parliament Square for more than half an hour. One of the planes developed engine failure and was forced to make an emergency landing on the Vérmező. The other two planes returned to Mátyásföld at about twelve noon.

Népszava, November 8, 1927.

"Lajos Kossuth and His Era"
The Hungarian Social Democratic Party Will Hold a

MEMORIAL MEETING

with this agenda item, at 9:30, Sunday morning, November 13, in front of the *Kossuth* statue to which it invites the working people of Budapest and its environs. The speaker will be Comrade Károly Peyer, Member of Parliament.
Let Us Spread the News for the Success of the Meeting!
With Fraternal Greetings,

The Hungarian Social Democratic Party

Népszava, November 12, 1927.

THE WORKERS' CELEBRATION BY THE *KOSSUTH* STATUE

...Many thousands gathered around the statue in the huge square, mostly men, our old guard on whom we can count on always and everywhere, in whom the Social Democratic conviction and the determined will for the achievement of a better future lives with a steely ardor. After 9:00 A.M. the first groups have arrived and the organizing group is in its place. This is a grand new structure in the Hungarian workers' movement which accomplishes the difficult task of maintaining order excellently well. They established a cordon around the statue and left a wide entrance. The way the masses found their place shows that this mighty army, which agreed to meet on Kossuth Square, was used to discipline.

Before the meeting got under way the conversations were mostly about the statue because most of the people saw the statue for the first time and all agree that the figures are sadly reminiscent of a funerary statue and that instead of the glorious shining of liberty and of the élan of progress, resignation and a sad discouragement sits on the statue of Kossuth and on all the other marble statues as well. It is understandable because they did have cause to be sad…they lament the oppression… they think about the restrictive legislation…this is heard from all sides.

The multitude is surrounded by a ring of policemen, policemen on foot and on horseback, the customary complement to workers' meetings, in the neighboring streets and everywhere. This police presence is an appropriate complement to the mood of the statue….The masses keep increasing. We place the red carnation wreath of our party on the pedestal of the monument.

Precisely at 10:30 A.M. the workers' choral groups, amalgamated into the Alliance of Hungarian Workers' Choral Groups, intoned the powerful chords of the "Let Our Song Ring Forth" which the audience listened to with heads bared. After the song comrade Árpád Szakasits steps to the podium. He welcomes the groups with the socialist greeting "Friendship" that has become extraordinarily popular during a short period of time. Many thousands of throats echo the greeting: "Friendship." He welcomes the people assembled for the memorial celebration in the name of the party leadership, which had called the meeting.

Kossuth is Celebrated by Those Who Fear His Ideas

The Memorial Address of Comrade Peyer

Then, accompanied by the deafening cheers and clapping of the audience, comrade Károly Peyer, parliamentary representative stepped on the podium and in a lengthy and inspiring oration praised Lajos Kossuth, the apostle with a fiery soul embracing the revolutionary ideals of March, of freedom for the people, and of democracy….

Then the assembled choral groups sing "Socialists Arise!" as the multitude begins to leave. The departure of the thousands of people is accomplished in perfect order. Dignified and proud comportment everywhere. The police have nothing to do. We must admit that the police behaved quite tactfully on this occasion even though there was no reason whatever for mounted police to disband the spectators gathered in front of the statue to inspect it more closely, only five minutes after the end of the meeting. Other than that there were no incidents of any kind and the workers returned home with the memory of a beautiful event and with the unbreakable conviction that, in spite of all oppression, the ideas of Kossuth about freeing the serfs will prevail....

Népszava, November 15, 1927.

Gömbös and Bethlen Claim That Nagyatádi Entrusted the Hungarian Peasant to Them

The statue of the late leader of the Smallholder Party, István Szabó Nagyatádi, erected in front of the Ministry of Agriculture was unveiled on Sunday forenoon in the presence of the members of the government and of smallholder deputations from a number of parts of the country....

Prime Minister Gömbös characterized Nagyatádi as a fighter for ideals, a proclaimer of the policy of unity, and a seeker for the harmony of social classes. He knew that the smallholders were a historic class and he turned to "Realpolitik" to provide land for the peasants. He (Gömbös) accepted Nagyatádi's call, and with that in mind "looks after the Hungarian peasant" and proclaims the Hungarian unity of fate.

The former prime minister, Count István Bethlen, endeavored to point out that when Nagyatádi first appeared in the Parliament, he ignored the daily political matters, that there was no hint of his affinity for agrarian socialism, and that he was concerned only with the problems of neglect suffered by the villages. His speech did not "cast a gauntlet into the face of society" and one could assume that, when public life was based on universal franchise, Nagyatádi would become one of the strengths of the nation. Nagyatádi's reform activities were brought to an end by the World War. He had no part in the preparations for the revolution. After the revolutions he had a lion's share in "re-establishing the peace of the villages" through the so-called land reform, and in bringing the village in harmony with the other social classes. Nagyatádi entrusted the people of the villages not only to Gömbös but to him (Bethlen) as well and he will honor this charge so that the people of the village not be misled.

There were several other festive orations and then wreaths were placed to the unveiled statue....

Népszava, November 22, 1932.

The Statue of István Szabó Nagyatádi Is Unveiled in the Presence of a Hundred Thousand People with Splendid Ceremonies

The admiration and generosity of his followers erected a statue to István Szabó Nagyatádi, one of the most characteristic figures of Hungarian public life after World War I. The bronze statue of the politically dominant figure of the smallholder class, financed from very many small contributions, was placed in the small park in front of the Ministry of Agriculture, across from the Parliament where István Szabó spent so many embattled days and where he fought so many bitter fights in order to bring the interests of the smallholder group and the traditions of Hungarian statehood into harmony. His statue was unveiled eight years after his death, in the presence of the head of state, members of the National Assembly, representatives of the capital city, thousands of smallholders, and with great festivity and pomp. Kossuth Square was decorated with banners and the surrounding buildings also displayed many colorful flags. By 10:30 A.M. there was no more standing room left in the square with most of the area occupied by the serrated ranks of smallholders and farmers, representing 2,714 villages at the unveiling ceremony of the statue of their former leader.

A few minutes before 11:00 A.M., a trumpet blast announced the arrival of Regent Miklós Horthy. The regent passed in review in front of the honor guard and proceeded to the statue where Prime Minister Gyula Gömbös and the entire government welcomed the head of state and introduced the Austrian Deputy Chancellor Winkler to him. Horthy and Winkler engaged in a friendly conversation. The regent then took his seat in the place reserved for him. On the left of the head of state sat Archduke József while Prime Minister Gyula Gömbös and the members of the cabinet sat on the regent's right. Count István Bethlen, János Mayer, the former minister of agriculture, and others were also on that side.

Budapesti Hirlap, November 22, 1932.

The Mighty Statue of Count István Tisza Was Dedicated with Historic Pomp

At noon on Sunday the monumental memorial statue of Count István Tisza was unveiled in a festive ceremony. The powerful creation of sculptor-artists György Zala and Antal Orbán was erected on Lajos Kossuth Square across from the entrance to the Upper House of the Parliament.

Lajos Kossuth Square was glorying in a display of banners and all the surrounding public and private buildings were richly decorated with flags. Already during the early forenoon hours untold thousands of people swarmed into the square to be present at the festivities.

In the area of the square, directly in front of the entrance to the Upper House a festive grandstand was set up. The principal figure of the memorial was covered by a huge national banner. On both sides of the statue a line of honor guards in ceremonial uniform stood at attention with liveried attendants from the cities and the counties, holding the flags of their municipalities, standing on the pedestal. In front of the principal entrance to the Parliament, Hungarian army infantry, artillery, and cavalry honor guards stood in a straight line.

Precisely at twelve noon the army band played the first notes of the national anthem. It was at this time that Prime Minister Gyula Gömbös, representing the regent at the festivity, arrived. He accepted the salute of the troops assembled on Lajos Kossuth Square and then proceeded to the grandstands taking the seat of honor. Now the approximately five hundred members of the united choruses opened the festivities by singing the national anthem....

A Deluge of Wreaths on the Pedestal of the Statue

Prime Minister Gyula Gömbös, accompanied by his staff, then descended from his seat of honor and went to the statue, placing the regent's enormous laurel wreath at the foot of the pedestal.

He said, "I am placing this wreath on behalf of His Highness. His Highness is profoundly distressed that an illness has prevented him from being present and performing this pious duty."

Prime Minister Gyula Gömbös silently paid his respects for some moments standing before the mighty bronze figure of Count István Tisza. He bowed his head and returned to his seat of honor among the enthusiastic cheers of the public....

Függetlenség, April 24, 1934.

The Body of Gyula Gömbös Was Placed on a Catafalque in the Dome Chamber of Parliament

All through Budapest....

The funeral cortege went along Rákóczi Avenue, the Grand Boulevard, Andrássy Avenue, Vilmos Császár Avenue, and Alkotmány Street to reach Parliament Square and stop before the main entrance to Parliament where it was received by Móric Putnoki, the sergeant at arms. The Dome Chamber was embellished with funerary decorations and the catafalque was erected in the rear of the chamber with two small tables at its side holding Gömbös's steel helmet, sword and decorations. After the funerary songs, Bishop Sándor Raffay offered a prayer and this was followed again be more funerary songs. The participants in the ceremony then went to express their sympathy to the members of the family. The Dome Chamber slowly emptied out and at 1:00 P.M. the main entrance to the Parliament was closed.

At 3:00 P.M. the doors were opened again and until 8:00 P.M. long lines filed before at the catafalque of the prime minister. On Friday the Dome Chamber will again be open to the public from 8:00 A.M. to 3:00 P.M.

Népszava, October 9, 1936.

FINAL PREPARATIONS FOR THE SATURDAY FUNERAL

At 8:00 A.M. on Friday the doors to the Dome Chamber were again opened so that the general public could view the catafalque of the late prime minister. A huge crowd was already waiting in front of the Parliament building and they were then admitted in rows of two abreast....

Népszava, October 10, 1936.

GÖMBÖS'S LAST JOURNEY FROM THE DOME CHAMBER OF PARLIAMENT TO THE KEREPESI ROAD CEMETERY

The Start of the Funeral Procession

...In the meantime the funeral procession lined up on Kossuth Square in front of the Parliament. In front mounted police in ceremonial uniforms, behind them two squadrons of hussars, then a battalion from the Ludovika Military Academy and a machine gun battalion. This was followed by a soldier wearing a steel helmet and carrying the prime minister's wooden grave post and he was followed by soldiers carrying the prime minister's decorations. Behind them a row of fourteen carriages carrying wreaths and then the delegation from Murga, carrying a small casket of dirt. Then came two soldiers leading Gömbös's horse covered with a funeral blanket. Lastly the hearse with the Gömbös family coat of arms on the doors.

The coffin was followed by the prime minister's family and a military honor guard. Behind them the regent and then the representatives of the foreign heads of states, members of the Habsburg family, Deputy Prime Minister Darányi with the presidents of the two houses of Parliament, then the ministers, the crown guards, the heads of the major courts and government offices, the Lord Mayor and other mayors, foreign ambassadors and ministers, diplomats, delegations, senior military officers, representatives, members of the Upper House, various delegations, disabled veterans, frontline fighters, then again a battalion of infantry, two batteries of artillery, two mounted police brigades, then the Turul Association, delegations from the rural organizations of NEP, university students, delegations from TESZ, various paramilitary youth formations and boy scout troops, and finally another mounted police brigade.

Népszava, October 11, 1936.

People by the Thousands from Budapest and from the Countryside Visit the *Rákóczi* Statue That Was Unveiled on Sunday

On Sunday Budapest woke up to a dazzling day. It appeared as though the weather wanted to create a proper setting for the great deferential festivities of the Hungarian nation in honor of the unveiling of the statue of the Ruling Prince Ferenc II Rákóczi. The lawns of Lajos Kossuth Square, covered with flowers and the thousands of banners gaily fluttering in the fresh morning breeze all underscored the significance of the day.

The multitude filled the square early in the morning. They included the colorful, gay dresses of the village people, numerous boy scouts in plumed hats, nice youngsters from the Budapest schools, burning with enthusiasm, students from the colleges and universities, veterans' associations, and paramilitary youth groups in military formation. The military was also present, a battalion of infantry, one unit from the artillery and one from the hussars, all in full festive uniforms. In the seats reserved for the invited guests sat the finest representatives of Hungarian society. The multitude of ancient, most beautiful, and valuable Hungarian ceremonial dresses was unforgettable and brought to mind the historic eras of the past: Hungary's great and glorious days. The assembly was made even more attractive by the purple pallia of the church dignitaries and by the magnificent military dress uniforms.

Nemzeti Ujság, May 5, 1937.

The St. Stephen Festive Year Begins with Dazzling Pomp

By Monday morning Parliament Square assumed a colorful pomp. The festive altar was erected at the entrance to the House of Representatives and two dates had been applied above the entrance: 1038–1938. Nine hundred years elapsed between the two dates, nine hard, glorious, frequently tragic but always heroic centuries of Hungarian history. These nine hundred years represent the entire life of St. Stephen's Realm. It began with his apostolic coronation and this is what we now celebrate just after the Eucharistic World Congress. To the left of the altar there is a canopy for the papal nuncio and there are grandstands erected all around for the spectators and guests. At 8:00 A.M. the festive procession started from the Castle Chapel with St. Stephen's right hand. Canon János Mészáros, the archiepiscopal vicar,

the guardian of the Sacred Relic led the procession.

There was a stand in the decorated entrance hall of the Curia where the prelates assembled and where the great sacred relic of the nation, the right hand of the first apostolic king, in its beautiful jeweled reliquary, was brought to. It is a picturesque scene, the assembly of cardinals, Hungarian ceremonial dress, festive dresses and national costumes, all around the Parliament as far as the eye can see. At 9:00 A.M. a trumpet blast announces the arrival of Cardinal Pacelli. The national anthem was played and reverential, glorious moments passed with the arrival of Regent Miklós Horthy and of his wife. The anthem was sung, then Canon Mészáros said a prayer by the Sacred Right Hand, and then the procession started from the Curia building toward the altar by the Parliament.

The Mass of the Prince Primate

The banners of the Castle Parish went first. The sun was shining brightly in the sky, the many-colored banners fluttered in the breeze, and the entire square shone with the dazzle of festivity and piety. The clergy walked in front of the relic and the Sacred Right Hand was carried after the prelates. Then came the crown guards and the military honor guard, followed by the cardinals with Prince Primate Jusztinian Serédi, as the highest ecclesiastic dignity of the host country, at their end. He was followed by the papal nuncio. In the meantime the distinguished lay guests line upon along the sides of the altar. Arriving at the altar, the prince primate donned his vestments, the choir sang psalms and then the silent mass began. During the mass, Cardinal Pacelli, the papal delegate, who this far had sat on his separate throne, descended from there and

went to the prayer stool placed in front of the altar and remained there until the Eucharist.

During the mass the choirs sang old Hungarian religious songs with the notes ascending to the high heavens, pleading for Hungarian justice and for a glorious fate for Hungary.

Friss Ujság, May 31, 1938.

A Nation's Compassionate Regret Accompany Pál Teleki on His Last Journey

A Lineup of Hundreds of Thousands from the Parliament to the Cemetery

...The coffin of the tragically departed prime minister was taken from the mortuary of the Kerepes Road cemetery to the Dome Chamber of Parliament on Sunday forenoon at 10:00 A.M. In the streets men stood with their hat in their hand wherever the hearse passed and black flags fluttered from the houses in the wind. On Lajos Kossuth Square, police in ceremonial helmets, drew a cordon before the huge gathering. The society of the country and every layer of society were represented and paid their pious respect to the memory of the great statesman. The façade of the Curia and of the Ministry of Agriculture were covered with a huge black shroud and flags of mourning fluttered all around the Lajos Kossuth Square. From the lions at the main entrance to Parliament all the way to the Dome Chamber the ground was covered with a black carpet and the walls of the Dome

Chamber were also covered by black hangings. Behind the catafalque an enormous white cross was displayed,...

Nemzeti Ujság, April 8, 1941.

THE FEAST OF FREEDOM WAS CELEBRATED WITH GREAT ENTHUSIASM BY THE NATION

Festivities in Front of the Petőfi *and* Kossuth *Statues*

The university and high school students organized the traditional March celebration again this year. After placing a wreath before the tablet affixed to the wall of the central building of the university, the youth made a pilgrimage to the Petőfi *statue and then to the* Kossuth *statue and, after placing wreaths at both statues, participated in the festivities taking place on the Szabadság Square. László Dizsóry, a Lutheran pastor, delivered a very effective speech in front of the National Banner with Relics....*

Magyar Nemzet, March 17, 1942.

ISTVÁN HORTHY WAS TAKEN ON HIS LAST JOURNEY ALONG A LINEUP OF TENS OF THOUSANDS OF PEOPLE

Thursday morning the Parliament and its environment were dressed in somber mourning pomp. On the buildings, as indeed on buildings throughout the city and the country, black funerary flags, black shrouds on the streetlights and black banners on all the lamp posts reaching from the top all the way to the ground fluttering in the wind. Black mourning draperies covered the façade of the Curia, of the Ministry of Agriculture, and, naturally, of the Parliament all facing the Kossuth Square. On the two sides of the lions guarding the main entrance a flame flickers in huge candelabra and from the open doors a black carpet extended out into the square.

Shortly after 9:00 A.M. Lajos Kossuth Square was occupied by police in ceremonial helmets. They drew a cordon around it and thereafter only those were allowed to approach the Parliament who had an invitation to the funeral ceremony. All traffic on the square stopped within minutes and the huge square emptied of passers-by but soon it was rapidly filled by military detachments, delegations and organizations participating in the funeral. Between the lion gate and the Alkotmány Street honor guard units of infantry, artillery, hussars, regular and mounted police, military bands, an honor guard from the air force, paramilitary youth formations, boy scouts and numerous delegations took their place....

The Funerary Procession

While the catafalque was dismantled in the Dome Chamber, the funeral procession took shape in the huge quadrangle of Kossuth Square. Half a squadron of mounted police was in front, then came the commander of the procession, then the mounted guards, one squadron cavalry, guards, half a battalion of infantry, a military band, soldiers carrying wooden grave posts, officials and employees of the Deputy Regent's Secretariat, the clergy and the church choirs led by László Ravasz. Then came

the coffin on a caisson and behind it the regent with his wife on his right and the young widow on his left.

The three of them were followed by the other members of the bereaved family, the heads of the Regental Cabinet Office, the head of the Regent's Military Office, the commander of the guards and the aides. On both sides of the coffin and of the family marched rows of guards and crown guards in full dress uniforms. Then came the representatives of foreign heads of state, then royal princes, the prince primate, the apostolic nuncio, Prime Minister Kállay, the presidents of the two houses of the legislature, members of the government, members of the diplomatic corps, crown guards, the highest government officials, the leaders of the army, the deputy chairs of the two houses, the secretaries of state, the leaders of the Ministry of Foreign Affairs, the deputy heads of the higher courts, and the generals. The Lord Mayor of

Budapest, the mayor, the chief of police, representatives and members of the Upper House, officials of the cabinet office and of the military office, high ranking government officials, delegations of military officers, the representatives of administrative bodies, various organizations, and delegations. At the end of the funeral procession came half a battalion of infantry, a detachment of air force cadets, and half a squadron of mounted police.

The funeral procession went along Alkotmány Street and Vilmos Császár Road to the arrival side of the Western Railway Terminal....

Népszava, August 28, 1942.

Tens of Thousands at the Budapest Memorial Service for Endre Bajcsy-Zsilinszky

National banners and black flags on the houses and the pealing of bells proclaim that the nation is burying a great departed, Endre Bajcsy-Zsilinszky, the leader of the national resistance movement who died a martyr's death. The metal coffin is placed on a catafalque in the open square and is surrounded by a sea of wreaths. Thousands of colorful Hungarian flowers accompany the martyr on his last journey. Behind the catafalque the façade of the Parliament is covered with black draperies up to the second story. In the middle of the façade there was a huge panel in the national colors. Next to the speaker's platform there are two loges of honor. In one of them Endre Bajcsy-Zsilinszky's widow and the members of the bereaved family, in the other one Béla Zsedényi and Prime Minister Béla Miklós Dálnoki....

To the right of the platform the members of the government, the mayor, city officials, and a number of the leading personalities of Hungarian public life took their place. Members of the resistance movement are also present, together with the leaders of the Hungarian democratic parties.

A military and police honor guard stands in the square and there is a cordon of boy scouts beyond which there is a huge multitude of the grieving public.

The ceremony begins with the national anthem performed by the full chorus and orchestra of the Opera....

After a short speech and prayer by Lutheran Minister Lajos Kemény, Prime Minister Béla Miklós Dálnoki spoke in the name of the Hungarian government....

After the prime minister, the national president of the Smallholder-Agricultural Worker- and Civic Party, Zoltán Tildy said good bye to the great departed of the party.

Then Ambassador Pushkin stepped to the podium and said:

"We gather at the catafalque of Endre Bajcsy-Zsilinszky to pay our pious respects to the memory of the heroic Hungarian patriot murdered by the fascist hangmen. Endre Bajcsy-Zsilinszky devoted his entire life to the battle for Hungarian democracy. He saw clearly the deadly danger that reaction, fascism, and their master Hitler's Germany meant for Hungary....

Árpád Szakasits said goodbye in the name of the Social Democratic Party to the great friend of the workers' party.

Gyula Kállai said goodbye to the departed in the name of the Hungarian Communist Party....

A funeral address was delivered by Imre Kovács, in the name of the National Peasant Party....

Péter Csaplár bid farewell to Endre Bajcsy-Zsilinszky on behalf of the Union Council and the Free Unions....

Finally, speaking for the Hungarian peasantry, B. István Szabó, state secretary for defense, bid good bye to Endre Bajcsy-Zsilinszky....

After the memorial addresses the ecclesiastic choir sang the hymn beginning with: "Our God is a strong fortress..." and the Opera chorus sang the "Appeal" The metal casket was taken from the catafalque to the music of Ferenc Erkel's "Hunyadi Funeral March" and was placed into the hearse while the funeral procession was being formed....

Kis Ujság, May 29, 1945.

Tens of Thousands of Budapest's Workers Dedicated the Kossuth Bridge

Tens of thousands of Budapest's workers gathered on the flag-decorated Lajos Kossuth Square Sunday morning to celebrate the most important technical achievement of Hungarian democracy, the ceremonial opening of Kossuth Bridge. The Allied Control Commission was also represented at the festivity. Admiral Trajnin represented the Soviet Union, Colonel Townsend appeared for the United States, and General Edgecumb was present for Great Britain. The participants at the festivity included all the members of the government, the leadership of the capital city, all democratic parties, youth organizations, the army, and the police.

Prior to the beginning of the festivity

a wreath was thrown into the Danube in memory of András Szabó, the heroic worker who lost his life while working on the bridge.

This was done from the center of the new bridge.

The national anthem was played and then Prime Minister Zoltán Tildy delivered a highly effective speech. He said, "This is a day of victory when the Hungarian government and the entire nation lower the flag in honor of the workers who had achieved this victory.

If everybody would work like the builders of the bridge and the peasants and everybody would be willing to endure the next few months this will be the happy home of all the workers."

Then comrade Ernő Gerő, the minister of transportation, spoke. He said: "Those who have built the Kossuth Bridge, will also rebuild the Ferenc József Bridge, and all the other bridges."

Then the "Appeal" was sung by the chorus of the Iron, and Gas Companies.

Népszava, January 22, 1946.

Zoltán Tildy Was Elected President by Acclamation—The President Introduces Himself to the People of Hungary

The People of the Country Celebrate

The masses of people billowing on the Kossuth Square presented an amazing sight. Thousands upon thousands of flags and placards carried by the workers and by the citizens of Budapest to cheer the republic and welcome the president of the republic and listen to the festive orations emphasizing the significance of the day. There was only one previous occasion when this many people assembled on the square, the autumn of 1918 when the second republic (*sic.*) headed by Mihály Károlyi was proclaimed. Now, there was not a square inch of empty space in the square with practically the entire population of Budapest squeezed together enjoying the warm sunshine, the precursor of spring. An unprejudiced spectator might have thought that Kossuth Square was the site of the May Day celebration by the workers. We must state that most of the participants came from the ranks of the workers' parties and the labor unions.

The celebration of the republic began at 2:00 P.M. Ferenc Nagy, the president of the National Assembly announced the results of the election for the presidency of the republic. Then a delegation of twenty-five, representing all the parties of the *Függetlenségi Front* [Independence Front], entered the Parliament and invited the president of the republic and the members of the National Assembly, to join the festivities.

After a speech by Ferenc Nagy, Zoltán Tildy, speaking from the steps of the Parliament, addressed the people of Budapest and the entire nation. He thanked the Allies for having liberated us. Then he pointed out that Hungarian democracy has already taken major steps and that it would continue its work in the future.

Népszava, February 2, 1946.

With Sincere Respect the Nation Honors Mihály Károlyi, the Hero of the October Revolution

Mihály Károlyi Is in the Hungarian Parliament Again!

The square in front of the Parliament is a colorful forest of flags. The gathering of the workers is mighty and impressive. Representatives of the factories, delegations of the labor unions, delegations of peasants and masses of youths are assembled here. Enthusiastic placards celebrate the great man, the distributor of land, on his return. The weather is gloriously bright and national and red flags are everywhere.

Led by Ferenc Nagy, the entire government is lined up on the steps leading to the Dome Chamber of Parliament. Mihály Károlyi is arriving and the eyes of the multitude of many thousands are focused on him. The grand old man of democratic Hungary walks with a buoyant steps toward the steps, among the cheers and clapping of the crowd.

Népszava, May 11, 1946,

The Construction Workers Will Not Tolerate It !

...Tuesday morning, about 11:00 A.M., several thousand construction workers, members MEMOSZ, marched under red flags, to notify the antiworker representatives in the National Assembly that

The Hungarian construction workers refuse to become the victims of the machinations of certain Smallholder Party representatives who wish to reestablish the past. They will not tolerate that they are not allowed to form new associations and do away with their present ones.

The justifiably rebellious mass, assembled in front of the Parliament sent a delegation to the prime minister....

Népszava, December 18, 1946.

HUGE DEMONSTRATION OF THE YOUTH OF BUDAPEST

It Is Our Purpose to Preserve Constitutional Order and Discipline—Said Imre Nagy in Front of the Parliament

...On the demand of the university students and workers assembled in front of the Parliament in the late afternoon hours, Imre Nagy appeared on one of the balconies of the Parliament. He addressed a brief speech to the gathering in which he said:

> Comrades, dear Friends!
>
> Let us have confidence in the future and in the strength and the endeavors which fill me and which are based on the prospect that we must have a future and a development of socialist democracy. I must again emphasize that above all we must remain calm.
>
> I heartily welcome those who are here. I have the greatest regard for the democratic youth of Hungary which with its democratic manifestation today and with its readiness for action wishes to promote the defeat of hindrances from the path of the further development of socialist democracy. Enthusiasm and the desire to act must be yoked to sobriety and a sense of responsibility. Lack of these might do great harm to our democratic achievements and to the results which our democracy has attained to date. There are people who will lead these developments and who will work for them. The possibility for developments lies in discussions and cleansing within the Party. For this reason the most important thing is to preserve our common sense. We must proceed on this path with a sense of responsibility and with sobriety and we will advance forward. Our goal is to preserve constitutional order and

discipline and it is on this path that we will go on and forward. Very shortly, within the next days, the Central Leadership will make the decisions which will create a solid basis for the interests of a free, independent, and socialist country for us all. The government will not delay these developments.

Dear Friends! I was called in order to give you my opinion. I, therefore, wish to declare my opinion! Listen to me! I believe that you have not been disappointed by my words! I have confidence, and you must have confidence in parliament to use constitutional means to eliminate obstacles and that the democratic perspectives, demanded by circumstances, will prevail. Long live the Party! Long live the People's Republic!

After Imre Nagy's speech the university students marched from the square singing. According to a late broadcast from the Kossuth Radio Imre Nagy held discussions with the leaders of the young people.

Reported Just before Going to Press

According to a report received just prior to going to press, a severe clash and the use of weapons occurred at the Broadcast Building. On the square by the City Park the marching multitude cast the *Stalin* statue off its pedestal.

Magyar Nemzet, October 24, 1956.

Meetings And Popular Celebrations on Constitution Day

Lowering the Flag on Lajos Kossuth Square and on Gellért Hill

The State Banner of the Hungarian People's Republic, which was displayed for two days in front of the Parliament on Lajos Kossuth Square in honor of the Constitution, was lowered from the flagpole with military honors on Wednesday forenoon. The Gellért Hill was the scene of a similar ceremony when by the Liberation Memorial the national banner and the red banner of the workers' movement were lowered with military honors.

Népszabadság, August 12, 1968.

Taking the Oath before the National Banner

The Celebration of Young Officers Taking Their Oath

In a ring of several thousand interested spectators on Wednesday morning at 10:00 A.M., in front of the Parliament on the Lajos Kossuth Square the command was given,

"Honor Guard attention! Eyes Right! Salute!"

General Lajos Czinege, the minister of defense and a candidate member of the Political Committee of the MSZMP [Hungarian Socialist Workers Party] had arrived. He received the report from Colonel Barna Kazai, walked by the tight row of the new officers of the armed forces and greeted the officers to be sworn in.

This was the first time that the public swearing-in of the graduates of the Lajos Kossuth Military Academy, the Maté Zalka Military Engineering School, the György Kilián Aviation Engineering School, and the Frigyes Karikás Military College took place in front of the National Banner.

...Included among those present were the high-ranking representatives of the Soviet troops temporarily stationed in Hungary with General K. I. Provalov at their head, the accredited foreign army and air force attachés, and foreign guests.

When the minister of defense arrived further commands were issued,

"Salute the National Banner!"

After the national anthem had been performed the orders of the minister of defense were read which, among other things, included the following,

You will be officers in the ranks of the Hungarian People's Army, of the Border Patrol, and of the Special Police who proudly claim the Kuruc of Rákóczi and the Hungarian soldiers of 1848 as their precursors, who consider the Hungarian internationalists who fought for soviet power and in the Spanish Civil War as their models, and who will follow the footsteps of the glorious Red Army and Red Guards of the Hungarian Soviet Republic. You will consider the patriots who fought shoulder to shoulder with the Soviet Army to liberate our country as your immediate predecessors. Be worthy of them and follow their noble example!

Then the young officers took their oath after which Lajos Czinege stepped to the microphone....

Népszabadság, August 22, 1969.

A New Segment of the Metro Has Been Opened

The construction of the capital city metro has reached an important goal on Friday. With festive ceremonies the segment between the Deák Square and the Southern Railway Terminal of the east-west metro line was opened for use by the public.

The festive inauguration ceremony began at 4:00 P.M. at the Lajos Kossuth Square metro station....

The president of the Közlekedési Építő Vállalat (Public Transport Construction Company) announced that the second segment of the east-west metro line was ready and that the service could begin....

Népszabadság, December 23, 1972.

The Country Has Celebrated

Mass Meetings, Reunions—Commissioning of Officers, Aquatic and Aerial Parades

On Tuesday forenoon, in the presence of several thousand interested spectators, the public commissioning exercises were held for the graduates of the Lajos Kossuth Military Academy, the Maté Zalka Military Engineering School, the György Kilián Aviation Engineering School, and the Frigyes Karikás Military College....

Those present included the commanding officers of the military training establishments and the families of the young officers. The festivity was attended by General B. P. Ivanov, the commanding officer of the Southern Army Group of the Soviet Army, temporarily stationed in Hungary, as well as Marshal S. M. Styemenko, the chief of staff of the unified armed forces of the Warsaw Pact nations, who was vacationing in Hungary. Lieutenant General Lajos Czinege, minister of defense, arrived at the site of the commissioning precisely at 10:00 A.M. He listened to the report of Major General Barna Kazai, then reviewed the line of new young officers, and greeted the soldiers. After the national anthem was played the orders issued by the minister of defense about the commissioning were read and then the young officers took an oath to faithfully perform the duties of their noble profession. Lajos Czinege made a speech and then the *Internationale* was played and the newly commissioned officers marched in parade formation in front of the National Banner....

Népszabadság, August 22, 1974.

Our Constitution Was Celebrated Throughout the Country with Lavish Programs

Inauguration of Officers on Kossuth Square in Budapest

...In the presence of many interested spectators trumpets blared on the square in front of Parliament. The military commander had arrived. He listened to the report of the commander of the honor guard, standing at attention behind their flag, and then greeted the members of the detachment. Then, to the music of the drums, honor guards carried the National Banner to the flag pole and then, while the national anthem was being played and the detachment stood at rigid attention, the banner was raised to the top of the flag pole. As the final act of the festivity the detachment and the band paraded before the banner with soldiers, policemen and worker guards standing at the base of the pole as honor guards....

Those present included Lieutenant General Nikolay Silchenko, the representative of the supreme commander of the combined armed forces of the Warsaw Pact in Hungary and Major General Nikolay Shevkun, a member of the military council of the Southern Soviet Army Group, temporarily stationed in Hungary.

Precisely at 10:00 A.M. there was a trumpet blast announcing the arrival of Lieutenant General Lajos Czinege, minister of defense, who received the report of Major General Barna Kazai, the Commander of the Lajos Kossuth Military Academy. He then reviewed the ranks of the honor guard battalion and greeted the young officers.

After the national anthem was played the orders of the minister of defense concerning the commissioning was read.

After the proclamation of the order the young officers took an oath that they would faithfully perform their noble duties. Lieutenant András Szabó read the words of the oath on behalf of the men and then Lajos Czinege delivered an address....

Népszabadság, August 22, 1984.

George Bush, the President of the United States Has Arrived to Our Country

Reception on the Kossuth Square

According to personal feelings people greeted George Bush, his wife and entourage with cheers, shouts of welcome, or booing when they mounted the podium erected in front of the *Kossuth* statue.

Bruno F. Straub greeted the guests in the name of the leaders of the Hungarian People's Republic and of the Hungarian people with respect and pleasure.

He attributed a symbolic significance to the fact that the greeting took place in front of the statue of Lajos Kossuth, in the square that bore his name. He reminded the audience that the historic events taking place in Hungary in the first half of the nineteenth century are referred to as the "Age of Reform" and that Lajos Kossuth was the principal figure of that era. There was a straight path that led from the "Age of Reform" to the 1848 revolution. The War of Liberation and the reprisals following its defeat caused severe losses to the country. The best of the survivors were forced into exile. This difficult period was eventually resolved with a Compromise which opened a path for the country's economic and social developments.

"There is again an 'Age of Reform' in Hungary. But, we believe that the historic sequence will be different. We are beyond our casualties and we have finally buried our dead with honor. Now there will be a Compromise. This is what the Hungarian people and every political-social force, feeling responsible for the country, expects."

Then the American president stepped to the microphones and, to the great pleasure of the gathering, waved the umbrella, held over his head, away and tore up and scattered his prepared speech saying that it would have been too long and that the people had already spent enough time in the rain waiting for him. His address was indeed very short and was received with considerable approval in spite of the improvised translation.

We are very happy to be here. Unfortunately we can be here for a very short time only, two evenings and one day. I am looking forward to the discussions with the leaders of this great country with pleasure. I will convey to them the greetings of the American people and the conviction of the citizens of the United States that we have to cooperate with Hungary, that we will cooperate with Hungary and that jointly with your leaders we can carry the reforms in your country forward.

I thank you for this reception and I hope that tomorrow you can listen to me in a dryer place.

The president of the United States stated that he was convinced that the rains will have long since stopped when he will still recall the warmth with which the people of Hungary had welcomed him. He thanked them and asked for God's blessings on Hungary....

Népszabadság, July 12, 1989.

The People Bid János Kádár Farewell with Deep Sorrow

With deep sorrow. Three words made trite by unimportant deaths and made cheap by routine obituaries but which came very much to everybody's mind who was in the lobby of the MSZMP KB [Central Committee of the Hungarian Socialist Workers Party] headquarters yesterday afternoon. Not only because tens of thousands of people (who knows how many?) stood solemnly in the several hundred meter line from the embankment of the Danube and the other end of Parliament, inching forward, to say goodbye to one of the most significant politicians of the most recent Hungarian history and not only because very few eyes remained dry standing in front of the old gold-colored coffin, decorated with silver ornaments....

The explanation was in the look on the faces. On the faces and in the eyes of people speaking in low tones, who started to assemble on the Kossuth Square before 3:00 P.M. On the faces of the soldiers and workers guards lining up since 2:00 P.M. there was no trace of the unemotional rigidity associated with formal parades and ceremonial uniforms. No such lack of feeling could be seen on the faces of the ten or twenty year-olds, the people in their thirties, forties, or who were in their sixth or seventh decade....

Népszabadság, July, 14, 1989.

Last Farewel to János Kádár

The story of the day of the funeral begins Friday night, at 2:15 A.M. That is when the long line of mourners comes to end and the doors of the headquarters of the Central Committee of the MSZMP are closed to be reopened at 7:00 A.M. for those who wished to bow their head at János Kádár's catafalque. By 10:00 A.M. the end of the multitude stands at the southern corner of the Parliament. Black dresses, white shirts, formal suits and everyday wear, military uniforms and miners' uniforms. Wreaths and bouquets. In front of the coffin some bow their head, some make the sign of the cross or only stop silently for a few seconds....

Népszabadság, July, 15, 1989.

We Are Facing the Founding of a Country Anew

Inauguration of Officers: Our Most Important Task Is the Defense of Our Country

Several thousands gathered Sunday forenoon on the Kossuth Square where 827 young army and border guard officers received their commission. At the festivity, organized with military pomp, those present included Bruno F. Straub, the chairman of the Presidential Council, the outstanding personalities of our public life, and, for the first time, the representatives of newly established parties and movements. After taking the oath, Lieutenant General Ferenc Kárpáti greeted the new officers. In his address he spoke about the role of the army in the evolution of society, about the improvements in the international situation, in the increased likelihood of demobilization and about the principal characteristics of the armed forces reforms....

Prior to the August 20 festivities, on Saturday afternoon, on Kossuth Square, in front of the Parliament and the National Banner of the Hungarian People's Republic was raised with military honors. The National Banner of the Hungarian People's Republic was raised with military honors on Gellért Hill.

Népszabadság, August 21, 1989.

The Thai Crown Prince Is Visiting Our Country

The Crown Prince Maha Vadjiralongkorn, was greeted in front of the Parliament with all the honors due to a head of state. He is the highest representative of the Kingdom Thailand abroad. On instruction from King Bhumibol Adulyadedj [Rama IX] the Royal Prince represents the Crown on visits abroad.

On the Kossuth Square Maha Vadjiralongkorn received the report of the commander of the honor guard lined up in his honor and then the national anthems of both countries having been played the hosts and the guests introduced their entourages to each other....

Népszabadság, August 29, 1989.

Hungary: A Republic

Enthusiastic Multitudes Welcomed the Historic Announcement

The Kossuth Square, in front of the Parliament, was the site of a historic event at noon on Monday, immediately after the noon-time ringing of the bells, Mátyás Szűrös, the president of the National Assembly and interim president of the republic, proclaimed the Republic of Hungary from the balcony of the Parliament. The announcement of the new structure and new name of the country was received with an enormous ovation, clapping for many minutes, and the festive blare of trumpets.

On the call of the National Assembly several tens of thousands gathered in the square. Those present included the officials of the National Assembly, numerous representatives, the members of the Council of Ministers, representatives of the social and mass organizations, the parties, the churches, and the heads of the foreign diplomatic missions.

Under festive ceremonies the National Banner was raised and military honor guards lined up in the square. The flags representing fateful turns in Hungarian history were taken to the National Banner.

The bells were still ringing and Mátyás Szűrös's speech was frequently interrupted by vivid demonstrations, clapping and cheering which demonstrated approval of the announcements. It was a few minutes after 12:15 P.M. when Mátyás Szűrös finished his talk and then the national anthem was played with many of the spectators singing along.

At the end of the festivity, Mátyás Szűrös, accompanied by Lieutenant General Ferenc Kárpáti, minister of defense, reviewed the lines of the honor guard, greeting the soldiers. After greeting the invited Hungarian attendees, Mátyás Szűrös greeted the heads of mission of the diplomatic corps. The festivity of the proclamation of the Hungarian Republic came to an end with the parade of the honor guard....

Tens of Thousands Throughout the Country Recall October 23, 1956

A series of commemorations were presented yesterday in Budapest and in several cities in the provinces on the thirtieth anniversary of the 1956 uprising. In the morning at section 301 of the cemetery on Kozma Street the remains of the revolutionary Ferenc Balázs, executed in 1957, was put to his final rest. In the afternoon the organizations of the October 23 Committee held commemorative meetings at several points of the city. At the Corvin Passage, at the Killián Barracks, and at the building of the Hungarian Radio. A place of remembrance was the central building of the Technical University, Bem

Square, and then Heroes' Square. During the evening hours they held the day's major program in front of the Parliament, on Kossuth Square. Several former inmates who were imprisoned after 1956 gave speeches from the steps of the Parliament. This was telecast live by [Hungarian] Television.

Commemorations on October 23

...Four forty-five P.M.: Groups carrying illuminated signs gather on the Kossuth Square in front of the Parliament. People continue to come from the metro and pass, with some hesitation, between the vendors of candles and books. The slogans of the illuminated signs are thundered from the loudspeakers. They advised the gathering that one of them said: "Communism never again!" The loudspeaker also announced that the environmentalists had arrived with a message on their sign, "Communist-free environment!" Around 5:00 P.M. it was announced, "They keep coming from the Bem Square."

Five fifteen P.M.: The commemorating crowd started off to Kossuth Square via the Margit Bridge.

five thirty P.M.: We were told that the world was changing, the policemen carry no weapons, the red star had fallen off their caps and they have the same armbands as we do. The words were received with loud clapping and was followed by another one, "We want a republic where even the police will be respected!"

Five thirty-six P.M.: It is announced that the members of the Association of Political Prisoners had arrived from the Heroes' Square. During the few minutes of their entry a Cyrilic letter poster is being read into the mike with an explanation that the script was very hard to read. The poster reads, "Russkies go home" The small group gathering in front of the steps to the Parliament kept repeating these words over and over again.

Six P.M.: Speaking for the October 23 Committee, Vilmos Bereczky said: "This day means freedom and democracy for the majority of Hungarians." He expressed his hope that the National Assembly to be elected would make October 23rd into a national holiday. He declared that this was the first occasion for unfettered celebration on the day the Republic was proclaimed.

Six fifteen P.M.: We could hear about the activities of Jenő Fónay performed thirty-three years ago. The assistant of Uncle Szabó, the leader of the Széna Square group, steps to the microphone and starts his speech with: "My dear brethren, Hungarians!..."

He recalled that the Communist Imre Nagy made the wishes of the Hungarian nation his own. This is why we must speak of the great day of the revolution, stopped by rifle fire, as a national holiday. The statement that the upcoming new ideas had to be fused with love and that we must love each other was received with great ovation. "Long live our national holiday, October 23," concluded Jenő Fónay's speech and with the line from the national anthem, "God bless the Hungarians!" he left the microphone.

Six forty P.M.: They announce the arrival of Gyula Obersovszky who was the editor in chief of the newspaper *Igazság* (Truth) published in 1956. He started his speech with a sentence he used many times on death row, "We will survive even if we perish." He was then thinking of the ones who would remember and not of surviving bodily. He also indicated that he was entitled to an apology from the authorities, primarily from the prime minister and from the minister of the interior. He also related a story where the principal character was his passport. "Why do I not have a passport to this day?" he asked. He then said that Gorbachev is aware of Hungary's interests more clearly than those here at home who claim to be patriots. He stated, "I look with warm feelings toward Moscow. I am worried for Gorbachev. I am worried for him and I support him. Our freedom is but an illusion until Moscow is not free as well." After mentioning the merits of the Soviet leader he emphasized the political greatness of Presidents Bush and Reagan. According to the speaker if such leaders had been at the head of the major powers in 1956, things would not have happened the way they did.

Seven P.M.: "Comrades!" was the way economist György Krassó, a founding member of the Hungarian October Party, addressed the crowd. He was soundly booed and hooted and then continued by saying, "'Comrades,' was the way a well meaning veteran politician started his address thirty-three years ago. He believed that being Hungarian was compatible with being a communist. Hundreds of thousands responded to him, 'we are not comrades, we are Hungarians.'"

The speaker then said that in October 1956 the people wanted to determine their own fate and paid no attention to the arrangements made by the great and small powers. Today they had no confidence in decisions made over the head of the people. Then he addressed the opposition: "Let us make peace with each other and let us ask our neighbors to assist and not impede the new conquest of our country which is based on the traditions of '56." He closed with, "Deliver us from evil."

Seven ten P.M.: Mária Wittner, disabled pensioner, sentenced to death in 1956, spoke of her years in prison, her humiliations and then turned to the Hungarian mothers urging them to raise good and moral patriots so that the completion of the work of 1956 not be marred by a flood of blood. Quoting Victor Hugo she said that death was a matter for God and others could make no claim for it. Finally she read a Petőfi poem entitled: "A nép nevében" (In the Name of the People) and asked when the time ever came that those speaking for the people asked the peoples' opinion.

Then Sándor Rácz, a machinist, the nominee of the Hungarian October Party for president, who was the president of the Greater Budapest Central Workers' Council in 1956, recalled the Russian intervention. Among repeated shouts of "Russians go home" the speaker complimented the youth on its courage and strength during the fights. Then he spoke of the importance of the Workers' Councils indicating that he was still their leader. Rejecting help from both East and West, he addressed the multitude and said: "You are the future of Hungary, because it can come only from Hungarian roots." In conclusion he voiced his confidence that the Republic would prove to be the governmental system of a free Hungary.

Seven twenty-five P.M.: They read the farewell letter of Benő Budavári, condemned to die which revealed that after an unsuccessful suicide attempt the writer went to his death with his head held high. His moral strengths is shown clearly at his last meeting with his family when he did not talk about himself but only of the survivors giving advice to all.

The memorial event concluded at 7:30 P.M. with the singing of the "Appeal." The message to be taken away by all was the slogan of the day: "Communism, never again!" Those present then sang the "Székely Anthem" and again echoed the: "Russians go home" slogan. The masses then slowly began to leave Kossuth Square.

Népszabadság, October 24, 1989.

The Blockade War Is Over

Subsequent to the Saturday afternoon street blockades and until the political breakthrough was accomplished the country lived between fears and hopes.

At the end of the week anxiety escalated, fearing that the deep social division might lead to confrontations. As seen in our paper, the ecclesiastical leaders counseled pacification and patience. Late in the evening on Saturday, moments of disappointment followed the special bulletin, announced on the radio, that an agreement had been reached between the cab drivers and the government. On Sunday morning, those guarding the barricades in the capital city, permitted the traffic to move through and both the streetcars and the buses resumed service.

Called by the MDF (Hungarian Democratic Forum) several thousands, according to one estimate as many as ten thousand, marched with police protection to the Parliament to assure the government of their support and urge it to persevere.

The pro-government demonstration of the afternoon was considered by János Palotás to have been a demonstration orchestrated by the government which endangered the peacefully demonstrating cab drivers who did not block the roads on Sunday. Palotás said that it was in vain that they asked for help from the national chief of police who said that they could not protect the cab drivers, waiting at major intersections, from the participants of the organized demonstrations. The government was blamed for this by all the organizations present....

Népszabadság, October 29, 1990.

ABSENT A CHANGE THEY WILL START AGAIN IN FEBRUARY

Thursday morning about five to six thousand participated in the demonstration in front of the Parliament where the milk producers protested against the economic policies of the government. At the same time the organizers of the demonstration handed out free milk, in six different areas of Budapest, to those who needed it.

Népszabadság, February 1, 1991.

FEW DEMONSTRATED WITH TORGYÁN

Remarkably fewer people participated in the FKGP (Independent Smallholder Party) demonstration than predicted and the day of wrath was converted into a day of possibilities. At the demonstration József Torgyán repeated his already innumerably often stated demands that the government step down, that there be a true change in system, that there be a new constitution and a new franchise and that petitions be circulated for making the representatives subject to recall.

Torgyán estimated the number of participants between two hundred and two hundred and fifty thousand people but the police, responsible for the safety of the demonstrators, estimated the number of participants to be between twelve and fourteen thousand....

The demonstration in two acts was scheduled and started on Saturday, at 10:00 A.M., at Heroes' Square. The party chief arrived in his green Volvo, accompanied by police, and joined the ones protesting the social tensions, "the starving retirees, the miserable condition of the young and the bitter fate of the peasants and workers." The speaker sharply criticized the government and the three top legal dignitaries, the president of the republic, the prime minister, and the president of the National Assembly who did not consider it possible to "meet the people and negotiate with them." After criticizing just about everybody, the economic transition power block, the Communists, the current politicians, etc., the party chief came to the conclusion that, "a new Mohács is threatening us which takes shape in the impotence and treachery of the government."

The second act of the demonstration took place in front of the Parliament where the demonstrators arrived on foot. In an address of almost one hour Torgyán just repeated what he had said already, that the government should resign and should yield power until September 1 to a government of experts. Then he detailed the twenty-point demands of the FKGP which among others included: "a true change in the system, the halt to transferring power and assets, proceedings against and bringing to account the looters and the despoilers of the people, a new franchise law, a new constitution, and the protection of the intelligentsia." The party chief also analyzed the media and claimed that the government exerted more control over them than even the Communists and that the media had taken up the cause of the enemies of the people....

The party chief then made those present vote in favor of the twenty points, but contrary to the original plans he did not transmit them in the Parliament....

Népszabadság, April 27, 1992.

Enthusiastic Demonstration in Favor of the Government

A demonstration planned for three days began Saturday evening in front of the Parliament. The goal of the protest demonstration, proclaimed by POFOSZ and other '56-er organizations was to make the presidents of the Hungarian Radio and Hungarian Television resign.

Jenő Fónay, the president of POFOSZ (Alliance of Hungarian Political Prisoners), and Gergely Pongrátz addressed the protesters. They forcefully criticized the program policies of the two media, considered to be anti-Hungarian. In his speech, Mr. Pongrátz threatened the capital city administration with unforeseeable consequences unless by October 23 all memorials and all street names identifiable as Soviet or Communist were removed in Budapest. "They can have one memorial where they came in and one where they left." This sentence of Pongrátz' was particularly well received.

The mood of the meeting was set by the rather vulgar tone with which the president of the republic was attacked by the speakers and the participants. As announced, several National Assembly representatives participated in the demonstration.

According to the original plan, the demonstrators should have accepted a joint announcement and then marched to the television station. The multitude, however, wanted to go immediately and therefore, singing Hungarian folk songs, moved to the Szabadság Square where they listened to additional speeches. They demanded that Hankiss resign. The spirit of the meeting was manifested by the repeated and rhythmical chanting of "Long live the government!" and "Long live Antall!" and by the rhythmic clapping accompanying the exclamations.

Népszabadság, August 24, 1992.

TENS OF THOSANDS DEMONSTRATE AGAINST THE MEDIA PRESIDENTS

At the Saturday demonstration of the Free Hungarian Information Committee the participants demanded the removal of the presidents of the radio and television and the establishment of free Hungarian media.

The demonstrators gathered in front of the Parliament. Here Feró Nagy sang a few songs, including one beginning with, "The comrades are dropping like flies...." Gyula Zacsek, the National Assembly representative of the MDF, asked the multitude to demonstrate with dignity, to hand over the troublemakers and provocateurs to the police and also reminded them that the demonstration had a single goal: making Csaba Gombár and Elemér Hankiss resign and establishing a free Hungarian radio and television. Gergely Pongrácz, the president of the World Association of '56-er Hungarians asked the demonstrators to be heard, "Let us show them that we are not a mob," he said.

Gyula Grosics was asked to chair the demonstration. Miklós Réti, MDF representative, on the twelfth day of his hunger strike, stepped to the podium and declared that the oppression and persecution of the Hungarian spirit was going on in the media and that this was due to the fact that one part of the citizenry had no roots and no national feelings. He declared that he would give up his hunger strike but that he was not giving up his principles and that henceforth he would work for the cause of the free Hungarian media with the tools of politics. He said that he had received a personal letter From József Antall, who emphasized the identity of their goals and asked the representative to give up his hunger strike. Miklós Réti asked Béla Győri, the dismissed editor of the Vasárnapi Ujság, *to do likewise. As an answer, Béla Győri read an announcement from the podium: he would stop starving.*

The list of the participating organizations was read and in this list we find the various '56-er organizations, regional organizations of the MDF and the KDNP (**Chriistina** Democratic People's Party), the '56-er circle of the MDF, the Közakarat Egyesület (General Will Association)....

Then the approximately ten to twelve thousand multitude started toward the Radio.

Népszabadság, September 21, 1992.

Charta Demonstration: Multitude with Flowers

At the Thursday evening demonstration of the Democratic Charta several thousands gathered for the "peaceful, dignified walk" to the *Petőfi* statue on March 15 square.

...According to the program the demonstrators would march from the *Petőfi* statue to the Kossuth Square in front of the Parliament, via the Duna Corso, Roosevelt Square, Zrínyi Street, October 6 Street, and Szabadság Square.

Népszabadság, September 25, 1992.

Commemoration on October 23

The President of the Republic was Prevented from Giving His Speech

An unexpected incident disturbed the thirty-sixth anniversary celebrations of the 1956 Revolution and War of Independence. At the commemoration in front of the Parliament on Friday afternoon a loud group of demonstrators, against whom the police took no action, choked off the words of the president of the republic and prevented him from delivering his speech. Árpád Göncz then deviated from the protocol and did not appear on the stage of the Opera House, where Prime Minister József Antall was to be the principal speaker....

Népszabadság, October 24, 1992.

Proposal for a Parliamentary Investigation

Condemnation of the Provocation of the President

There is no calming the political storm raised by the incident which occurred in front of the Parliament on the afternoon of the twenty-third. As known, a group of about two to three hundred skinheads prevented the president from delivering his speech. Noted public figures raised their voice in protest immediately after the incident occurred. On Saturday the government issued a statement about the event and so did the Ministry of the Interior and the BRFK (Budapest Police Chief Captaincy).

According to the capital city police no illegal event took place at any of the memorial sites that would have been subject to immediate intervention. Protests were raised by the participating political parties, organizations, and private persons. Imre Mécs, speaking to our paper, indicated that he would ask for the establishment of a parliamentary fact-finding committee. Similar

action is being prepared in the house by Socialist minority leader Zoltán Gál.

(*From our correspondents.*)

In an announcement sent to the MTI, the government expressed its regrets that because of the demonstration and behavior of one part of the audience the president of the republic was unable to deliver his speech. The government announcement also pointed out that no event occurred on the square that would have endangered public safety. The announcement from the press office of the prime minister stated that at the same time the government most vigorously rejects the insinuations and accusations in the press and from other sources which refer to the responsibility of the government in connection with the disturbance and which go so far as to assume that there was a conscious government organizing activity behind the event....

Népszabadság, October 26, 1992.

Ten Thousand Teachers Demonstrated

The teacher's organizations and the KKDSZ organized a protest and cautionary demonstration. Yesterday afternoon at 3:00 P.M. in front of the Hungarian Academy of Sciences, the demonstration began with a large gathering and then the group marched to the Parliament to deliver their petition to György Szabad, the president of the National Assembly. The petition asks the representatives of the National Assembly not to support the government proposal to delay action. It calls upon the government of the Hungarian republic and on the parties assembled in Parliament to ensure that when the law on the 1994 annual government budget was drafted and debated, they would live up to their obligations under the Public Employees' Act and make certain that the financial guarantees of the institutional organizations be enacted.

Népszabadság, June 2, 1993.

HUNGARY REMEMBERS 1956

...At the wooden grave marker erected on the steps of the Parliament the members of the government and the president of the republic lit candles to the memory of the victims and thousand of others did likewise in other parts of the Kossuth Square....

Népszabadság, October 25, 1993.

JÓZSEF ANTALL WAS ESCORTED ON HIS LAST JOURNEY

On Saturday Prime Minister József Antall was buried in Budapest and a great many showed their respect during the solemn funeral service. Until the early morning hours approximately a quarter of a million mourners marched by the coffin placed on a catafalque erected in the Parliament. During the morning first the officials of the MDF and then the foreign statesmen coming to the funeral bowed their head before the catafalque. They included the vice president of the United States, the former prime minister of the United Kingdom, the "Iron Lady," and the high ranking officials of foreign countries near and far. Their being present at the same time, on the day of mourning, made it possible for them to review the major events of the world and to hold bilateral meetings.

György Szabad, the president of the National Assembly, declared to the assembled multitude that the late prime minister wished to create a Hungary based on national and democratic principles. Speaking for the Hungarians of the world, the writer András Sütő said that after Antall's accomplishments fear would no longer force the Hungarians beyond the borders to avoid the discussion of awkward problems. Pál Bolberik, the titular abbot performing the religious ceremony recalled the day when the dying man asked him to come to his bedside and told him that he wanted a Christian Hungary. A military honor guard accompanied the coffin, placed on a gun carriage, to the National Pantheon in the cemetery on Fiumei Road, where the representatives of the churches said good bye to the deceased head of government....

At twelve noon the bells were rung and six soldiers of the Republican Guard Regiment placed József Antall's flag-draped coffin onto a catafalque erected at the main entrance to the Parliament....

Népszabadság, December 20, 1993.

Demonstration against the Tuition Ordinance

Approximately four thousand people participated yesterday on Kossuth Square in the demonstration called for by the National Association of the Hungarian University and College Students to protest against the tuition. In their petition, handed in at the office of the prime minister, the student organizations demanded the revocation of the current tuition ordinance, the declaration that the new regulations were null and void, the raising of the student financial support, and the lowering of the dormitory fees....

Approximately four thousand people gathered on Kossuth Square. Balázs Várkonyi and Katalin Liebmann read the list of the organizations and parties supporting the demonstration. A number of people at the demonstration waved red and white striped Árpád flags....Calls of "Down with the government and down with Horn" were repeated regularly.

Népszabadság, October 2, 1996.

The Country Remembered the Revolution

On Wednesday morning, on Kossuth Square in Budapest the banner of the Hungarian Republic was raised with military honors. Immediately afterwards, also in front of the Parliament, a new '56-er Monument was dedicated, the Flame of the Revolution. It is the work of the sculptor, Mária Lugossy....

Népszabadság, October 24, 1996.

Workers in the Meat Industry Demonstrate in Front of the Parliament

...The approximately three hundred workers of the Szekszárd Meat Processing Company, who demonstrated yesterday in front of the Parliament, turned to the prime minister and to the president of the National Assembly for assistance in their fight against the labor-offensive and illegal regulations introduced in their work place....

The Workers from Szekszárd Demonstrated in Front of the Parliament

The approximately three hundred demonstrators arrived in six buses yesterday, a little before 3:00 P.M., to Kossuth Square and the placards they carried made it clear with Hungarian and German inscriptions what they thought of the increasingly poisoned situation in Szekszárd. The placards read: "Gyula, the Gunther carries the votes!" "More bread. More rights!" and "The Schlegel exploits even the poor man!" The workers tested the speaker system prior to the speeches and, while they listened to the leaders of their union, frequently engaged in a shouting match with the [ruling] party sympathizers who came to watch the demonstration. The latter were more concerned with the assessment of the government activities and this bothered the people from Szekszárd, shivering in the icy weather....

Népszabadság, February 18, 1997.

Pál Kovács Caused an Accident Near the Parliament Building

Mihály Dézsi, the spokesperson for the BRKF told the MTI that at 9:15 A.M. Tuesday morning a private automobile hit a policeman in the parking area in front of entrance seventeen to the Parliament building. He stated that according to the police report the car was owned by Dr. Pál Kovács, Member of Parliament and former minister of public welfare.

The driver of the car wished to stop there but the policeman advised him that a reception was going to be held for Herzog Roman, the president of the German Federal Republic and that therefore there was no parking in that area. The driver and the policeman got into an argument. The driver of the car suddenly sped away and the left side view mirror of the car knocked the policeman down causing injuries which took eight days to heal....

Népszabadság, February 26, 1997.

MIÉP: Everybody Should Resign

On the call from the MIÉP (Hungarian Justice and Life Party) **a few thousand people participated in the general solidarity assembly called for last night for the Kossuth Square where the twenty item list of demands of István Csurka's party were announced....**

Népszabadság, February 28, 1997.

Tractors on Kossuth Square

On Tuesday the agrarian demonstrations slowing all traffic continued throughout the country. The participants held their authorized demonstration in the capital city as well. Eight trucks, guided by police, arrived in front of the Parliament. The demonstrators handed their petition to Zoltán Gál, president of the house....

Potatoes Were Sold for One Forint in Pest

The farmers of the communities surrounding Budapest, Alsonémedi, Bugyi, Ócsa, Aporka, Kiskúnlacháza, Majosháza, Makad, Ráckeve, and Szigetbecse demonstrated yesterday with almost a hundred tractors and other agricultural machinery in front of Parliament. The tractors demonstrated in the morning by closing off one of the traffic lanes on the lower Danube embankment and in the afternoon they demonstrated in front of the Ministry of Agriculture with eight vehicles. The delegation representing the farmers of the nine communities delivered a petition to Zoltán Gál, the president of the National Assembly. In the petition the farmers demanded, among other things, the enactment of a business federation act, the creation of an agrarian support system that was independent of sectors, the enactment of a prohibition of the sale of productive land to foreigners, and the introduction of ordinances protecting the internal agrarian markets. The tractors started toward the Kossuth Square, in a slow tempo, at about 2:00 P.M. and the approximately hundred people walking behind them were soon joined by a group of permanent demonstrators who rapidly grasped the initiative and, with varying intensity, demanded the resignation of the government....

Népszabadság, March 12, 1997.

POLICE ACTION AGAINST THE DEMONSTRATORS

Harsh police action, injuries, arrests—these were the characteristics of the Metész demonstration held in Budapest in spite of a court injunction

...The police prevented the demonstrators gathered at the Heroes' Square to march, as an organized parade, to the Parliament. The multitude was dispersed; Gyula Zacsek, the organizer of the capital city demonstration, was arrested and many of the ones resisting the administrative actions were asked for identification and several were taken into custody. The latter included Gergely Pongrátz, the president of the World Association of '56-er Hungarians, who hit a policeman with his car....

Népszabadság, November 4, 1997.

Peace March of Many Thousands in the Capital City

"We demand that the MSZP (Hungarian Socialist Party) fulfill its role in maintaining the peace, stop the Milošević genocide, and the NATO attacks," was the theme at the antiwar demonstration organized on Sunday in the capital city. Several thousand people participated in the event organized by the recently-established Peace in the Balkans movement....

Népszabadság, May 10, 1999.

The Holy Crown Is in the Parliament

...On Saturday, the first day of the year 2000, the Holy Crown and the coronation regalia were moved with festive ceremonies from the National Museum to the Parliament....

Viewing the Crown on Kossuth Square

...Two enormous projection screens were erected next to the main entrance to the Parliament, but they were not placed high enough so that they could not be seen from the more distant points of the square, not even standing on tiptoes. The square itself was illuminated with large spotlights and thus the screens became useless. Alkotmány Street was closed off, ropes were strung along the sides and it was impossible to cross the street. The multitude still waited patiently for the crown to appear....

Népszabadság, January 3, 2000.

The Millennial Year Has Come to an End

The festivities on August 20th officially brought the Millennial Year to an end. On Monday the National Banner was raised in front of the Parliament. At the centralized national commemoration, held at this place, Prime Minister Viktor Orbán emphasized, "Hungary has accomplished what few could do: it became what it wanted to become, a free, independent, strong and growing country." As part of the ceremony 212 young people, 185 men and 27 women were given officer's commission.

Népszabadság, August 21, 2001.

Opening of the Kossuth Memorial Year

Árpád Göncz, the former head of state, stated at the opening of the Kossuth Memorial Year on Kossuth Square that we must watch with careful diligence if the essentially European type of freedom that was the moving force in 1848–1849, and was serving the interests of the country, was getting stronger. We must be careful that we do not abrogate social equality, equality before the law, and the laws of humanity and freedom of thought and speech. At the opening ceremony in 2002 of the one-year-long series of festivities honoring the two-hundreth anniversary of Kossuth's birth and arranged by the SZDSZ (Alliance of Free Democrats), Gábor Kuncze, the president of SZDSZ, declared that the liberals also had a tradition and that in the fight for freedom they resisted the crown, the excesses of the church, and the Communist oppression. He believed that the dictatorship no longer existed, but that dictatorial activities continued. According to Kuncze, the forces trying to eliminate liberalism from Hungarian political life had to be repressed.

Népszabadság, November 8, 2001.

Remembering the Heroes of 1956

...On October 23rd the National Banner was raised on Kossuth Square with military honors and to the singing of the national anthem. This was the act initiating the national festivities to commemorate the forty-fifth anniversary of the 1956 revolution and the twelfth anniversary of the proclamation of the Hungarian Republic....

Népszabadság, October 24, 2001.

Demonstration of Firemen on Kossuth Square

"The fireman saves—save the fireman," "We help everybody—who will help us?" "Can we bring you out? Would you go in for him on a salary of 153 forints gross?" It was with signs like these and black ribbons, reflecting great desperation, that firemen marched to the Parliament at noon on Thursday to protest against the discontinuation of hazard pay....

In the interim the Ministry of the Interior "counter-demonstrated" on the other side of the Kossuth Square. They displayed the position of the ministry, concerning the demonstration, on a large screen. Its basis was that for more than half a year the trade union had blackmailed the ministry, over and over again, with demands which could not be met legally and that the leadership misled not only public opinion but its own membership as well. The ministry held the firemen in high esteem and was pleased to work with men who are faithful to their oath and are willing to risk their life on behalf of their fellow citizens.

After the speeches a truck brought a coffin onto the square in which they placed—buried—the papers dealing with the hazard pay supplements. The firemen stood as an honor guard next to the coffin for the next seventy-two hours.

The leaders of the trade union organizing the monster demonstration counted on 1,500–2,000 participants but in the end, according to official tabulation, about 1,000 showed up. We have asked several firemen whether the rumors coming from a number of counties about the off-duty firemen being called back to work for the time of the demonstration and that it was forbidden for them to participate were true, but those asked did not offer any concrete information and only said that they had also heard about the rumors....

Népszabadság, November 9, 2001.

Orbán Transfers from a Rocket to a Train

There was a large and disciplined multitude on the Kossuth Square and the fears, suggested by the government-friendly press, that the "concerned left wing" would organize a provocation did not materialize. The participants in "the greatest national gathering in Hungarian history" cheered the head of government and Orbán repeated his Tuesday speech about his fears for the "middle-class future" but in somewhat milder tones. In his speech, in the Vigadó in February, the head of government likened the country to a rocket while now he said it was like a railway station where everybody could select their own train. The greatest controversy was about the size of the multitude with the master of ceremonies estimating the number of attendees first as one and a half million and then as two million, the police estimating the number at one and a half million, The Duna TV at one million, and the public space administration at 300–400 thousand....

Népszabadság, April 15, 2002.

Never Before Seen Multitude on Kossuth Square

"There are always people who hate but they can win only if you hate them too. This is why we believe in the force of love and cooperation," announced Prime Minister Viktor Orbán on Saturday at the election meeting of Fidesz and MDF in which, according to police estimate, about one and one half million people participated. A number of noted public personalities, sports figures, and entertainers also participated.

People behaved decorously....

Magyar Nemzet, April 15, 2002.

Blockade on the Bridge, Demonstration on the Square

"It has started, Erzsébet," was the message received yesterday morning by a man who called our editorial office. Another office worker was called by mobile telephone to come and demonstrate on Kossuth Square. The program director of Pannon Radio had mentioned on Wednesday that it was incomprehensible to him why the people protesting the destruction of the ballots last July did not arrange a demonstration similar to the earlier taxi cab blockade. Thursday morning members of the Lelkiismeret '88 group blocked the Erzsébet Bridge. The blockade, lasting for hours, practically brought the traffic in the capital city to a halt. The Lord Mayor, trying to negotiate, had to be rescued by the police who then dispersed the protesters with force and removed the cars from the bridge. A few hundred protesters then marched to the Kossuth Square where they were met by a police cordon because they had not received permission for their demonstration. The politicians kept away from the demonstration but Imre Makovecz, a founding member of Szövetség a Nemzetért (Alliance for the Nation), which is under the directorship of Viktor Orbán, appeared in the multitude and declared that the events made him recall '56 with the difference that now the demonstrators were beaten and slashed while in '56 some of them were shot. A live broadcast from Pannon Radio, reported and manipulated the news of the events and urged on the audience at the demonstration of whom several were arrested by the police. There were no serious atrocities until late afternoon although there were a number of minor encounters. The forces endeavoring to maintain order were standing face to face with the slightly larger mass of people for a long time and then started to force the group away from the square. Fidesz makes the coalition government responsible for what happened because it resisted the wishes of the people in the matter of recounting the votes. At the same time Tamás Deutsch, the new parliamentary leader of the [Fidesz] party representatives, called the demonstration illegal and urged both sides to remain calm....

Népszabadság, July 5, 2002.

Are the Vote Counters Disappearing?

...On Thursday two demonstrations in the capital city demanded a recount of the votes. At the gathering on the Kossuth Square, László Grespik, the former head of the Capital City Administrative Office, spoke and György Budaházy, one of the organizers of last week's blockade of the Erzsébet Bridge, read a proclamation. In the evening on Március 15 tér (March 15 Square) in Budapest, the organizers, the Civic Circle of Veszprém and the Christian Civic Circle of Balaton, announced through bullhorns that this demonstration was the first regime-changing meeting of the second regime change and also announced that their intent was to recapture the area before the *Petőfi* statue from Gábor Demszky. The multitude of several thousand was joined by the people who had demonstrated a few hours earlier on Kossuth Square....

Demonstrations for a Recount

Several hundred people participated yesterday in a demonstration on the Kossuth Square demanding a recount of the votes of the April elections. The peaceful, previously announced and thus legal gathering was free of any violence. Among others, László Grespik spoke and claimed that the concerns about the irregularities, which may have occurred during the elections, were legitimate. György Budaházy, one of the organizers of the Erzsébet Bridge blockade of the past week, read a proclamation on behalf of the managers of that event. In this proclamation they demanded not only that the votes be counted again but also that all persons who in any way, openly or secretly, supported Communist oppression be removed from Parliament and from public life. The demonstrators departed at 7:15 P.M. to join the demonstration on the Március 15 Square....

Népszabadság, July 12, 2002.

Kossuth Memorial Meeting in Budapest

"With cooperation, faith, and strong determination the third republic could make Kossuth's dreams into reality," said Prime Minister Péter Medgyessy on Saturday, at the memorial gathering in front of Parliament held as the closing act of the Kossuth Memorial Year. The head of government emphasized that in the person of Kossuth the nation could remember a statesman who knew that a republic has a leader and not commander, who is willing to enter into a discussion and does not object to being assessed, who takes responsibility for the nation, who does not specify the conditions of power but who creates the opportunities for advancement....

Minister of Education Bálint Magyar and Minister of Culture Gábor Görgey discussed Kossuth's historic achievements. They emphasized that Kossuth recognized the need for the Hungarians to cooperate with the nations of the Carpathian Basin and that the countries along the Danube had to strive together to find the path to salvation. Görgey emphasized that Kossuth, improperly and incorrectly, in deep desperation called Artur Görgey, the commander in chief, a traitor after the Világos surrender even though they had agreed that the tragic end was inevitable. Minister Görgey said, "My ancestor, albeit deeply hurt, knew that Kossuth symbolized the War of Liberation and that even in spite of major disagreements they agreed on all the basic issues."

Demonstrators Disrupted the Festive Oration

The festive oration of the prime minister was disrupted by demonstrators in front of the Parliament. About fifty to sixty persons gathered in the early afternoon, hours before Medgyessy's scheduled appearance, in the area of the Kossuth Square where earlier the Lelkiismeret '88 Group held its demonstration demanding the recount of the votes. During the speech of the head of government they continuously shouted, whistled, and booed. They joined in calling him a traitor and, among other things, repeated over and over again, "Let the government perish" and "Let's have Orbán back!" Some of them tried to mingle with the people festively gathered in the middle of the square, but the security guards, in civilian clothes, promptly removed them from the gathering. In an announcement sent to the MTI on Sunday the Lelkiismeret '88 Group stated that the speech of the prime minister was disrupted by the Lelkiismeret '88 Group, by the World Council of '56-er Hungarians, by the Hungarian Revisionist Movement, and by several civic circles.

Magyar Nemzet, September 29, 2002.

Children in the Parliament and in Front of It

...Yesterday an artificial skating rink was opened in the parking area of the Parliament. Until January 2, the children could use it free of charge and the adults do not have to pay for using it after eight in the evening. The establishment and operation of the artificial skating rink cost fifty million forints and the cost was borne by the Szerencsejáték Rt. (Game of Chance, Inc.).

Népszabadság, December 23, 2002.

Solidarity with the Children

...On Children's Day the Parliament and its surroundings were the site, for the first time, for children's programs organized by the Red Cross and by the Alliance of Large Families. There were entertaining presentations and handicraft workshops. A number of other organizations also arranged play activities for the children, including the mentally and physically challenged ones....

Népszabadság, May 26, 2003

They Recalled Ferenc Rákóczi

A memorial service and the placement of a wreath were performed on the three hundredth anniversary of the beginning of the Rákóczi War of Liberation, in Budapest, by the equestrian statue of the prince on Kossuth Square....

Népszabadság, June 18, 2003.

A Charity Clash

Several hundreds were anxious to see the handball battle on Kossuth Square in front of the Parliament building between Dunafer, the women's champion team, and the select team of employees of the Parliament. The ladies won 19 to12 and the goal of the meet was to focus attention on the fight against breast cancer and the importance of participating in the screening process. Every year, in Hungary, 5,700 women are diagnosed with breast cancer and 2,300 die of this disease. The most important feature in the fight against cancer is early diagnosis. This is why it is so important to have as many as possible participate in the screening process.

Népszabadság, June 20, 2003.

Petition of Comrades in Misfortune

Saturday afternoon a peaceful demonstration was held on the Kossuth Square by the Sors-Társak Egyesület (Comrades in Misfortune Association) representing the victims of the apartment mafia in whose name a petition was handed to representatives of the Ministry of the Interior.

Népszabadság, June 23, 2003.

Employees of the Radio Protested on Kossuth Square

A group of about eighty, mainly from artistic ensembles of the Hungarian Radio demonstrated yesterday in front of the Parliament. The participants protested the changing of the work rules.

Népszabadság, June 24, 2003.

Antigovernment Demonstration in Budapest

…Yesterday, in the late afternoon, at the second demonstration of the day several thousands, many more than at the earlier demonstration, gathered at the Erzsébet Bridge. They were summoned by the Szabad Magyarországért Mozgalom (For a Free Hungary Movement), the World Alliance of '56-er Hungarians, the Jobbik Magyarországért Mozgalom (For a Better Hungary Movement), the Magyar Polgári Szalon (Hungarian Civic Salon), and the Trianon Társaság (Trianon Society). The occasion for and the message of the demonstration were the same as for the morning one. According to the proclamation calling for a demonstration the march was for a "Day of Awakening," for "The Stolen Regime Change" for the cessation of privatization, for the elimination of the mafia, and against the country being debased into "A World of Matrix." The multitude marched to the Parliament yelling slogans such as, "Perish Medgyessy," "We Want a Hungarian Government," "Trianon Must Perish," and "Ria, Ria, Ria Hungaria." Along with the '56-er [tricolor with a hole in the middle] and Árpád [red and white striped] flags, there was a gallows with a sign "D–209" [referring to the prime minister's past as a Communist intelligence agent]. Budaházy and the members of the Nemzeti Front (National Front) marching with him sang the "Wake up Hungary" song well known from MIÉP television material. They arrived to Kossuth Square for speeches and a program at the time we went to press.

Népszabadság, July 5, 2003.

The Magyar Cetelem Bank
Presents
Budapest
Public Space Films and Music

Festival
On Giant Screens

13:00–14:30 Children's Movies

14:15–16:00 Hungarian Movies

16:30–19:00 Theater on Film

19:30–22:00 Classical Music on Film

Attendance of the Festival Is Free

July16–August 1, 2004
Kossuth Square

Népszabadság, July 3, 2004.

Demonstrations at the *Károlyi* Statue

"We don't want a second Trianon, we don't want the geographic and territorial Trianon of the twentieth century to be followed by an ethnic and national Trianon in the twenty-first century," declared István Hiller, the president of the Hungarian Socialist Party, at the major gathering organized in memory of the Fall-Aster Revolution, Friday afternoon, by the Parliament, at the statue of Mihály Károlyi. He reminded the listeners that it was eighty-six years ago, at this time of year that the Fall Aster Revolution succeeded and that the idea of a Hungarian republic was born.

Also yesterday there was a silent demonstration on the Kossuth Square by ten members of the Hungarian Democratic Forum, which condemned the Fall Aster Revolution memorial meeting by the government parties. The demonstrators carried signs which said, "The Károlyi government financed István Tisza's murderers" and "Move the *Károlyi* statue to the Romanian border."

A counterdemonstration with about five hundred participants was organized by the For a Better Hungary Movement and other affiliated organizations. They protested against the elevation of Mihály Károlyi, the former president of the republic into a "national symbol" and paraded under flags of the national tricolor, Árpád stripes, and black color [symbolizing grief].

At the end of the demonstrations there was some trouble. The people departing from the MSZP-SZDSZ meeting were insulted by the Better Hungary followers and some of them were pelted with tomatoes and eggs....

Népszabadság, October 30, 2004.

They Continue to Demonstrate and to Negotiate

Several thousand farmers and a few people, well known from extreme right-wing movements, assembled in front of the Parliament with the four tractors which the police allowed to enter the square. There were a number of witty or coarse signs, condemning the government and the ministry, a goat, a donkey, an inflatable bull, as well as unhappiness and emotions. The farmers drafted a fourteen-point petition in addition to the demands for the disbursement of the agrarian support at the earliest possible moment....

Népszabadság, February 23, 2005.

Demonstration Followed by Messages

...After the major meeting on the Kossuth Square on Saturday, the farmers announced another meeting for Sunday but during the night they agreed to the Friday night ultimatum of the government and desisted from organizing further demonstrations. Consequently there were only a few hundred people gathered in the square on Sunday forenoon, but the negotiations did not continue....

Instead of a Blockade, Apples from Spain? Civic Anger and Common Sense of the Farmer

...SUNDAY MORNING a group of several hundred people gathered on Kossuth Square. Those massed on the square waved red-white-green flags and showed signs of the Honfoglalás 2000 Egyesület (Conquest 2000 Association) and of the Civic Circle of Fonyód. The demonstrators were told that the Sunday demonstration had been called off.

Népszabadság, February 28, 2005.

A Multitude of a Million Issued a Wake-Up Call

...Viktor Orbán, president of Fidesz, announced yesterday at the mass meeting of the Alliance on Kossuth Square that the election on April 9 will not be the usual quadrennial event.

He said, "The past, in a new garb and repackaged tries to steal back in. The ones who made the country go into debt and to the verge of bankruptcy, who served foreign interests over Hungarian ones, and who did not want to hear about free elections and democracy." He urged the audience not to allow themselves be intimidated with threats, alarming rumors, and prophecies, nor with paper sculpture. The latter "threat" was in reference to an election portrait of Ferenc Gyurcsány displayed on a high rise in the capital city. Orbán insisted that he believed that on April 9 truth would prevail again. He asked the audience to remember that the *Stalin* statue had weighed sixty-five tons and was backed by the army of an empire, yet it could be pulled down. "Now we must only put a paper sculpture in its proper place." The participants in event, which went under the name of the Day of Hungarian Solidarity, completely filled Kossuth Square and the neighboring streets. According to information received from Fidesz, more than 1.5 million people participated.

Magyar Nemzet, April 3, 2006.

From the Bridge to Kossuth Square

...The organizers of the demonstration called the "Day of Truth," summoned to protest the restrictive ordinances of the Gyurcsány government at 5:30 P.M. today on Kossuth Square, gathered more than twenty thousand signatures. The organizers of the event, defined by them as a civilian one, handed a representative of the head of government a petition labeled, "What Does the People Want?" The call for action over the internet asked a number of questions: "Will you be able to pay your electric and gas bill? Will you be able to continue to pay your mortgage with the higher interest rates? Are you sure that you will keep your job? Will you be able to afford to continue with your education? Are you hoping that your children will get an education? Do you agree with the rise in medicine prices and the cost of medical visits? Are you expecting the visit from the commando overseeing the APEH increase in assets? If your answer is NO! Join us."

Kossuth Square was occupied on June 22, in spite of the "No Stopping" signs set up on Monday....

Népszabadság, July 4, 2006.

Alarms on the "Day of Truth"

"The civilian sphere is the force that can control the political powers to be" was what one of the speakers at the "Day of Truth" demonstration told the audience of a few hundred people assembled on Kossuth Square yesterday afternoon, armed with trumpets, whistles and "Historic Hungary" pins. At the demonstration, organized on the internet in opposition to the restrictive package of the Gyurcsány government, the Better Hungary Movement was represented by its rowdies and the Munkáspárt (Labor Party) by a letter from its president, Gyula Thurmer.

Népszabadság, July 5, 2006.

Megamovie on Kossuth Square

The Budapest Public Space—Movie—Music Festival is going full blast this week on Kossuth Square in front of the Parliament. This is the third year that the open air megamovie program has become available and every performance can be seen free of charge through the generosity of the Cetelem Bank.

Children's movies and cartoons begin every day in the afternoon at 4:30 P.M. for one and one half hour after 6:00 P.M. music and dance movies can be seen; after 8:00 P.M. major movies are shown and after 10:00 P.M. we can become acquainted with one of the rarely seen silent classics of Hungarian movie making. This year they can be seen under much improved technical conditions the screen having been enlarged to sixty-two square meters twice the previous size....

Népszabadság, July 17, 2006.

Cultural Saturday

The Kossuth Square demonstration called for the end of the week, during the lull in campaigning, is becoming a cultural event, but if the police will attempt to disperse the peaceful multitude, the organizers will urge resistance, according to a statement of the leaders of the demonstration....

Magyar Nemzet, September 17, 2006.

"You F.....ed It Up! Let's Go, Dance, Feri!"

Prime Minister Ferenc Gyurcsány's admissions having become publicly known a nationwide movement was triggered. A multitude began to assemble in front of the Parliament late on Sunday evening. The demonstrations lasted all day yesterday. By Monday evening increasing numbers assembled and there were gatherings all around the country.

"You fucked it up, you fucked it up," was among the things said rhythmically, over and over again by the several thousand people gathered in front of the Parliament after unknown people provided the press with a tape of a speech by Prime Minister Ferenc Gyurcsány presented at the two-day meeting of the MSZP parliamentary representatives held on May 25–26 in Balatonöszöd. The people marching to the Parliament demanded the resignation of Ferenc Gyurcsány and of the government, the dissolution of parliament, and the scheduling of new elections. The police were present in great strength with József Petrényi, minister of justice and public protection, and Péter Gergényi, the chief of police of Budapest, also being present. In the end the police did nothing except to make sure that order was being maintained. In an announcement Gergényi stated that the previously unannounced gathering would not be dispersed. His argument was that in times of elections and campaigning, political meetings could be held without previous permission and therefore the police did not consider the present demonstration to be illegal....

Magyar Nemzet, September 18, 2006.

Hundreds of Large Families Demonstrate in Front of the Parliament

Hundreds of families demonstrated against the Gyurcsány package in Budapest on the Kossuth Square, the event being organized by the National Association of Large Families.

Endre Szabó the president of the association stated that they protested because the ordinances of the government make the existence of the families impossible.

Népszabadság, September 18, 2006.

Demonstration on Kossuth Square

A Cordon of Police Protects the Parliament

...By evening six to seven thousand people gathered on Kossuth Square and demanded with increasing force the resignation of the government. Several groups broke through the police cordon and advanced all the way to the protective cordon erected just outside the wall of the Parliament.

Népszabadság, September 19, 2006.

Demonstration: Day 3.

The multitude on the Kossuth Square broke through the outer cordon.

The group of four to five hundred grew to about ten thousand by the early evening hours in front of the Parliament. Unscheduled speakers followed each other and in the intervals popular music was played. The mood was both tense and relaxed....

According to the MTI [news agency], at the time we went to press, a mass of ten thousand demonstrators broke through the outer cordon and reached the inner cordon on Kossuth Square. Several orators spoke of a "moral revolution" and regularly warned that nobody should be deceived by "provocations coming from deep down."

Népszabadság, September 20, 2006.

"As Though These People Would Not Come on Their Own"

Saturday evening, about 7:30 P.M., about six to eight thousand people gathered on the Kossuth Square and in the area of the Parliament behind the reconfigurable crowd control railings unusually great police preparations could be seen. While the demonstration proceeded in its usual fashion a line of trucks arrived and the police lined up along the barrier.

The demonstrators watched the activity with great interest and the announcement that pictures of the speakers had appeared on police posters caused annoyance (the information was incorrect and it was the picture of vandals who were wanted by the police).

Among the visuals we must mention the coffin ornamented with pictures of Ferenc Gyurcsány, Gábor Kuncze, and László Keller. On the oak the "mourners" appended an inscription reading, "For you there will be no resurrection!..."

The Kossuth Square commander of the spontaneously formed "National Guard" rose to speak and asked the "wholesome and Hungarian" youths to report for duty at the *Rákóczi* statue. Between the orations poems were recited. A number of people cast their political demands about the dismissal of Gyurcsány into verse and then gladly gave impromptu interviews to the reporters of the numerous foreign TV companies. At the very edge of the square chickens were roasted, there was free coffee and mineral water and there were long wavy lines of people in front of the tents. There were no disturbances by 8:00 P.M. and this was the same every evening since Monday....

A Call for an Uprising Is Announced on Kossuth Square

Society was called to rise up by the Hungarian National Committee—2006 (MNB), which took the responsibility for the series of demonstrations on Kossuth Square....

Népszabadság, September 21, 2006.

Only the Field Kitchen Had a Permit

The field kitchen is operated with a permit from the public health authorities but other hygienic restrictions are not observed very much on Kossuth Square.

In any activity involving more than two hundred people there has to be one toilet for every forty women and one toilet and one pissoir for every eighty men. According to the regulations of the public health authorities, issued to the organizers of the activity there also have to be facilities for hand washing, for keeping the area clean, and for the removal of the waste materials. Because it is not clear whether the Kossuth Square, "inhabited" since a week ago was an incidental event or the occupation of a public space, the public health officers did not know who was responsible for the enforcement of the hygienic regulations....

Népszabadság, September 22, 2006.

A Variety of Ideologies on Kossuth Square

The Desire to Change the Government Moved Multitudes of a Hundred Thousand Across the Land

Just like on previous days several thousand people gathered on Kossuth Square in Budapest in the early evening hours. The peaceful demonstrators are harangued by self-appointed, but organized, speakers. Some read poetry, some prayed in the defense of democracy....

Magyar Nemzet, September 22, 2006.

Saturday, Kossuth Square

Ten to eleven A.M.: There are several hundreds on the Kossuth Square....

Eleven to noon: Orations begin on the podium erected on Kossuth Square. The organizers had decided that only those could speak who had asked to do so in writing and had submitted, in general, what they were going to say....

Volunteers clean vegetables at the Magosz tent. Lunch is being prepared.

Noon to one P.M.: The police arrest a man who is trying to start a fight among the assembled people.

Two to three P.M.: Demonstrators dressed as wranglers march toward the Parliament.

On Kossuth Square there is a brisk trade in national flags and ribbons in national colors. There is a long line in front of the field kitchen.

Three to four P.M.: There are more than five thousand demonstrators....

Five to six P.M.: The multitude had increased to approximately twenty thousand on the Kossuth Square....

After the Recsk commemoration, László Tőkés, a bishop of the Reformed Church [in Transylvania], declared that in his opinion the head of government had no moral basis to condemn the demonstrators in the street....

Six to seven P.M.: Imre Pozsgay, an emblematic figure of the later Kádár period, speaks on the Kossuth Square. Followed by Mátyás Szűrös....

Seven to eight P.M.: Opinions vary about the number of people on the Kossuth Square and estimates range from twenty to fifty thousand....

Népszabadság, September 24, 2006.

After the Seventh Day, Still on the Square

Even though Gábor Demszky, the Lord Mayor, cautioned the capital city to be prepared for even greater demonstrations, the seventh day of demonstrations passed in a carnival mood on Kossuth Square where demonstrators in very large numbers demanded the resignation of the prime minister and of the government until 1:30 A.M.

The demonstrators and the speakers continued their activities but the mood remained a very peaceful one. This was shown also by the reduction in the number of police in front of the Parliament and the fact that they were no longer carrying shields....

Népszabadság, September 25, 2006.

The Protests Continue

...There were thousands on Kossuth Square again to convince the government to resign and similar demonstrations were held in the country as well.

One group of the demonstrators on Kossuth Square demanded the establishment of an interim government, the calling of a national assembly to draft a constitution, and the immediate start of negotiations....

Népszabadság, September 26, 2006.

The Field Kitchen Is Proscribed and Removed

Summarizing their night-time experiences, the Public Health Service declared that it was a divine miracle that there had not been a mass poisoning. After reports by the population and by the demonstrators no food may be distributed on Kossuth Square.

At night Kossuth Square presents a very different picture, at least from the perspective of public health. While the day time inspectors found everything in reasonable order, allowing for the pervasive stench, after an inspection on Wednesday night all food distribution was stopped in the square. The field kitchen, standing in front of the Parliament, was packed up and towed away and the illegal food merchants also had to leave....

Yesterday, in the square, the demonstrators could use ten portable toilets instead of the former two. Glasses and plates could be used only once and there was free mineral water. The regional inspectors admitted that there was not much that could be done about people relieving themselves wherever they wanted to. In the meanwhile, the organizers asked the homeless to ask for food in front of the Lord Mayor's office because the Lord Mayor had announced that food would be provided.

Népszabadság, September 29, 2006.

Concerts and Theater in Front of the Parliament

The field kitchen was closed yesterday on Kossuth Square. The demonstrators organized a cultural program for the times between the campaigns and today there will be a theater performance. The demonstrators who had been arrested were called political prisoners by the organizers and they were expecting the representatives of an international human rights organization to assist in their release. They also invited Lech Wałesa....

Magyar Nemzet, September 29, 2006.

There Will Be No Early Elections

...At a Fidesz mass meeting, yesterday afternoon, Viktor Orbán announced a Yes, Hungary Charter movement before eighty to one hundred thousand supporters. The goal of the charter is to make the country overcome the moral crisis. For this reason they will be present on the Kossuth Square every afternoon between 5:00 and 6:00 to stand up for justice. "We will be here," "We will be here," was yelled rhythmically on Kossuth Square....

Népszabadság, October 7, 2006.

Hundreds of Thousands Hold a Protest Meeting on Kossuth Square

According to estimates about 300,000 protesters marched in response to Fidesz's invitation to Kossuth Square yesterday, where Viktor Orbán, the president of the opposition party, declared that in view of the crisis his party did not demand new elections but did demand that the government parties place a new prime minister and a coalition government of experts at the head of the country. Orbán launched the "Yes, Hungary Charter" the signatories of which can say, "Yes to the reestablishment of morality, to every Hungarian regardless of gender or religion, to national unity, to the defense of the national patrimony, democracy, the dignity of the president of the republic, and the oaths taken." The president of the party declared that they asked the people to stand forth for justice, just like the opposition representatives in the Parliament who will stand on the square every afternoon between 5:00 and 6:00 until the government departs....

Magyar Nemzet, October 7, 2006.

Fidesz Initiates a Criminal Proceeding against Gyurcsány

On the basis of the Criminal Code 177/B Fidesz initiated criminal proceedings against Ferenc Gyurcsány, because the prime minister "failed to bring matters of public interest to the public, falsified data of public interest, and thereby violated the criminal code's stipulations pertaining to the mishandling of public data." This is what János Áder, the vice president of the National Assembly stated at the mass meeting sponsored by Fidesz on Saturday on Kossuth Square. "Gyurcsány, get out," "resign," and "to jail, to jail," the assembled yelled rhythmically....

Népszabadság, October 9, 2006.

Kossuth Square: Who Is in Charge?

"The Capital City Public Area Inspectorate cannot act in areas where programs come under the Right of Assembly Act," declared the director of the inspectorate after the organization came under fire from several directions. It was accused of doing nothing while Kossuth Square evolves into a continuous bazaar. The police, which was also charged with passivity, announced that they will do what they are capable of....

Népszabadság, October 10, 2006.

Kövér: "There Is No Place to Retreat"

"Ferenc Gyurcsány is through. From a moral and political perspective he is a non-person and the whole government will depart with him. The only question remaining is whether they will be able to steal the remainder of the national assets" stated László Kövér, the president of the Fidesz board, yesterday before tens of thousands of people on Kossuth Square. According to the politician "we have no place to retreat to until this so-called left wing criminal gang does not disappear...."

Gyula Grosics, the goalkeeper of the legendary Golden Team, also spoke and urged the departure of the head of the government and of the cabinet. Between the speeches poetry and folk songs were broadcast from the Fidesz stage.

Magyar Nemzet, October 10, 2006.

Soldierly Discipline on Kossuth Square

"We must defend the country, the state, and the citizens at the risk of our life. Can we expect the same from the state and from the leaders of the state?" was heard at the warning demon-

stration of the Fegyveres és Rendvédelmi Dolgozók Érdekvédelmi Szövetsége (Protective Alliance of the Armed and Public Safety Workers).

The armed and public safety workers held a spectacular, dignified, disciplined and well organized one hour warning demonstration on Saturday morning in front of the Parliament. FRDÉSZ, representing the police, the military, the fire fighters, the customs officers, the prison guards, the border guards, the civilian protective bodies, and the national security personnel, made up of a hundred members from each of the above organizations, a total of eight hundred, march to the beating of drums, as an "expanded brigade" to the Kossuth Square from the Szalay Street all the way to the grassy area in front of the Kossuth statue. In view of the particular situation only members of the press were allowed to enter the area surrounded by a cordon. From outside the cordon a number of people, clapped and shouted, "we are with you," "we are Hungarians," as they watched the event with great interest.

Magyar Nemzet, October 16, 2006.

Lapid: "The Entire Kossuth Square Must Be Cordoned Off"

The stalemate on Kossuth Square continues: the demonstrators do not leave and threaten resistance. According to some unsubstantiated news a political decision had been made that the demonstrators could not stay on Kossuth Square on October 23. The police are helpless....

Népszabadság, October 18, 2006.

After Ultimatums, between Cordons

The antigovernment demonstrators may stay on Kossuth Square at the time of the October 23 official festivity. The number of participants will not be controlled, the square will be divided into two areas with cordons, they are reserved for the demonstrators, will undergo a security check in the morning of the 23rd and may be entered only after the security inspection. This was announced late yesterday afternoon by László Bene the national police chief. The demonstrators promised that they would not disrupt the festivities....

Népszabadság, October 21, 2006.

Behind Closed Gates, with Dignity

The next day, on October 23, those who wished to see the festive raising of the National Banner and the salute to the flags of the neighboring countries on Kossuth Square, found out that they could not do so. The immediate area around the Parliament was cordoned off and the square was emptied. The demonstrators who were there were evicted at dawn by the police stating that the demonstrators had failed to keep the agreement about the demonstration. Some demonstrators agreed, others denied it.

The camp of the revolutionaries remained in place in the morning in front of the Parliament but was hidden from the foreign guests by posters of historic photographs and by the grandstand. On Kossuth Square all the flags of the states saluting the memory of the revolution were raised and every leader of a delegation placed a wreath on the 1956 Monument....

Népszabadság, October 24, 2006.

In the Absence of Jurisdiction: No

After the police declared that the Kossuth Square was an operational area, its lack of authority became manifest in connection with the acceptance of the Magosz tractor demonstration. The present situation is that the farmers may not demonstrate at the Parliament....

Népszabadság, October 28, 2006.

BIOGRAPHICAL NOTES

Áchim, András (1871–1911). Politician, parliamentary representative. Founder of the Magyarországi Független Szocialista Parasztpárt (Independent Socialist Peasant Party of Hungary), 1906. Editor and publisher of the *Paraszt Ujság* (Peasant Newspaper) from 1906 on. An argument with the sons of Endre Bajcsy-Zsilinszky, led to an exchange of shots and he was killed.

Aczél, György (1917–1991). Politician. A member of the Communist Party, he held a number of political positions. His most important role was the leadership of cultural life and he was its highest decision maker. In this he set the tone for the whole period from the middle 1960s until 1985.

Áder, János (1959). Jurist, politician, parliamentary representative, president of the National Assembly. After 1988 a member of Fidesz (Fiatal Demokraták Szövetsége—Association of Young Democrats). A delegate of the Ellenzéki Kerekasztal (Opposition Round Table) and, after 1993, the vice president of the party. President of the National Assembly from 2002 to 2006. Head of the Fidesz party representatives in parliament. After 2006 again the Vice President of the National Assembly.

Ady, Endre (1877–1919). Poet, publicist, journalist. His volume entitled *Új versek* (New Poems), published in 1906 is of historic significance in Hungarian literature. He was a leading figure among the writers grouped around the journals *Nyugat* and *Holnap*. His poetic innovations, transmitting the influence of French avant guarde and symbolism, and his first liberal and then radical political views made him the subject of constant attacks and criticism.

ANDRÁSSY, GYULA, SR. (1823–1890). Count, politician, prime minister, joint minister of foreign affairs. Because of his position in the 1848–1849 War of Liberation, he was forced to live in emigration until 1857. Deák Party representative with a major role in the creation of the Compromise. Became prime minister in 1867 and held this position until 1871 when he was appointed joint minister of foreign affairs. The most significant achievements of his foreign policy activities were the Berlin Congress of 1878 and the creation of the Dual Alliance in 1879.

ANDRÁSSY, GYULA, JR. (1860–1929). Count, politician, minister, writer on political science. Son of Gyula Andrássy, Sr. Liberal Party representative, 1894–1895. Minister of personal service to the king, 1906–1910; minister of the interior and then, in 1918, the last minister of foreign affairs of the Austro-Hungarian Monarchy. One of the leaders of the royalist opposition he played a role in the attempts of Charles IV to regain his throne.

ANJOU ruling dynasty. The family was of French extraction. A scion of its Neapolitan branch, Charles Robert became king of Hungary after the death of the last male ruler of the House of Árpád in 1301. He ruled under the name of Charles I until 1342. His son, Louis I, The Great, was the ruler of Poland as well, after 1370. After Louis I died in 1382, his daughters, Maria and Hedvig (Jadwiga) inherited the thrones.

ANTALL, JÓZSEF (1932–1993). Politician, prime minister, historian. Director of the Semmelweis Museum of the History of Medicine. He was also instrumental in the change of regime as one of the delegates of the Opposition Round Table. Beginning in 1989 he was the president of the Magyar Demokrata Forum (Hungarian Democratic Forum) and, after the free elections in 1990, prime minister of Hungary.

APPONYI, ALBERT (1846–1933). Count, politician president of the House of Representatives, minister. A member of several parties (Egyesült Ellenzék (United Opposition) Szabadelvű Párt (Liberal Party), Függetlenségi és 48–as Párt (Independence and '48-er Party), etc., representing all of them in succession in the Parliament. Considered one of the foremost orators of the time. President of the House of Representatives, 1906–1910. Minister of religion and public instruction. Chairman of the Hungarian peace delegation in 1919–1920, and Hungary's delegate to the League of Nations, 1925–1933.

Árpád Dynasty Ruling dynasty in Hungary between 1000 and 1301. Named after Prince Árpád from whom they descended. The first one to bear the title of king was St. Stephen (1001–1038) who is viewed as the founder of the state of Hungary. The dynasty had twenty-three successively ruling members of whom the most important ones were St. Ladislaus I (1077–1095), Coloman the Learned (1095–1116), Andrew II (1205–1235), Béla IV (1235–1270). Because of the internecine fights within the family, the death of Andrew III, meant that the male line had come to an end.

Bajcsy-Zsilinszky, Endre (1886–1944). Politician, journalist. A founding member of the Magyar Országos Véderő Egyesület (Hungarian National Defense Forces Association) in 1918, the Fajvédő Párt (Race Defense Party) in 1923, and the Nemzeti Radikális Párt (National Radical Party). Since 1936 a member of the Független Kisgazdapárt (Independent Smallholder Party) and a contributor to a number of newspapers including *Szabadság, Szabad Szó,* and *Magyarország).* President of the Magyar Nemzeti Felkelés Felszabadító Bizottság (Hungarian National Uprising Liberation Committee). For this activity the fascist Arrow Cross condemned him to death and hanged him on Christmas Eve, 1944.

Balassi, Bálint (1554–1594). Baron, poet. A major figure in the second period of the Hungarian Renaissance. His importance in the history of literature is due to his creation of love poetry in Hungarian. One of his innovative verse forms were known as the "Balassi Stanza." His poems about military life was also important. Most of his work can be found in the *Balassi Codex.*

Báthory, Stephen (1533–1586). Prince of Transylvania and king of Poland. A follower of John Sigismund and after the latter's death prince of Transylvania (1571–1586). King of Poland after 1576. In domestic politics he endeavored to create a strong, centralized administration while in foreign policy he tried to create an anti-Ottoman organization, with the help of the Holy See. This organization was to be anti-Habsburg as well. He was preparing a campaign for the occupation of Moscow to be followed with the occupation of Constantinople.

Batthyány, Lajos (1807–1849). Count, politician, prime minister. After 1830 a member of the Upper House. Leader of the opposition at the 1832–1836, 1840, and 1844 diets as a Liberal Party politician. One of the founders of the Védegylet (Defensive Association) in 1844. The first Hungarian constitutional prime minister from March 17, 1848, to the end of September, 1848. Arrested in Pest in January 1849, he was accused of high treason, sentenced to death and executed on October 6.

Beöthy, Algernon (1839–1900). Notary public, National Assembly representative. After 1868 notary public of County Bihar. Member first of the Balközép (Center-Left Party) and then of the Liberal Party. National Assembly representative from 1875 and notary of the House of Representatives until 1891.

Berzeviczy, Albert (1853–1936). Historian, president of the Hungarian Academy of Sciences, National Assembly representative, minister, and president of the House of Representatives. Minister of religion and public education in the István Tisza government, 1903–1905. After his resignation he became the president of the Hungarian Academy of Sciences, of the Kisfaludy Association, and of the Hungarian section of the Interparliamentary Union.

Bethlen, István (1874–1946). Count, jurist, politician National Assembly representative, prime minister. He served as a representative of the Liberal Party (1901–1903), the Independence Party (1904–1913), and of the Constitution Party (1913–1918). One of the major organizers of the counterrevolutionary forces in 1918–1919 and the leader of the Antibolshevik Committee (ABC). The founder of the Keresztény Nemzeti Egyesülés Pártja (Party of Christian National Unification) in 1919. Prime minister after 1921. He held several portfolios in his own government. During his administration he stabilized the Horthy regime and he was also responsible for the creation of the understanding with the Social Democratic Party, the so-called Bethlen-Peyer Pact.

BIERMANN, ISTVÁN (1891–1937). Politician. Member of the Hungarian Social Democratic Party after 1912 and then one of the founders of the Kommunisták Magyarországi Pártja (Party of the Communists in Hungary). Held a number of offices during the Soviet Republic. He was arrested in October 1919 and then interned. In a prisoner exchange he departed for the Soviet Union where he became the director of the Dnyepropetrovsk metal works.

BOKÁNYI, DEZSŐ (1871–1940). Writer, journalist, translator, sculptor, commissar. Member of the Hungarian Social Democratic Party, 1894–1919. Editor of *Népszava* after 1895. Founding member and president of the Construction Workers' Orgnization (MÉMOSZ). Became a member of the National Council in 1918, and Commissar for Labor and Public Welfare under the Soviet Republic in 1919. Commanding officer of the Third Division of the Red Army. Sentenced to death in December 1920, he was exchanged to the Soviet Union in 1922 where he continued to be politically active until he became a victim of Stalin's purges.

BŐHM, VILMOS (1880–1949). Diplomat, politician, minister. Member of the Hungarian Social Democratic Party, 1913–1919. State secretary for defense in the Károlyi government, 1918–1919. He was responsible for the demobilization of the soldiers returning from the war and then he was the minister of defense in the Berinkey government in 1919. During the Soviet Republic first he was commissar of social affairs and then commissar of defense. He was also commander in chief of the Red Army and then ambassador to Austria during the summer of 1919. Returned from emigration in 1945 joining the right wing of the Social Democratic Party. Ambassador of the Hungarian Republic in Stockholm, Oslo, and Copenhagen, 1946–1948. When the Social Democratic Party and the Communist Party fused in 1948 he resigned and emigrated to Sweden.

BUKOVICS, GYULA (?–1914). Architect. Opened his office around 1870 and was one of the founders of the Magyar Mérnök és Építész Egylet

(Hungarian Engineer and Architect Association). The Ministry of Agriculture, built in Italian Renaissance style, is considered to be his greatest work. He also participated in the planning of the New York Palace and of the Andrássy Courtyard which is today the Zoltán Kodály Museum, located on the Kodály Circle and which was built according to his designs.

Bush, George Herbert Walker (1924). Politician. President of the USA. Congressmen from Texas, 1967–1971, UN representative, 1971–1973, president of the Republican National Committee 1973–1974, director of the CIA 1975–1977. Vice president of the USA, 1981–1982, and then president of the United States, 1989–1993.

Büchler, József (1886–1958). Politician, union leader. Member of the Hungarian Social Democratic Party, 1900–1948. At the time of the Soviet Republic he was one of the representatives of the Revolutionary Governing Council in 1919 and was forced into emigration, 1920–1922. Returning home he became first secretary and then general secretary of the Socialist Democratic Party until 1939 and the party's parliamentary representative, 1931–1935. Member of the Provisional National Assembly in 1948 and president of the National Bank, 1945–1948. Sentenced to prison for life in 1950. Rehabilitated in 1956 and worked on the reorganization of the Social Democratic Party at the time of the revolution.

Ciano, Gian Galeazzo (1903–1944). Count, Italian politician, minister of foreign affairs. Served as a diplomat in Rio de Janeiro. Became Italian consul in Shanghai and married Mussolinis's daughter Edda. Returning home he became minister of press and propaganda in 1935 and then his father in law appointed him Minister of Foreign Affairs in 1936. He also enjoyed the support of the royal family. After 1939 he essentially ruled occupied Albania. During World War II he became the Italian ambassador to the Vatican. He voted against Mussolini at the meeting of the Fascist Grand Council in July 1943 but followed the Duce to Salo after Mussolini escape. Sentenced to death for treason in January 1944, he was executed.

CORVIN dynasty in Hungary, 1458–1490. Its only ruler was Matthias Corvinus (1443–1490), the son of János Hunyadi, celebrated for his fight against the Ottomans. His marriage to Beatrix of Aragon produced no offspring and therefore he wanted to secure the throne for his natural son János Corvin, but after his death the estates elected Vladislas II from the Jagiellon dynasty as king of Hungary. The name of the family is derived from its coat of arms which contains a raven holding a ring in its beak.

CZINEGE, LAJOS (1924–1998). General, parliamentary representative, and minister. Member of the Hungarian Communist Party and its successor the Hungarian Workers' Party, 1945–1956. He held numerous political offices. At the time of the 1956 Revolution he was a member of the HWP's Central Committee's Military Committee. He was one of the founders of the Hungarian Socialist Workers' Party and participated in the organization of the Workers' Guards. Parliamentary representative, 1958–1967, and a member of the Central Committee of the HSWP, 1959–1988. Minister of defense, 1960–1984, and deputy chairman of the Council of Ministers, 1984–1987.

CSÁKY, ALBIN (1841–1912). Count, politician, minister. Parliamerntary representative after 1865 and Lord Lieutenant of Szepes (1867–1888) and Sáros Counties. Liberal Party minister of religion and public instruction (1888–1894). During his tenure he issued the so-called Naming Ordinance in 1890 and this was the beginning of the fight over ecclesiastic policy. Became a dissident from the government party in 1898, but returned to the party in 1899 and became its vice chairman. He was also in the Upper House and was its president in 1900–1906 and 1910–1912.

CSURKA, ISTVÁN (1934). Writer, politician, parliamentary representative, party president. One of the founders of the Magyar Demokrata Fórum (MDF) [Hungarian Democratic Forum] in 1987. Member of the party's presidium in 1988 and its vice president in 1991–1992. Expelled from the MDF in 1993 because of internal dissentions he founded the Magyar Igazság és Élet Pártja (MIÉP) [Party of Hungarian Justice and Life] and is its president to this day.

Dálnoki, Miklós Béla (1890–1948). Lieutenant general and prime minister. Military attaché in Berlin in 1933–1936 and then chief aide-de-camp to the regent and head of the Regent's Military Office after 1942. When the fascist Arrow Cross took over in October 1944, Dálnoki joined the Red Army and on October 17, 1944, issued an unheeded proclamation asking that "all military activity against the Russian army come to a stop and that the weapons should be turned against the German army." An independent member of the Provisional National Assembly in December 1944 and then prime minister of the provisional government until November 1945.

Deák, Ferenc (1803–1876). Jurist, politician and minister. Deputy Lord Lieutenant of County Zala after 1932 and the parliamentary representative of the county after 1833 and in 1839–1840. In the diet he was one of the leading personalities in the liberal reform opposition. Because of the bloody riots during the 1843–1844 parliamentary elections he withdrew his candidacy and participated in legislative activities only after March 20, 1848. He was the minister of justice in the Batthyány government and his major achievement in this position was the preparation of the legislation eliminating all traces of feudal tenure. He resigned in September 1848 but continued to participate in the work of the National Assembly. When the Bicske meeting, on January 3, 1849, resulted in impasse he withdrew to his estate at Kehida. During the 1850s he was the leading figure in passive resistance. In the 1861 diet he was the leading member of the Felirati Párt (Petition Party). It was his "Easter Article" published in the *Pesti Napló* in 1865 which was the first major step toward the Compromise. He had a major role in working out the legal and political background for the Compromise but refused to take a post in the Andrássy government in 1867. In the parliament he remained the president of his party, the Deák Party.

Demszky, Gábor (1952). Politician, Lord Mayor. Staff member of *Világosság* (Light), 1976–1981 and the editor of *Hírmondó* (Courier). Participated in the publication of the samizdat papers *Máshonnan beszél?* (Speaker from Elsewhere) and *Magyar Zsidó* (Hungarian Jew). He played an important role in the change of system and was one of the founders of Szabad Kezdeményezések Hálózata (Network of Free Initiatives) in 1988, and of the liberal party, the Szabad Demokraták Szövetége (Alliance of Free Democrats) which evolved from it. Lord Mayor of Budapest since October 1990. Elected to the National Assembly he resigned because of a conflict of interest and he also resigned from his membership in the European Parliament.

DINNYÉS, LAJOS (1901–1961). Politician, parliamentary representative, prime minister. Member of the Agrarian Party and then, from 1919, of the Smallholder Party. Parliamentary representative until 1939. Returned to political life after the party was reorganized in 1945 and became a member of the Provisional National Assembly. Minister of defense after 1947 and then prime minister. After the fall of his second government, in December 1948, he became the director of the National Agriculture Library and Documentation Center. At the time of the 1956 Revolution he was a member of one of the ad hoc national committees and then, in 1958, became one of the vice presidents of the National Assembly.

EÖTVÖS, JÓZSEF (1813–1871). Baron, writer, politician and minister. His political career began with the 1832–1836 diet where he belonged to the liberal opposition in the Table of Magnates. After 1840, he was one of the editors of *Budapesti Szemle* (Budapest Review). At the 1843–1844 diet he was one of the leaders of the centralist opposition and regularly published political essays in the *Pesti Hirlap* (Pest News) after 1844. In the 1848 Batthyányi government he was the minister for religion and public instruction. He resigned in September and then, with his family, fled to Munich. Returning in 1853 he participated in the activities of the Hungarian Academy of Sciences as one of the vice presidents after 1856. He became its president after 1866. Member of the Kisfaludy Society and a Deák Party representative in parliament. In the Andrássy government, established after the Compromise, he served as minister of religion and public instruction until 1871. His ministry was responsible for the introduction of universal mandatory education and the equal rights legislation for the Jews.

EÖTVÖS, KÁROLY (1842–1916). Politician, writer. Participated in the Almásy-Nedeczky conspiracy in 1864 and was sentenced to confinement in a fortress. After 1867 he worked as a county attorney and also served as editor for the *Pesti Napló* (Pest Journal),1872–1875, and *Egyetértés* (Concord), 1900–1902. He was a parliamentary representative, first in the Deák Party (1872–1875), then as an independent (1878–1884) and again as an independent (1887–1910) favoring the National Party of Work. In 1883 at the anti-jewish Tiszaeszlár blood libel trial he served as a defense attorney and was successful in getting his clients acquitted.

Eszterházy, Pál (1785–1866). Prince. Politician, diplomat, minister. Ambassador to Dresden (1810–1814) and then to The Hague (1814–1815). He then became ambassador to the Holy See and finally to London (1815–1842). Minister to the king (April–September 1848). A senior member of the conservative group during the Age of Reform and then, during the Batthyány government. After his resignation he lived in London where he was participating in the newspaper campaign against Kossuth.

Fadrusz, János (1858–1903). Sculptor. Worked in the Zayugroc woodcarving institute after 1875 and, during his military service in Prague (1879–1883) he became acquainted with the Czech sculptor Josef Václav Myslbek. Later in 1886 he received a scholarship to work in the workshop of Victor Oscar Tilgner in Vienna, and then continued his studies at the Vienna Art Academy as a student of Edmund von Hellmer. By this time he had produced a number of portrait sculptures, but he became nationally known for his work known as *The Crucifix* (1891). One of his early major commissions was the equestrian statue of Maria Theresa in Pozsony [Pressburg] (1892–1896) and then he worked on the *King Matthias Corvinus* statue in Kolozsvár [Cluj] (1894–1902). He produced the two allegorical statues for the Curia, presently the Ethnographic Museum (1893). During the rebuilding of the royal castle in Buda, he produced the two Atlas figures (1897) and the two lions guarding the entrance (1901–1902). His significant sculptures also include the equestrian statue of Béla Wenckheim (Kisbér, 1901), the *Wesselényi* statue (Zilah, 1902), the Tuhutum Memorial (Zilah, 1902), and the equestrian *Tisza* statue (Szeged, 1904).

Falk, Miksa (1818–1908). Publicist. A correspondent of the Vienna *Wanderer*, a liberal newspaper (184–1867). Then he worked with István Széchenyi (1858–1860). After the Compromise he became the editor in chief of the *Pester Lloyd* and also wrote a number of items anonymously for the *Budapesti Hirlap* [Budapest News]. He was Queen Elizabeth's teacher of Hungarian and later published his memoirs about this experience under the title of *Erzsébet királynéről. (Visszaemlékezések)* [About Queen Elizabeth. Recollections]. He was also a parliamentary representative, first in the Deák Party and later in the Liberal Party.

Fényes, László (1871–1944). Newspaperman. Worked as a reporter from 1894. Joined the *Az Est* (The Evening) in 1910. He was elected as an independent parliamentary representative but was emotionally close to the bourgeois radicals and to Count Mihály Károlyi's independentists. Consequently, during the Fall Aster Revolution he became a member of the National Council and a Commissioner of the National Guard. He was a defendant in the Tisza proceedings but was acquitted for lack of evidence. Later he became a correspondent for the Socialist paper *Népszava*. In 1926 he was forced to emigrate.

Ferenc József (Francis Joseph) (1839–1916). Emperor of Austria and king of Hungary. Took the throne on December 2, 1848, following the abdication of Ferdinand V. The initial period of his rule was shaped by the defeat of the 1848–1849 Revolution and its consequences. The legal basis for the actions were laid down in the Olmütz Constitution, published on March 4, 1849. He ruled as a neo-absolute ruler until 1867. Following the defeats in the wars with the Kingdom of Sardinia and Prussia he was forced to change his political orientation and reached a Compromise with the Hungarians in 1867. The new state structure, the Austro-Hungarian Monarchy, permitted a broader framework for development and this period was referred to in retrospect, after World War I, as the "happy times of peace." In domestic policies he endeavored to preserve these parameters while all throughout his rule his foreign policies were directed toward increasing the Monarchy's influence in the Balkans and in strengthening the ties with Germany. His figure became a symbol of the period.

FÓNAY, JENŐ (1926). Engineer and politician. Member of the Magyar Szabadság Párt (Hungarian Freedom Party) after 1946 and he worked as an engineer at the Erőműtervező Iroda (Power Plant Design Office) from 1953 to 1956. During the 1956 Revolution he was a leading figure of the Széna Square freedom fighter group. For this activity he was sentenced to death in 1958 but the sentence was commuted to life in prison. He was released in 1963 and became a founding member of the Történelmi Igazságtétel Bizottság (Historic Justice Committee) in 1988 and after 1989 was also the president of the Magyar Politikai Foglyok Szövetsége (Alliance of Hungarian Political Prisoners). He was also the vice president of the Magyarok Világszövetsége (World Association of Hungarians), 1992–1995.

FRIEDRICH, ISTVÁN (1883–1951) Politician and prime minister. Served as state secretary for defense in the Károlyi government during the Fall Aster Revolution in 1918. Arrested during the Soviet Republic as a leader of one of the major counterrevolutionary groups. After his escape he played an important role as a member of the "White House" group in overthrowing the Peidl government in August 1919. He became the prime minister in the next government from August 7 to November 25 and then became the minister of defense in the Huszár government in 1920. He resigned from the Keresztény Nemzeti Egyesület Párt (Christian National Association Party) and established a new party which fused with a group under the leadership of Gyula Andrássy, Jr. It became known as the Szövetkezett Keresztény Ellenzék (Associated Christian Opposition) in 1922. Parliamentary representative until 1939. Indicted for the murder of Tisza but he was acquitted by the court.

FÜREDI, RICHÁRD (1873–1947). Sculptor. He studied in Budapest and became one of the representatives of academism. He did mostly portrait sculptures and funerary monuments. He was instrumental in establishing this art form in Hungary.

GÁL, ZOLTÁN, SR. (1940). Politician. Taught at the HSWP Political College (1970–1974) and became deputy minister of the interior (1987–1989). In 1990 he became the minister of the interior. As a politician he first belonged to the Hungarian Socialist Workers Party (1964–1989) and then to its successor, the Hungarian Socialist Party (since 1898) and served as parliamentary representative for both parties. Between 1994 and 1998 he served as president of the National Assembly.

Garami, Ernő (1876–1935). Journalist, politician and minister. Member of the Hungarian Social Democratic Party (1898–1918) and editor of its organs, *Népszava* [People's Voice] (1905–1918), and *Szocializmus* (1908–1914). One of the chief theoreticians of the party. Member of the National Council and minister of commerce in the Károlyi and Berinkey governments (1918–1919). Emigrated during the Soviet Republic. Published the *Jövő* (Future) in Vienna (1921–1923) and then became a correspondent for *Népszava*.

Garbai, Sándor (1879–1947). Journalist, politician and president of the Governing Council of the Hungarian Soviet Republic. Member of the Hungarian Social Democratic Party leadership (1901–1919). Played an important role in the franchise struggles. Consequently he became the vice president of the Franchise Bloc in 1917. After the Fall Aster Revolution became the head of the National Domiciliary Council in 1919 and, during the Soviet Republic, he was the president of the Revolutionary Government Council in 1919. He was also the president of the Allied Central Executive Committee and, later, the minister of education in the Peidl government. Following this he was forced to emigrate.

Gerő, Ernő (1898–1980). Politician. During the Soviet Republic he functioned as a Communist politician and worked in the Alliance of Young Communist Workers. Following the collapse of the "Commune," he was arrested but as a result of a prisoner exchange he went to the Soviet Union where he was active in the Comintern. He returned home in 1944 and became a leader of the Communist Party and the second in command in the evolving Stalinist Rákosi regime. Had numerous political offices including several ministerships. From 1949 to 1952 president of the Népgazdasági Tanács (National Economic Council) 1949–1952 and then the deputy chairman of the Council of Ministers

(1952–1953). After the changes in 1953 he became first deputy prime minister. During the revolution of 1956 he was stripped of his offices and fled to the Soviet Union. Returning in 1962 he was expelled from the Party for his earlier activities.

Gombár, Csaba (1938). Sociologist, political scientist. Worked as a political associate in the Central Committee of the Young Communist Alliance (1963–1966). He then taught philosophy at the Budapest Technical University (1966–1968). Subsequently a senior research fellow of the Institute of Social Science of the Central Committee of the HSWP (1968–1989). Later he was President of the Hungarian Radio.

Gorbachev, Mikhail Sergeyevich (1931). Politician and head of state. Member of the Soviet Communist Party since 1952. Secretary responsible for agrarian matters (1970) and member of the Central Committee (1971) and of the Supreme Soviet (1974). Also elected to the Politburo of the Soviet Communist Party (1979) where under his patron, Iuri Andropov, he kept moving up in the Party hierarchy. After Constantin Chernenko's death, Gorbachev became the first secretary of the Communist Party and the president of the Soviet Union. The changes he initiated led to the end of the Cold War and to the collapse of the Soviet Union. He received the Nobel Peace Prize in 1990. After the failed coup in August 1991 he resigned from the presidency of the Soviet Union on December 25, 1991.

Gömbös, Gyula (1886–1936). Military officer, politician and prime minister. Worked in the ministry of defense after 1918 and in 1919 became the president of the Magyar Országos Véderő Egylet, MOVE (Hungarian National Military Association). During the Soviet Republic he was secretary of state for defense in the Szeged counterrevolutionary government. Became a Smallholder parliamentary representative in 1920. He was considered one of the confidants of Horthy and had a major role in defeating the attempts of the king to resume his throne (October 1921). Became a member of the Egységes Párt (Unified Party) in 1922 but resigned and formed his own party, the Magyar Nemzeti Függetlenségi (Fajvédő) Párt in 1923 (Hungarian National Independence [Race Defense] Party). In 1928 he returned to the government party and was made secretary of state for defense again. He was minister of defense in the Bethlen and Gyula Károlyi governments after 1929. Prime minister from 1932 to 1936, he developed a domestic program of 95 points. His foreign policy favored Italy and Germany.

Gömbös, László (1926). Sculptor. He was in a Russian forced labor camp between 1944 and 1948. Until his rehabilitation in 1957 he worked as a laborer and then as a lathe operator. He studied at the Academy of Fine Arts under Sándor Mikus and Pál Pátzay (1957–1963). His major works are the memorial statue of Béla III (Szentgotthárd, 1983), *Victims of the Fusillade* relief (Budapest, Kossuth Square, 1996), and the Victims of '56 Memorial (Kerepesi Road cemetery, 2000).

Göncz, Árpád (1922). Writer, translator, politician and head of state. Trainee in the Országos Földhitelintézet (National Land Credit Institute) in 1939 and then worked in the Teleki Pál Munkaközösség (Pál Teleki Work Panel). Member of the Independent Smallholder Party in 1945 and was the editor of *Nemzedék* (Generation). Until the dissolution of the party he was its parliamentary secretary and general secretary. At the time of the 1956 Revolution he was active in the Magyar Parasztszövetség (Hungarian Peasant Alliance) and then in the Magyar Demokratikus Függetlenségi Mozgalom (Hungarian Democratic Independence Movement). For his activities he was sentenced to life in prison in 1958. Released on amnesty in 1963. After 1965 worked as a writer and translator. One of the founding members of the Szabad De-mokraták Szövetsége (Alliance of Free Democrats) and of the Történelmi Igazságtétel Bizottság (Historic Justice Committee). Parliamentary representative after 1990 and from August 3, 1990 until 2000 president of the Republic of Hungary.

Görgey, Gábor (1929). Writer, minister. Worked in the National Theater (1950–1951) and after he returned from his forced expulsion to the countryside in 1951, he became a staffer for the *Magyar Nemzet* (Hungarian Nation) from 1959 to 1994. He was a script editor for the Pannonia Film Studio and also worked as a literary supervisor in the Szeged National Theater (1982–1988). Became the minister of the national heritage (2002–2003) and then became the prime minister's chief cultural adviser.

Gyurcsány, Ferenc (1961). Economist, politician, and prime minister. Member of the Communist Youth Alliance (KISZ) and after 1981 a secretary in the alliance. In 1989 he was the vice president of the Demokratikus Ifjusági Szövetség (Democratic Youth Alliance), the the successor to the alliance (1989). He represented a more radical reform direction and when he resigned, he became the president of the youth organization, Új Nemzedék (New Generation). After he finished his studies he worked in business. Became a member of the Hungarian Socialist Party in 2000 and then became the chief councilor to prime minister Péter Medgyessy in 2002. Minister for children, youths and sports (2003–2004) and after the prime minister resigned he became Hungarian prime minister in September 2004. In 2007 he took up the presidency of the Hungarian Socialist Party. He resigned from his positions in March 2009.

Hankiss, Elemér (1928). Sociologist. Research Associate of the National Széchenyi Library (1953–1962) and then the senior research associate of the Institute of Literary Scholarship of the Hungarian Academy of Sciences (1963–1975). Later he worked at the Szociológiai Kutatóintézet (Institute of Sociology) of the academy. He lectured at a number of domestic and foreign universities. His area of research was the sociology of values and political sociology. After regime change he was the president of the Hungarian Television.

Hauszmann, Alajos (1847–1926). Architect. Studied first at the Buda-pest Technical University and then Bauakademie in Berlin. Became a full professor at the Technical University in 1872 and then the chief of the architectural team in charge of the Royal Castle (1891). Honorary member of the Hungarian Academy of Sciences after 1924. One of the most active and influential representative of historicism in Hungarian architecture.

Helfy, Ignác (1830–1897). Journalist and politician. Worked in Kossuth's office in 1848–1849 and then emigrated to Italy (1854). As editor of *Alleanza* (1859–1867) he published Kossuth's very controversial Danubian Confederation plan (1862). In his paper he attacked the Compromise and, returning home in 1870, he became the leader of the '48-

er Party and then of the Independence Party. He was also their parliamentary representative. He edited for publication Kossuth's writings in emigration.

Hentzi, Heinrich (1785–1849). Austrian general. Commander of the Royal Castle in Buda in 1849, directed artillery barrage at Pest during the siege by the revolutionary Hungarian troops. Taken prisoner, he died of his wounds. In 1852 Francis Joseph had a statue erected at the castle which became the subject of repeated protests on the part of the Hungarians. The ruler paid no heed to these objections.

Herczeg, Ferenc (1863–1954). Writer and publicist. Correspondent of the *Budapesti Hirlap* (Budapest News) from 1891, *Az Újság* (The News) from 1903, and the *Magyar Figyelő* (Hungarian Observer) from 1911. In 1894 he started and edited the literary weekly *Új Idők* (New Times). Member of the Petőfi Society from 1893 and its president until 1920. Was a member of the Kisfaludy Society since 1893 and was the vice president of the Hungarian Academy of Sciences (1919–1922, 1929–1931, and 1945–1946). In politics he was first a member of the Liberal Party and its parliamentary representative and after World War I was a major supporter of irredentist, revisionist policies. It was for this reason that he was elected president of the Revisionist League in 1919. His novels were among the most popular of the times and his plays were performed frequently.

Hock, János (1859–1936). Priest, writer, and politician. Parliamentary representative after 1887, first in the colors of the Liberal Party, then in the National Party and finally in the Justh Party (1910). In 1918 he became the president of the National Council and had to emigrate during the Soviet Republic. While abroad his publicist activities were consistently anti-Horthy and therefore, after he returned to Hungary in 1933, he was indicted and sentenced to prison. Pardoned and released in 1935.

Hóman, Bálint (1885–1951). Historian, politician, and minister. Director of the University Library from 1915 and of the National Széchenyi Library after 1922. Director general of the Hungarian

National Museum after 1923. As an historian his primary area of interest was the Middle Ages. Professor of medieval Hungarian history at the Budapest University, now Eötvös Loránd University (1925–1931). Minister of religion and public instruction (1932–1942). As a politician he favored the German orientation. Consequently, in 1946, he was sentenced to life in prison as a war criminal.

Horn, Gyula (1932). Politician, prime minister. Member of the Magyar Dolgozók Pártja (Hungarian Workers' Party) since 1954. At the time of the 1956 Revolution he was a member of the paramilitary Worker Guard but his role at that time is still not clear. Worked in the Ministry of Finance (1954–1959) and then in the Ministry of Foreign Affairs. Had diplomatic assignments and later worked in the Foreign Affairs Department of the Central Committee of the HSWP (1969–1983). State secretary for foreign affairs after 1985 and then minister of foreign affairs in the Németh government (1989). One of his most noted actions was the removal of the Iron Curtain at Sopron which he did jointly with the Austrian minister of foreign affairs, Alois Mock, in June 1989. He was instrumental in opening the borders. After regime change he became one of the founding members of the Hungarian Socialist Party, served as a parliamentary representative and became prime minister of Hungary (1994–1998).

Horthy, István (1904–1942). Engineer, deputy regent. Miklós Horthy's older son. Worked first as an engineer in the machine works of the Hungarian State Railways Machine Factory (MÁVAG) and became its director in 1938. Became president of Hungarian State Railways (MÁV) in February 1940. State Secretary after 1921 and was elected by parliament as deputy regent on February 19, 1942. In politics he favored the British orientation. During the war he served on the eastern front as a reserve fighter pilot in 1942. On August 20, 1942, during a reconnaissance sortie near Alexeyevska in the Ukraine his plane crashed and he was killed.

Horthy, Miklós (1868–1957). Naval officer, regent of Hungary. Aide de camp to Emperor Francis Joseph and during World War I served as commander of the battleship *Habsburg* and later of the *Novara*. He was responsible for the suppression of the mutiny in Cattaro (Kotor) in February 1918. Minister of defense in the Szeged counterrevolutionary government in July 1919 and then became the commander in chief of the National Army cooperating with the irregular Prónay-Héjjas formations. Elected by parliament as regent of Hungary on March 1, 1921, thus proclaiming the peculiar arrangement, the kingdom without a king. It was during his regency that the Bethlen government consolidated the political and economic situation with a constitutional government and a regular state administration. His regental authority was enlarged repeatedly (1933, 1937) and in 1942 his son István was elected deputy regent to assist him in his work. In foreign policy he favored the Italian-German line. After his failure to get Hungary out of the war, the fascist Arrow Cross coup, with German help, forced him to resign in October 1944. Was a witness at the Nuremberg War Crime Trials and then lived in exile in Portugal.

Horvát, Boldizsár (1822–1898). Politician, jurist, and minister. During the War of Liberation he was a liberal member of the legislature and after the revolution's defeat he was put in jail by the Austrians for his activities. He was a member of the Chief Justice Council in 1861 and then he again became a representative of the Deák Party. One of the founders of the Földhitelintézet (Land Bank) and later its legal affairs director. Minister of justice in the Andrássy government (1867– 1871). Retired in 1878 and spent his time in writing. Became a member of the Kisfaludy Society (1887) and of the Hungarian Academy of Sciences.

Horvay, János (1873–1944). Sculptor. He started his studies at the School of Applied Arts and then studied in Vienna (1889–1895). Following this he went on a study tour to Paris, to Italy and to the United States. His work was largely limited to funerary monuments and memorial sculptures in the academic style.

Hunyadi, János (1405?–1456). Military leader, politician, and governor. Father of King Matthias Corvinus. Served in the Hungarian court of King Sigismund of Luxemburg and followed him on his campaign in Italy. After this he was made governor of Szörény County (1439–1446) and during the reign of Vladislaus I he became voivode of

Transylvania, captain of Nándorfehérvár (Belgrade), and Lord Steward of Temes (1441–1446). Gained triumphs in the fight against the Ottomans. He became the regent during the minority of the new King Ladislaus V (1446–1452). Then he became captain general of Hungary and manager of the royal revenues. Because of his great power a baronial league was created to oppose him. Died from the plague three weeks after the Nándorfehérvár (Belgrad) battle against the Ottomans which on July 22, 1450, ended in Hungarian victory.

Hültl, Dezső (1870–1946). Architect. A student of Alajos Hauszmann at the Budapest Technological University and worked with him in the Royal Castle building administration office until 1902. Receiving a doctorate in 1906 he was the first Hungarian architect to have a Ph.D. degree. He taught at the university from 1898 until 1940, receiving his full time appointment in 1913. Dean of the Architectural and Engineering School (1917–1919), he became the president of the University (1930–1932). He designed his buildings in neo-Renaissance and neo-baroque style but after the 1930s introduced functional elements in a novel style. His most important projects were the Pajor Sanatorium on Vas Street, the building of the Farmers' Insurance Association on Kálvin Square, the Capital City Commercial Arts College on Mester Street (1912), the Naphegy Sports Club of the Hungarian National Savings Bank, the hospital on Péterfy Sándor Street, and the apartment house belonging to the Hungarian Academy of Sciences on Károly Boulevard.

Jászi, Oszkár (1875–1957). Publicist, social scientist, politician, and minister. One of the founders (1900) and later editor of the *Huszadik Század* (Twentieth Century) which published essays on the modern social sciences. A member of the Társadalomtudományi Társaság (Social Science Association) from 1901. In politics he emphasized the importance of a general and secret franchise and of land reform and also took a stand against forceful Hungarization. Later one of the founding members of the Országos Polgári Radikális Párt (National Bourgeois Radical Party) and its president in 1914. Front-line reporter between 1915 and 1917 and then one of the founders of the National Council. Had a significant role in the Fall Aster Revolution in October 1918. A minister without portfolio in the Károlyi government in charge of the nationality affairs. In order to preserve the Monarchy he worked out a federal system known as the Eastern Switzerland. After the government fell he was forced to emigrate and lived from 1925 in the United States where he became a professor of political science (1925– 1942).

JÓKAI, MÓR (1825–1904). Novelist. Even though he was an attorney, after the success of his first novel (1846) he devoted his life to literatrure. Under the influence of Petőfi he voiced republican sentiments and served as a national guardsman in the War of Liberation. After the collapse he had to go into hiding and returned to Budapest only in 1850. He became a parliamentary representative of the Határozat Párt (Decision Party) in 1861 but joined the Liberal Party in 1875. A collaborator on a number of periodicals. Member of the Kisfaludy Society after 1860 and of the Petőfi Society, after 1876. He became a director of the Hungarian Academy of Sciences after 1892. For a long time the most widely read and most productive Hungarian writer, the most eminent representative of Hungarian romantic prose. Initially worked in the French romantic style but later developed his own particular romantic style. Being the most popular Hungarian publicist he was asked by Crown Prince Rudolf in 1885 to edit the Hungarian version of the *Osztrák-Magyar Monarchia irásban és képben* (The Austro-Hungarian Monarchy in Words and Pictures).

JÓZSEF, ATTILA (1905–1937). Poet. His first volume of poetry: *Szépség koldusa* (The Beggar of Beauty) was published in Szeged in 1922. Three poems were published in *Nyugat* (West) in 1923. In 1924 he published a poem "A lázadó Krisztusért" (For the Rebellious Christ) and was indicted for blasphemy. For his poem, "Tiszta szívvel" (With a Pure Heart), the dean of Szeged University, Antal Horger, forced him to drop out. His second collection of poems was published in 1925 including the poems "Nem én kiáltok" (I'm Not Shouting) and "Nincsen apám se anyám" (I Have Neither Father Nor Mother). Politically he was a socialist and in 1927 joined the illegal Communist Party and became a member of the Hungarian Socialist Worker Party as well. His illness progressed and he committed suicide in 1937. He is considered to be one of the most influential Hungarian poets of the twentieth century.

József, Ágost (1872–1962). Royal prince. Grandson of Palatine József. Austrian archduke, field marshal of the Hungarian army, royal governor. A descendant of the Hungarian branch of the Habsburg-Lotharingian dynasty. His wife, Augusta, was the daughter of the Austrian Princess Gisella and the granddaughter of Emperor Francis Joseph. On his own request the emperor transferred him to the Hungarian army and he also studied law at the University in Budapest. During World War I he fought first on the Serbian front, then in Galicia and later on the Italian front. He became a lieutenant general in 1916 and then the new ruler, Charles IV, appointed him commander in chief of the eastern front. The opposition wanted him to be appointed palatine for the coronation ceremony but the government party gave this appointment to István Tisza. At the end of World War I, in October 1918, he was the commander of the troops in the Balkans, a field marshall and eventually the commander in chief of the entire Hungarian army. He was also the plenipotentiary Hungarian palatine. After the Fall Aster Revolution he asked Mihály Károlyi to form a government and under the Soviet Republic he was being watched closely. After the fall of this system, on August 7, 1919, he declared himself to be regent and appointed István Friedrich as prime minister. He also supported the attempts of Charles IV to regain his Hungarian throne. On protests from the Entente he was forced to resign and confirm Miklós Horthy as commander in chief of the Hungarian National Army and later as regent. During the Horthy era he and his wife were the leaders of society until 1944 when they had to emigrate.

Justh, Gyula (1850–1917). Politician. Independence Party parliamentary representative after 1884. President of the party after 1891. As a politician he came out for ecclesiastic reforms, was active in opposition motions, including the "obstruction." President of the House of Representatives (1905–1909). Cooperated with the bourgeois radicals and the Social Democrats in the franchise question. Became cochairman of the United Independence Party where he supported Mihály Károlyi's bourgeois radical line.

Kádár, János (1912–1989). Politician, prime minister. Member of the illegal Hungarian Communist Party after 1930 and was repeatedly arrested for Communist activities during he Horthy era. Minister of the interior after World War II (1948–1950) but was found guilty in a show trial and sent to prison (1952–1954). At the time of the 1956 Revolution he was a minister in the Imre Nagy government (October 30– November 4). On November 4 he switched to the Soviets. Established the Hungarian revolutionary worker-peasant government in Szolnok and came to Budapest with the Soviet soldiers on November 7 to reestablish the Communist dictatorship. In the period that bears his name (1956–1988) he was the political leader of the country and held numerous positions, including generall secretary of the HSWP, chairman of the Council of Ministers, and prime minister (1956–1958 and 1961–1965). The politics associated with his name (Kádárism) are a matter of debate at the present time.

KÁLLAI, GYULA (1910–1996). Politician, journalist, prime minister. Became a member of the illegal Communist Party in 1932. After World War II he was a member of the Hungarian Communist Party and then of the central leadership of the Hungarian Workers' Party until 1956. Worked as a state secretary in the Propaganda Ministry, until 1947 and then became the minister of foreign affairs in the Dobi government (1949–1951). Deputy minister of education until 1956 and then minister of culture (1957–1958) and then minister of state (1958–1960). Had a number of additional political offices. Chairman of the Council of Ministers (1965–1967), which made him functionally the prime minister. He was also the president of the National Assembly (1967–1971).

KÁLLAY, MIKLÓS (1887–1967). Politician, prime minister. Parliamentary representative from 1919, first of the Egységes Párt (Unified Party) and then of the Nemzeti Egység Párt (National Unity Party). In 1937 he became a life member of the Upper House. Political state secretary in the Ministry of Commerce (1929–1931). Minister of agriculture in the Gömbös government (1932–1935). Prime minister of Hungary (1942–1944) and minister of foreign affairs (1942–1943). Wanted to expand the options and loosen the ties with Germany, reduce the participation in the war and eliminate the deportation of Jews. After 1945 active in émigré-movements.

KÁROLYI, ALAJOS (1825–1889). Count, diplomat. After 1845 served as a diplomat in a number of cities including Berlin, St. Petersburg, and

Rome. Secretary of the embassy in London in 1853 and later ambassador in Berlin (1860–1866). In this capacity he cooperated in the preparations for the Prague peace treaty. During Andrássy's service as minister of foreign affairs, Károlyi was again ambassador in Berlin and played a major role at the Berlin Congress in 1878. Following this, he was ambassador in London (1878–1888).

KÁROLYI, MIHÁLY (1875–1955). Count, politician, prime minister, president of the republic. Parliamentary representative after 1905 in the Independence Party and the '48-er Party. President of OMGE the National Hungarian Economic Association (1909–1912). In 1916 he established the Károlyi Independence and '48-er Party and after 1917 was the president of the Franchise Bloc. Days before the victory of the Fall Aster Revolution the National Council was formed under his leadership and he became successively prime minister and president of the republic (November 16, 1918). Resigned after the Vix Ultimatum leading to the rise of the Béla Kun regime. He was forced to emigrate in 1919. He was active in Social Democratic movements. After 1947 Hungarian ambassador in Paris. In 1949 resigned protesting the show trial of the Communist László Rajk and died in exile.

KERNSTOCK, KÁROLY (1873–1940). Painter, graphic artist. He started his studies at the School for Applied Arts and then became a pupil of Simon Hollósi in Munich. He then matriculated at the Julian Academy in Paris (1893–1895). Returning home he became a pupil at the Benczúr Master Class (1896–1899) and in 1906 made another visit to Paris. The early phase of his career is characterized by critical realism and then, under the influence of the Nagybánya group, he experimented with open air elements on his realistic canvases. His later paintings are characterized by postimpressionists features. He became one of the trend-setting representative of the artist group known as the Eights. After his emigration to Berlin (1919–1926) his work in Hungary reflects Etruscan influences. He also made copper engravings.

KISFALUDI STROBL, ZSIGMOND (1884–1975). Sculptor. He started his artistic training at the School for Applied Arts as a pupil of Lajos Mátrai and Antal Loránfi. He then studied with Alajos Stróbl, spent time in

Vienna and in Budapest worked at the School of Design with Béla Radnai. Won the Rudics Prize in 1912 which gained him recognition. The esthetics of the German sculptor, Adolf Hildebrand and the academic approach had great influence on his work.

Kiss, Ernő (1799–1849). General. Commander of the 2nd (Hannover) Hussar Regiment after 1845. After the revolution started, he fought against the Serbian insurgents. After the Battle of Pákozd he was a member of the mission negotiating peace with the pro-Habsburg ban of Croatia, Josip Jellačić. He was promoted to major general of the Hungarian army in December 1848. Became the commander of the National Supreme Military Command attached to the Debrecen government and on several occasions acted for the minister of defense. After the collapse of the War of Liberation he was jailed and then sentenced to death for his military activities. On October 6, 1849, he was executed in Arad.

Klauzál, Gábor (1804–1866). Politician and minister. Part of the liberal opposition at the diet during the Age of Reform as the representative from Csongrád County (after 1832). Became one of the leaders of the diet. He was the minister of agriculture, industry, and commerce in Batthyány government in April 1848. Following the outbreak of the War of Liberation he resigned and withdrew from public life. He reappeared only at the 1861 and 1865 national assemblies as a supporter of the Deák's Petition Party.

Kocsis, András (1905–1976). Sculptor. Started his studies at the Schol of Applied Arts in 1923 as a student of Lajos Mátrai, doing ornamental sculpture. He then worked with János Pásztor (1914–1928) and finally became a pupil of Zsigmond Kisfaludi Strobl (1928–1931). After the end of World War II he became very active as a sculptor of memorials.

Kossuth, Ferenc (1841–1914). Engineer and politician. As the son of Lajos Kossuth he grew up in emigration where he became a secretary in the Magyar Nemzeti Igazgatóság (Hungarian National Directorate) after 1859. Returning to Hungary in 1894 he exploited his father's popularity and became the parliamentary representative of the Independence and '48-er Party. Later he became its president. Became the minister of commerce in the Wekerle government (1906–1910) but also kept the presidency of the Independence and '48-er Party (1909–1913).

Kossuth, Lajos (1802–1894). Politician and statesman. He started his political career at the end of 1932 at the Pozsony diet as a representative and it was at this time that he started publishing the *Országgyűlési Tudósítások* (Reports of the Diet). In 1836 he followed this publication with the *Törvényhatósági Tudósítások* (Municipal Reports). He was sentenced to prison in a fortress for his journalistic activities and, upon his release in 1840 started publishing a newspaper, the *Pesti Hirlap* (Pest News). His political articles led to a confrontation with István Széchenyi. In order to promote economic progress he organized the first Hungarian industrial products exhibition in 1842 and established the Magyar Kereskedelmi Társaság (Hungarian Commerce Association) and was also one of the founders of the buy Hungarian movement, the Védegylet (Society for Protection) in 1844. The "Opposition Declaration" drafted by him in 1847 became the official policy of the Opposition Party. At the 1847 diet, as the representative of Pest County, he was already considered to be one of the leaders of the opposition. He became minister of finance in the Batthyány government after the March 1848 revolution. It was on his recommendation that the National Defense Commission was established on September 15, which took over management of the country, under his leadership, after the resignation of the government. On his initiative the House of Habsburg was dethroned on April 14, 1849, and he was elected as governing president of Hungary. During the waning days of the War of Liberation he turned power over to General Artúr Görgey on August 11, 1849 and escaped to Turkey. During his exile he was continuously active in politics hoping the European political situation would make it possible to reestablish the independence of Hungary. He worked out plans for the future of the country, such as the Danubian Federation and condemned the Compromise in the "Cassandra Letter" in 1867. He continued to send instructions to his Independence Party adherents which condemned the politics of the prevailing system, urged the more consistent protection of the nation's interests, and the support of democratic changes. In 1889 he lost his Hungarian citizenship, based on an earlier ordinance. His funeral in Budapest became a major patriotic demonstration.

Kovács, Béla (1908–1959). Politician and minister. State secretary for internal affairs in the Provisional Government established in Debrecen in 1944 and later minister of agriculture in the Tildy government (1946–1946). General secretary of the Smallholder Party. For this reason and for being a leader of the right wing, he was arrested in February 1947 and was taken to the Soviet Union. Minister of agriculture in the Imre Nagy government established in October 1956 and a strong supporter of the reorganization of Hungarian agriculture.

Kovács, Imre (1913–1980). Writer, sociologist and politician. Finished his studies at the Budapest University and, through the Pro Christo College became involved in village research. His first significant research work was done in the village of Kemse and the results were published in his first major work: *Az elsülyedt falu a Dunántúlon* (The Sunken Village in Transdanubia) in 1936. Because of a law suit initiated against him he could not finish his studies and worked as a publicist and politician. He became one of the founders of the progressive Márciusi Front (The March Front) movement in 1937 and of the National Peasant Party in 1939. In connection with this he wrote a book, *Kivándorlás* (Emigration), in which he pointed out the need for a land reform. Towards the end of War War II, in the summer of 1944, he represented his party in the Magyar Front Intéző Bizottság (Executive Committee of the Hungarian Front). Later he was elected its general secretary and he became a parliamentary representative. After the arrest of Béla Kovács he became a member of the Independent Democratic Party and in 1947 was forced to emigrate. After 1951 he worked in Washington, D. C. as a staff member of the Free Europe Committee.

Kozma, Lajos (1884–1948). Architect, craftsman, and graphic artist. He studied at the Technical University in Budapest and, after a study tour of France, he worked in Béla Lajta's architectural office (1910–1913). He became a teacher at the School for Applied Arts and was one of the founding members of the Budapesti Műhely (Budapest Workshop) in 1913. In the early stage of his career Transylvanian folk art exerted a major influence on his work and later he was considered one of the most important representatives of the Hungarian Secession. During the Horthy era he worked primarily as an architect and home decorator. The villas and apartment houses designed by him generally were in a modern style with the influence of functionalism being prominent. His furniture designs gained both domestic and foreign recognition and his original style is now known as "Kozma baroque." He also designed scenery for theaters. After World War II he taught at the College of Applied Arts and at the Technical University.

Krassó, György (1932–1991). Politician. Member of the Communist Party (1946–1952) and at the time of the 1956 Revolution participated in the attack on the Hungarian Radio building and in the opposition movements. For these activities he was sentenced to prison and was released in 1963 by amnesty. Around 1980 he became a lecturer at the Hétfői Szabadegyetem (Monday Free University) and also published a samizdat paper: *Magyar October* (Hungarian October) in 1982. In 1985 he became a staff member of Radio Free Europe in London and of the BBC. Returning home in 1889 he founded the Magyar Oktober Párt (Hungarian October Party) but did not gather enough votes to participate in Parliament.

Kun, Béla (1886–1938). Politician and publicist. During World War I he was captured on the Russian front. After 1917, he published *Szociális Forradalom* (Social Revolution) and was one of the organizers of the Bolshevik revolutionary activities of the Hungarian and foreign prisoners of war. Returning home he was one of the founders of the Hungarian Communist Party and became the commissar for foreign affairs in the government of the Hungarian Soviet Republic, which was established on March 21, 1919. In fact, he was the leader of the country and one of the commanders of the Hungarian Red Army. After the fall of the regime he was forced to emigrate. Became a member of the Executive Committee of the Moscow-based Comintern (1921–1936) and of a member of its presidium (1928–1935). In 1938 he became a victim of Stalin's purges.

Kuncze, Gábor (1950). Politician, president of the party, and minister. One of the major politicians in the Szabad Demokraták Szövetsége (Alliance of Free Democrats), a liberal party established after the change of regime. He was a parliamentary representative of the party after 1990. Minister of internal affairs in the Horn Socialist-SZDSZ coalition government and deputy prime minister (1994–1998). He was president of the SZDSZ from 1997 to1998, and from 2001 to 2007.

LANDLER, JENŐ (1875–1928). Jurist and politician. As a politician he supported the railway worker's strike in 1904 and became one of the leaders of the streetcar drivers' strike in 1906. Became a member of the Social Democratic Party in 1908. A member of the National Council in October 1918 and then had a part in the formation of the Hungarian Soviet Republic in which first he was commissar for commerce and then commissar of internal affairs. He was one of the leaders of the Red Army's campaign in Eastern Slovakia. After the collapse of the regime he had to emigrate and continued his political activity abroad.

LECHNER, JENŐ (1878–1962). Architect and historian of architecture. He completed his studies at the Budapest Technical University and then worked in the architectural design workshop of Alajos Hauszmann. From 1905 he taught at the university in 1905 and in 1928 he became a professor at the College of Applied Arts. In one phase of his career he designed according to the classical style (the Rezső Square church) but also accepted tasks of restoration of old buildings.

LÉKAI-LEITNER, JÁNOS (1895–1925). Publicist, writer, and politician. He was a member of the left-wing Galilei Circle and of Ottó Korvin's anti-militarist movement. He was arrested for an attempt to assassinate István Tisza in October 1918. At the time of the Soviet Republic he was in charge of the industrial education section of the Commissariat of Public Instruction. After the fall of the regime he was forced to emigrate and, after 1922, lived in New York where he continued to write socialist, revolutionary articles under the pseudonym of John Lassen.

LENIN, VLADIMIR ILYICH (1870–1924) Soviet politician and head of state. Member of a Marxist circle in 1889 and then became one of the members of the illegal organization, League of Struggle for the Emancipation of the Working Class (1893). He was arrested and banished to Siberia because of his political activities (1897). After his sentence was over, traveled in Russia and took up exile in the West, where in 1903 he was instrumental in splitting the Russian Socialist Labor Party into the Leninist Bolshevik and the Menshevik factions. He was active in the the work of the Central Committee of the party. He returned briefly to Russia during the ill fated 1905 revolution only to live in Western exile again. On hearing about the liberal March 1917 Revolution he returned to Russia and in his *April Theses* he emphasized the importance of a socialist revolution. After the Bolshevik Revolution of November, he became the chairman of the revolutionary Council of Commissars. As head of government he wanted to make the Russian revolution into a world revolution. By accepting the humiliating Brest-Litovsk Peace Treaty with Germany and the other Central Powers, he ended the World War for Russia but triggered the Civil War. In domestic policies he endeavored to end the civil war and following victory, he announced the New Economic Policy to prevent the economic collapse of the country. He had a major role in the formation of the Soviet Union in 1922.

Lónyay, Menyhért (1822–1884). Count, politician, and prime minister. He was close to the centralist group of József Eötvös and was one of the right-wing liberal opposition representatives in the diet after 1843. During the War of Liberation he was a councilor in the Ministry of Finance and then the state secretary for finance in the Szemere government. Returning from emigration in 1850 he was one of the founders and then president of the Földhitelintézet (Land Bank). Minister of finance in the Andrássy government after the Compromise (1867–1870). Later he became joint minister of finance (1870–1871). When he became prime minister (1871–1872) he was attacked for his policies and his integrity and was forced to resign. After 1871 he was also the president of the Hungarian Academy of Sciences.

Lovászi, Márton (1864–1927). Politician, publicist, and minister. Editor of the daily *Magyarország* and after 1901 the parliamentary representative of the Independence Party. Later one of the key decision makers of the his party. As a supporter of Mihály Károlyi he became a member of the National Council in October 1818 and the minister of religion and public instruction in the Károlyi government. Returning from emigration he became the minister of foreign affairs in the

Friedrich government in 1919 but was again forced to leave. In emigration he consistently attacked the consolidating Horthy regime.

Lugossy, Mária (1950). Goldsmith, glass designer, and sculptor. Studied art in the Goldsmith Department at the College of Applied Arts (1969–1973). On graduation she became a member of the Continuing Education Institute (1973–1975) and afterwards of the Széchenyi Literary and Art Academy (after 1993) and of the Glass and Sculpture Section of the Hungarian Sculptors' Association. Until 1992 she was also in charge of the Medal Section of the Hungarian Association of Fine and Applied Arts. Her art is characterized by a series of linked periods of creativity and by a wealth of creative thinking. In the beginning of her career she worked mostly with metals but later she used plastics, minerals, optical glass and other new substances with increasing emphasis on stones. This is how she developed multilevel, organic and geometric forms which are characteristic of her work. She was also an active participant in the Győr Statuary Artist Settlement. The principal goal of the group was the improvement of the city's appearance.

Makovecz, Imre (1935). Architect. Studied at the Budapest Technical University (1953–1959) and then worked as an architect at the Budapesti Városépítési Tervező Vállalat (Budapest Urban Building Design Company) (1959–1962). From 1971 until 1982 he was teaching at the Magyar Építőművészek Szövetségének Mesteriskolája (Master School of the Hungarian Architecture Alliance). He also became the vice president of the board of trustees of the Országépítő Alapítvány (Nation-building Foundation). At about the same time he was the principal architect of the Pilisi Parkerdőgazdaság (Park and Forest Estate of Pilis). The creation of Hungarian organic architecture is viewed as his principal achievement. The Austrian Rudolf Steiner and the American Frank Lloyd Wright had a major effect on his work. The spaces designed by him were adapted to the human form and included mythology and the wealth of forms derived from the early Hungarians. He used natural materials adapting both his techniques and his materials to the environment.

MÁLNAI, BÉLA (1878–1941). Architect. During his studies he was a pupil of Ödön Lechner and Béla Lajta. Following this he designed, in cooperation with Gyula Haász, one of his most significant creations, the building of the former Czech-Hungarian Industrial Bank at Nádor Street 6. During the Soviet Republic he was appointed to the Chair of Industrial and Economic Architecture at the Budapest Technical University. After the fall of the regime the offer was withdrawn. During the later part of his career he was designing primarily eclectic works, such as one of the apartment houses on Kossuth Square. He also worked as an editor at the journal *Ház* (House) and designed scenery for the Vígszínház (Gayety Theater).

MARTON, LÁSZLÓ (1925). Sculptor. He started his studies at the Hungarian Industrial Arts College in 1940 and studied later at the College of Applied Arts as a pupil of Pál Pátzay and Béni Ferenczy (1946–1952). His work was also influenced by Aurél Bernáth and István Szőnyi. The majority of his works were for public display. His early period is characterized by massive forms, heavy and of expansive vitality. Later he moved toward the smaller plastic forms and his statues preserve the classical sculptural recognition of the human body. Even later, after 1970, his works reflect the signs of expressivity.

MÉCS, IMRE (1933). Politician. During the 1956 Revolution he had a major role in organizing the National Guard and was in the resistance. For these activities he was sentenced to death but this was commuted to life in prison. After his release in 1963 he worked as an engineer. After 1975 he participated in the activities of the democratic opposition and after 1988 became a founding member of the Alliance of Free Democrats and of the Történelmi Igazságtétel Bizottság (Historic Justice Committee). He was a parliamentary representative of his party from 1990 to 1998.

MEDGYESSY, PÉTER (1942). Politician, prime minister, and businessman. Official in the Ministry of Finance and then minister of finance in the Lázár and Grósz governments (1986–1987). Following this he was the deputy chairman of the Németh government in charge of financial matters (1987–1990). He was also a member of the Central Committee of the Hungarian Socialist Workers Party. He became prime minister as a non-party Hungarian Socialit Party candidate in 2002 and announced the One Hundred Day program of the government. It was during his prime ministry that Hungary joined the European Union. When his former activities as an internal security agent became known he was the subject of numerous attacks, but his fall in 2004 was due to internal conflicts within the coalition parties.

Mészáros, Lázár (1796–1858). Honvéd general, politician, and minister. Participated in the Napoleonic wars as a soldier in the Imperial Army (1813–1815) and then, as a follower of István Széchenyi he became involved with the reform opposition. Became the minister of defense in the Batthyány government. He was promoted to major general and became a member of the National Defense Committee in October 1848. He then became the commander of a division in Upper Hungary and was made a lieutenant general in April 1849. In July 1849 he was the commander in chief of all Hungarian armed forces and chief of the general staff. After the collapse of the War of Liberation he had to emigrate and was executed in absentia in 1851.

Mezőfi, Vilmos (1870–1947). Journalist and politician. In the 1890s he worked for several newspapers and was a member of the Social Democratic Party. In 1900 he founded the Újjászervezett Szociáldemokrata Párt (Newly Organized Social Democratic Party) which was linked to the agrarian socialist movement and, in opposition, supported the Independence Party.

Mikoyan, Anastas Ivanovich (1895–1978). Soviet political leader. Member of the Bolshevik Party after 1915 and after the Civil War became one of Stalin's allies and close associates. A member of the Communist Party of the Soviet Union's Central Committee (after 1923) and then functioned as a commissar in several areas. He was the deputy chairman of the Council of Commissars and a member of the Politicalburo (1930–1966). After World War II he held a number of political offices of which the most important was that of deputy prime minister (after 1946). He also became one of the confidential advisors of Khrushchev (1955–1964). He played an important role in the developments of the 1956 events in Hungary and in the Soviet intervention and retribution.

Nagy, Imre (1896–1958). Politician and prime minister. Became a member of the Hungarian Section of the Communist Party in Russia in 1918 and after his return to Hungary joined the Hungarian Social Democratic Party. Forced to emigrate, he assumed some political offices in the Soviet Union. After World War II he again returned to Hungary where he was elected to the Central Committee of the Hungarian Communist Party and also to its Politburo. He became minister of agriculture (1944–1945), minister of the interior (1945–1946) and then minister of food supplies (1950–1952). In 1948 he was the president of the National Assembly. In 1952 he first became minister of produce requisitioning and collection and then deputy prime minister. After the change of policies in the post-Stalin Soviet Union, he became prime minister (1953–1955) but because of his "New Course" reform policies he was forced to resign and was stripped of his Party membership. During the 1956 Revolution he became prime minister again (October 24–November 12). During his days in power he reestablished the coalition system in government and in foreign policy he sought the removal of the Soviet troops from Hungary and the recognition of Hungary's neutrality. After the defeat of the revolution, the Kádár government had him indicted for these activities and a kangaroo court sentenced him to death. He was executed on June 16, 1958.

Nagyatádi Szabó, István (1863–1924). Politician. One of the founders of the Kisgazdák Szövetsége (Alliance of Smallholders) in Somogy County and also of the *Magyarországi Kisbirtokosok Szövetsége* (Alliance of Smallholders of Hungary). He was also a parliamentary representative (1908–1918). Became the founding president of the Országos és '48-as Függetlenségi Gazdapárt (National and '48-er Independent Peasant Party). Became minister of economy in the Károlyi government after the Fall Aster Revolution. Was a minister in a number of governments after the collapse of the Soviet Republic. After the 1920 elections he was considered one of the most important Hungarian politicians. It was during his official tenure that the land reform, associated with his name, was implemented. He became the president of the Unitfied Party in 1922.

OBERSOVSZKY, GYULA (1927–2001). Writer and publicist. In 1954 he was a member of the Cultural Section of the Alliance of Hungarian Newspaper Writers, but soonafter he was fired from jobs and expelled from the Party. The day after the outbreak of the 1956 Revolution he began to publish a new newspaper, *Életünk* (Our Life) and also became a member of a freedom fighter group active in the hospital on Péterfy Sándor Street. For these activities he was sentenced to death after the defeat of the revolution but the sentence was commuted to life in prison due to great international pressure. After his release in 1964 he again worked as a publicist and was also one of the founding members of the Historical Justice Committee (1988).

ORBÁN, ANTAL (1887–1940). Sculptor. He studied in Budapest, Munich, Paris, and Brussels and then worked in the atelier of György Zala. He later worked for silver and ceramics factories as a designer and model maker. He also taught at the Industrial Arts College after 1919.

ORBÁN, VIKTOR (1963). Politician and prime minister. One of the founders of Fidesz (1988) and represented this party in the negotiating team known as the Ellenzéki Kerekasztal (Opposition Roundtable) in 1989. After 1990 a Fidesz representative in parliament and the head of the group party representatives in the National Assembly until 1993. He became the president of the party (1993–2000). While he was prime minister (1998–2002) Hungary joined NATO (1999). One of the most important politicians in the party, he was its candidate for the prime ministry in 2006 and, in 2007, he again became the president of the party.

PACELLI, EUGENIO (1876–1958). Cardinal and pope as Pius XII. He was ordained in 1899 and then became involved in diplomatic activities. Became nuncio in Munich and Berlin in 1920. Returning to Rome he was made a cardinal by Pius XI and worked as state secretary in Vatican after 1930. Elected Pope in 1939 he chose the name Pius XII. Protested against the war and against persecutions in several encyclicals and emphasized the importance of peace. He condemned the events taking place in Eastern Europe after World War II and those Catholics who were willing to cooperate with the Communist regimes.

PÁSZTOR, JÁNOS (1881–1945). Sculptor. Studied at the College of Applied Arts as a pupil of Lajos Mátrai. In 1903 he became a student at the Julian Academy in Paris. His works such as *Bucsúzkodás* (Saying Goodbye) include folk genre pieces and he was also considered one of the best Hungarian representatives of academism. During the Horthy era he was one of the most active creators of public space statues and memorial sculptures. He was killed in Budapest during an Allied bombing raid in 1945.

PERCZEL, DEZSŐ (1848–1913). Politician and minister. Parliamentary representative of the Liberal Party and then minister of the interior in the Bánffy government (1895–1899). His activities during his ministry were designed to restrain worker and nationality activities. President of the National Assembly on two occasions (1899–1901 and 1903–1905). In this capacity he supported István Tisza in the latter's attempts to curb opposition (1903–1904). After Tisza's fall he retired and later became a founding member and president and parliamentary representative of the National Party of Work (1910).

PETŐFI, SÁNDOR (1823–1849). Poet. His first volume of poetry was published in 1844 with the title of *Versek* (Poems) and then he became the assistant editor of the *Pesti Divatlap* (Fashion Magazine of Pest). He played an important role as one of the March youths at the time of the outbreak of the 1848 Revolution. His poem *Nemzeti Dal* (National Song) written at this time, became one of Hungary's symbols of resistence to foreign domination. His political ideas were based on republican principles, much under the influence of the French Revolution. Consequently he believed that national independence could be achieved only if universal freedom were introduced at the same time. During the War of Liberation he became a National Guardsman and then joined the army of Józef Bem in January 1849. He was missing in action in the battle of Segesvár on July 31, 1849. The beginnings of his literary activities were characterized by a folksy, natural simplicity. Of considerable merit are his descriptions of nature, his love poetry and his poems with a political bent.

PEYER, KÁROLY (1881–1956). Politician and minister. One of the participants in the labor movement and then, after 1906, an official of the

Általános Munkásbetegsésegélyző Pénztár (General Workers' Health Mutual Bank). He then became the secretary of the National Alliance of Iron and Metal Workers. He was one of the leaders of the Social Democratic Party and, during the Fall Aster Revolution, commissioner of mines. During the Soviet Republic he was a member of the Szövetséges Központi Intéző Bizottság (Federated Central Executive Committee) and in the August 1919 he became minister of the interior in the Peidl government. In the Friedrich and Huszár governments he was minister of labor and public welfare (1919–1920). The Bethlen-Peyer Pact, instrumental in consolidating the political stability of the regime, was one of his significant accomplishments (1921). One of the leading politicians of the right wing of the Social Democratic Party, he was the parliamentary representative of the party from 1922 until 1944. He was expelled from the left-dominated party in 1947 and as a result of the political changes in the country, he was forced to emigrate.

Pintér, Béla (1925–1992). Architect. Studied at the Budapest Technical University (1944–1951) and then worked as a design architect. In recognition of his accomplishments, he was rewarded with the Ybl Prize on two occasions: in 1958 and 1978.

Podmaniczky, Frigyes (1824–1907). Baron, politician, and writer. Notary of the Upper House of the Pest National Assembly in 1848. Served during the War of Liberation as captain of hussars and as battalion commander. After the collapse of the revolution he was demoted to private. Later a parliamentary representative as a liberal politician and vice president of the National Assembly in 1861. After 1889 he was the president of the Liberal Party. He was the vice president of the Capital City Public Works Council and worked to make Budapest into a metropolis (1873–1905). He was instrumental in arranging for many improvements, including roads and embankments. As the director of the National Theater he played a major role in the cultural life of Budapest (1875–1885).

Pongrátz, Gergely (1932–2005). Revolutionary activist. During the 1956 Revolution he was one of the leading fighters in the Corvin Passage after October 25, 1956. He was one of the negotiators with General Gyula Várady and insisted that the revolutionaries would not lay down their arms until the Soviet troops left Hungary. They also demanded the independence of the country, the renunciation of the Warsaw Pact, the disarming of the secret police, the AVH, and the creation of a multiparty system. After November 1 he was the commanding officer in the Corvin Passage and frequently demonstrated against the political activities of Minister of Defense Pál Maléter. In spite of this he was successful in cooperating with the soldiers of the Kilián barracks. The attack of the Soviet troops, beginning on November 4, forced him to move part of his contingent to Víg Street and there he resigned his command. At the end of November he escaped from Hungary and in emigration he was an anti-Kádár regime activist and participated in several exiled veteran '56-er organizations. Returned home after the change of regime in 1990 and established the Pesti Srácok Alapítvány (Pest Youth Foundation). Politically he was radically right wing and a committed anti-Communist. One of the founders of the extreme right-wing Jobbik Magyarországért (For a Better Hungary) movement.

Pozsgay, Imre (1933). Politician and minister. First deputy minister of culture (1975) and then minister (1976–1980). After this he became minister of culture (1980–1982). Member of the communist Hungarian Workers Party and its successor, the Hungarian Socialist Workers Party (1956–1989). After the change of regime he was a member of the Presidium of the new Hungarian Socialist Party, until he resigned from the party in 1990. After 1997 he served as an advisor to the Hungarian Democratic Forum and also taught at several Hungarian universities.

Preisich, Gábor (1909–1998). Architect. Studied at the Budapest Technical University (1927–1930) and then opened an architectural office with Mihály Vadász (1933). After World War II he participated in a number of rebuilding projects and then became an associate in the Építéstudományi és Tervező Intézet (Architectural Science and Design Institute) and in the Magasépítési Tervező Intézet (MATI) (High Rise Design Institute). He was also head of the Department of House Planning at the Budapest Technical University. He was in charge of the Urban Planning Department of the Capital City Council and then became the chief architect for Budapest (1953–1955). He was a member of the Hungarian Academy of Sciences.

RÁCZ, SÁNDOR (1933). Politician. At the time of the revolution in 1956 he was the president of the Greater Budapest Central Workers' Council and demanded that Imre Nagy be set free by his Soviet captors. Later he negotiated with the government and also with the Soviet military leaders. He was arrested on December 11. After he was set free, in 1963, he maintained opposition activities against the Kádár regime. He participated in the organization of the Historical Justice Committee in 1988 and then became a member of the Independent Smallholder Party in 1993. Since 2003 he is the honorary president of the World Alliance of Hungarians.

RÁKÓCZI, FERENC II (1676–1735). Prince. The son of Ferenc I Rákóczi and Ilona Zrínyi and later the stepson of Imre Thököly. He refused to lead an insurrection in 1697 and was willing to take charge of the organization of the estates only after 1698. For this activity he was arrested in 1701, but he managed to escape to Poland. In 1703, he called the population of the country to arms and this made him the leader of a war of liberation. He was first elected prince of Transylvania, in 1704, and then, at the Diet of Széchény he was elected ruling prince. In foreign policy he represented the French direction and, after the dethronment of the House of Hapsburg in 1707, he suggested a number of potential rulers. The deteriorating military situation forced him to negotiate abroad. In the meanwhile his military commander signed the compromise Peace of Szatmár of 1711 which was rejected by Rákóczi. Consequently he remained in exile and finished his life in Rodosto (Tekirdagˇ), Turkey, where he lived after 1720.

RÁKOSI, MÁTYÁS (1892–1971). Politician and minister. Member of the Hungarian Social Democratic Party after 1910 and one of the founders of the Hungarian Communist Party in 1918. During the Soviet Republic he was commissar for commerce and a member of the Revolutionary Governing Council. He was also elected to the Central Control Committee of the Governing Council, in July, 1919, and then he became the Commander in Chief of the Red Guard. After the collapse of the regime he emigrated and became one of the secretaries of the Executive Committee of the Comintern in 1921. Returning home he was active in the illegal Communist movement and was arrested in 1924. In 1940 he was freed and was allowed to go to the Soviet Union where he became one of the leaders of the Hungarian Communist emigration, decimated by Stalin's purges. Returning to Hungary in 1945 he was general secretary of the Hungarian Communist Party and became minister of state in November. After 1947 he was deputy prime minister. In1948, after the two Marxist parties were forcefully fused by the Communists, he was elected general secretary of the "new" Hungarian Workers' Party. He also had a number of political functions. After 1949 he was the president of the Államvédelmi Bizottság (National Security Committee) and after 1952 he was the president of the Council of Ministers. He was the leading Stalinist politician of the era which carries his name. After the death of Stalin in 1953 he was forced out of power. In 1955 he was able to assume a leadership role for a brief period of time but he was forced to resign in 1956 and departed to the Soviet Union. In 1962 he was expelled from the Party.

RÁTH, KÁROLY (1821–1897). Attorney, Lord Mayor. In 1841 he started to work as a notary in the Court of Appeals and then fought in the War of Liberation. Then he worked as an attorney and was invited to the National Judges' Conference (1860). After the Compromise he served in parliament and then became the deputy president of the Royal Court of Appeals (1871). He became a member of the Upper House of parliament and the Lord Mayor of Budapest (1873). His position was primarily representational and the effective leader of the capital city was the mayor Károly Kamermayer.

RÉVAI, JÓZSEF (1898–1959). Politician, minister, and publicist. One of the founders of the Hungarian Communist Party in 1918. He was a correspondent of the *Vörös Ujság* (Red News). During the Soviet Republic he was a member of the Budapest Central Workers' Council and emigrated after the collapse of the regime. During the Horthy era he participated in the activities of the illegal Communist Party and for this activity he was sentenced to prison in 1930. After he was released he went abroad. He returned in 1944 and became a member of the Provisional National Assembly in Debrecen and then of the National Supreme Council. He was also a parliamentary representative and a member of the Central Leadership and of the Politburo (1945). He was the editor in chief of the Communist Party's daily *Szabad Nép* (Free People) and then became minister of education (1949–1953). Subsequently he became deputy chairman of the Presidential Council. One of the chief ideologists of the Communist system he was instrumental in introducing the Communist interpretation of history to Hungary.

Ribbentrop, Ullrich Friedrich von (1893–1946). German politician, diplomat, and minister of foreign affairs of the Third Reich. Member of the German National Socialist Workers' Party after 1932. He became Hitler's foreign policy expert. He was ambassador in London (1936–1938) and then became minister of foreign affairs to implement Hitler's foreign policy ideas (1938–1945). During his ministry he signed the notorious non-aggression pact with Molotov in 1939. He labored to increase the cooperation between Germany and her allies. For his activities he was sentenced to death as a war criminal at the Nürnberg War Crimes Trial and was executed.

Ripka, Ferenc (1871–1944). Politician and Lord Mayor. At the beginning of his career he worked as a newspaper man and published in *Fővárosi Lapok, Magyar Újság, Hazánk, and Gödöllő és Vidéke*. Subsequently he became an official in the Ganz and Company iron and machine works (1894) were he rose to the position of section head. He was also a member of the Capital City Justice Committee (after 1906) and in 1912 he was appointed president of the Gas Company. As a politician he was a member of the Civic Party (1924) and then he was appointed Commissioner of Budapest by Horthy. He was Lord Mayor of Budapest from 1925 to 1932. During his tenure the Capital City Act was enacted (Act 18 of 1930) and his major accomplishment was the organization of the fiscal system and the balancing of the budget. He did much to encourage tourism and, for this reason, established the St. Stephen Week.

Róna, József (1861–1939). Sculptor. He started his studies as an apprentice in a cabinet making shop and then worked as an assistant in a sculptore's atelier. He then became a student in the Vienna Zumbusch Master School (1882–1885). He had his first major success in Berlin where for one of his works he was awarded a scholarship to Rome (1985). He was widely recognized and won the Gold Medal in Antwerp for *Utolsó Szerelem* (Last Love) and the top prize in Paris. He was a member of the Benczúr Society.

Rothermere, Lord Harold Sidney Harmsworth (1868–1940). British newspaper magnate and politician. In 1896 he and his brother established the very popular *Daily Mail* and in 1903 they established the *Daily Mirror.* During World War I he became Minister of Aviation in 1917. His newspapers were enormously popular and made him the third richest man in Great Britain by 1926. He visited Hungary for the first time in 1927 and then became the most important and influential supporter of Hungary's revisionist goals. In his famous article "Hungary's Place in the Sun" in the *Daily Mail* on June 21, 1927, he pointed out to international public opinion the injustices suffered by Trianon Hungary. In his papers he promoted an alliance with Germany and was one of the principal supporters of the first fascist party in Great Britain.

Rudnay, Béla (1857–1932). Chief of police and political genealogist. He worked in the administration of Nyitra County as deputy clerk and then as chief magistrate (1880) and then as county recorder (1887). After 1893 he was parliamentary representative in the Liberal Party and also became Lord Lieutenant of Hont and Nógrád Counties (1894). He was then appointed national police chief of Budapest in 1896 and later, during the Fejérváry government, he was the royal commissioner for Budapest. Became a representative for the new National Party of Work in 1910. He was active in genealogical research and regularly published his findings.

Rudolf (1858–1889). Hapsburg archduke, crown prince, only son of Francis Joseph destined for a military career. He was promoted regularly becoming a Field Marshal (1883) and then Inspector of the entire infantry (1888). His political views could be considered liberal. He consistently came out in opposition to the politics of the Taffe era and was considered to be a supporter of French-British orientation. His views known to his friends in Hungary made him very popular there. In addition to his official duties he was active in ornithology, ethnography, and journalism. Committed suicide with his mistress on January 30, 1889.

Schickedanz, Albert (1846–1915). Architect and painter. He studied art and architecture in Karlsruhe and Vienna. Returning to Budapest he worked with Antal Skalnitzky and Miklós Ybl. Following this he shared an architect's office with Ferenc Fülöp Herzog. He became one of the noted representative of eclectic architecture in Hungary. He also engaged in painting and in applied arts and taught at the Budapest College of Applied Arts (1880–1902).

Sipőcz, Jenő (1878–1937). Attorney and Lord Mayor of Budapest. Prosecuting attorney after 1915 and interim commissioner for Budapest in 1919. Elected mayor of the capital city in September 1920. A number of significant reforms characterize his tenure, such as the end to exclusively male officials and the city taking over the utility companies. He developed better transportation and better school and health services. He also promoted tourism. He was the target of numerous attacks and was accused of defalcation but was reelected twice. In 1934 he was promoted to Lord Mayor.

Somogyi, Árpád (1926–2008). Sculptor. Prior to his formal advanced studies he learned modeling in the studio of Ferenc Medgyessy (1943–1945). Following this he studied at the Hungarian Fine Arts College (1948–1953) where his teachers included Béni Ferenczy, Pál Pátzay, and Ferenc Medgyessy. His art was characterized by realistic spirituality and he liked to depict peasants. He also carved numerous busts and small figures. His works reflect calmness, balance, solidity, and closed compositions.

Stalin, Josip Vissarionovich (1879–1953) Soviet politician and head of state. In 1898 he became a member of the local Georgian Social Democratic organization and was banished to Siberia in 1902 for his political activities. In his absence he was elected to membership in the Russian Social Democratic Workers Party's Caucasian Association Committee. After his escape from Siberia he joined the Bolshevik faction of the party in 1904 and during his internal exile was one of the founders of the Bolshevik newspaper *Pravda* (1912). His first leading article in the paper was signed Stalin. In the new Bolshevik government formed in Niovember 1917 he became the Commissar of Nationalities in the Council, of Commissars and was also elected to the Party's Politburo in 1919. Following this he was also the general secretary of the Central Committee of the Russian Communist Party (1922). After Lenin's death he gradually eliminated the Leninist group within the Party thus strengthening his own position. To consolidate his position he initiated a "revolution from above" (1929). In domestic policies he initiated the planned economy and promoted the development of heavy industry. He had a major role in the establishment of the GULAGs and in arranging for the political show trials. In foreign policy he endeavored to end Russia's isolation and then urged an antifascist coalition and also involved the Soviet Union in the Spanish Civil War on the side of the republicans (1936–1938). Just prior to World War II he made an alliance with Germany, the Ribbentrop-Molotov Pact. During the war he assumed supreme command over the armed forces and also the chairmanship of the Council of Commissars (1941). His strategic decisions were very costly in manpower but the Allied forces were victorious and then he used the victory to legitimize his system of government. He managed to gain domination of Eastern Europe as a result of the wartime international conferences.

Steindl, Imre (1839–1902). Architect and Budapest Technical University professor. He started his studies at the József Polytechnic Institute and later studied at the Vienna Fine Arts Academy. His teachers included Eduard van der Null, August von Siccardsburg, and Friedrich von Schmidt. After he returned he started to teach at the Technical University in 1869. His architectural style was characterized by historicism and moved from the Renaissance to the Gothic. He worked much on the repair of historic buildings. He is considered as the most influential architect of the Francis Joseph era who was a decisive factor in the Hungarian eclecticism after the Miklós Ybl period. In recognition of his work he was elected a corresponding member of the Hungarian Academy of Sciences in 1898.

Straub, Ferenc Brúnó (1914–1996). Biochemist, academician, and chairman of the Presidential Council. Taught at Szeged University after 1937 and became the chairman of the Department of Biochemistry in 1945. He then became the director of the Biochemical Institute of the Semmelweis Medical School (1948) and the president of the Section of Biological Sciences of the Hungarian Academy of Sciences (1960–1967). He was also the vice president of the Hungarian Academy of Sciences. As a politician he was a member of the Hungarian Communist Party and then of the Hungarian Workers' Party (1948–1956). In 1985 he was elected to parliament as an independent and, in 1988 he was elected as the last chairman of the Hungarian People's Republic's Presidential Council. After the change of regime this position disappeared and he retired completely from public life. His researches focused on enzymes, muscle function, protein synthesis and cellular respiration.

Stróbl, Alajos (1856–1926). Sculptor. He started his artistic studies at the Vienna Industrial Arts College as student of Otto König and continued his studies at the Academy with K. Zumbusch (1876–1880). Recognition came to him for his *Perseus* statue in 1882 and thereafter he was the most popular sculptor of memorial statues and an outstanding representative of the typical nineteenth century memorial sculpture. His work was sensitively realistic. He also taught at the College of Fine Arts.

Suslov, Mikhael Andreyevich (1902–1982). Soviet politician and ideologue. Member of the Communist Party after 1921. He was first secretary of the Rostov Territorial Party Committee (1937–1939) and then held the same position at the Stavropol Committee (1939). During World War II he was instrumental in arranging deportations of the indigenous populations in the Caucasus and in Lithuania. He was appointed a member of the Central Committee in 1941 and then became its secretary. He was also editor in chief of *Pravda* until 1950. He played an important role in the defeat of the 1956 Hungarian Revolution, backing the Soviet military intervention and supporting the appointment of János Kádár as general secretary of the Hungarian Communist Party. Later, as a follower of Brezhnev he was a member of the group that arranged for Khrushchev's fall in 1964. As the party ideologue he rejected any divergent policies.

Sütő, András (1927–2006). Transylvanian writer. He studied first at the Nagyenyed Reformed College and then at the Kolozsvár Reformed Gymnasium. Following this he enrolled in the Division of Directing of the Kolozsvár István Szentgyörgyi College of the Performing Arts (until 1949). He then worked as editor in chief of the weekly paper *Falvak Népe*. He was also a Romanian parliamentary representative (1965–1977) and the vice president of the Romanian Writers' Association (1974–1982). In 1980 the publication of his works and the staging of his plays were forbidden in Romania and he was constantly harassed by the Securitate, the Romanian secret police, as a person opposed to the regime. One of the founders of the Digitalis Literary Academy in 1998. On the basis of his literary activities he was considered as one of the leaders among the contemporary Hungarian writers.

Szabad György (1924). Historian and politician. He first was an apprentice at the National Archives and then taught at the Loránd Eötvös University in the Department of Modern History. He is currently professor emeritus. He started his political career in the Smallholder Party (1945–1946) and, after the change of regime he became one of the founders of the Magyar Demokrata Fórum (Hungarian Democratic Forum) and was a member of its presidium (1989–1994). He was a parliamentary representative and the president of the National Assembly (1990–1994).

Szakasits, Árpád (1888–1965). Publicist, politician, president of the republic, and chairman of the Presidential Council. A correspondent of *Népszava* (1908) and during the Soviet Republic he was a section head in the Commissariat for Internal Affairs in 1919. Politically, he was the secretary of the Social Democratic Party (SZDP) and then became the president of the National Association of Construction Workers (1928–1938). Within the party he represented the group willing to cooperate with the Communists. Minister of state in 1945–1948 and was also minister of industry in 1948. After the fusion of the parties he became the president of the Hungarian Workers' Party and in August 1948 he became president of the republic. He then became the chairman of the Presidential Council (until 1950). On the basis of trumped-up charges he was sentenced to life in prison in 1950 and was rehabilitated in 1956. After the revolution he again became politically active as a member of the Central Committee of the Hungarian Socialist Worker Party.

Szalay, László (1813–1864). Historiographer and politician. As a university student he joined circle of friends around József Eötvös and then worked as junior clerk with Ferenc Kölcsey. He became a librarian at the Hungarian Academy of Sciences after 1837 and then, in 1840, became the secretary of the national committee charged with producing a criminal code. Delegate in the diet of 1843–1844 and there he was one of the important members of the central group of the pro-reform opposition. After 1840 he was also the editor of *Budapesti Szemle* (Budapest Review) and later he also edited the *Pesti Hirlap* (1844–1845). Because of his work he can be considered to have been one of the theoreticians of the Centralists in formulating the theoretical issues before the 1848 legislature. After the revolution he became the head of the codification section of the Ministry of Justice in the Batthyány government. He represented the Hungarian government at the imperial meeting in Frankfurt and later in Paris and London as well. After the collapse he lived in emigration until 1855. Returning home in 1861 he was again elected to parliament.

Szamuely, Tibor (1890–1919). Politician and publicist. Member of the Hungarian Social Democratic Party and during World War I he was captured on the Russain front. After the Bolshevik Revolution he worked with Béla Kun in Moscow. Returning home he became a member of the Central Committee of the Hungarian Communist Party and then deputy commissar for defense and commissar for education during the Soviet Republic. He then became the political commissar of the Budapest Red Army group. It was under his administration that the terrorist group known as the Lenin Boys was organized. This group forcefully requisitioned and committed various acts of violence. The number of their victims is estimated at 399–600. After the fall of the Soviet Republic he was forced to flee and lost his life while trying to escape.

Szántó, Béla (1881–1951). Politician and official. One of the representatives of the left-wing SZDP opposition and during the Fall Aster Revolution he became one of the leaders of the Military Council in Budapest. He than became one of the founders of the Hungarian Communist Party and during the Soviet Republic he became commissar for defense and one of the organizers of the Red Army. After the collapse of the regime he was forced to emigrate and became one of the members of the Profintern and of the Comintern. He later worked for Radio Moscow and for the Soviet Information Bureau. Returning home in 1946 he became one of the leaders of labor union movement and then became ambassador first in Belgrade and then in Warsaw.

Széchenyi, István (1791–1860). Count, politician, and minister. He initiated a number of civilizing and infrastructural improvement activities using European models. He introduced horse racing in 1822, created a Danube and Balaton steam ship navigation system, began an organization for the regulation of rivers and flood control. In order to establish a permanent connection between Pest and Buda he was the moving power behind the construction of the Chain Bridge. One of his best known contributions was the creation of the Hungarian Academy of Sciences in 1825 and the opening of the National Casino in 1827. As a politician in the first half of the nineteenth century he became one of the leaders of the national liberal reform movement and in his political program he was favoring moderate reforms under the leadership of the aristocracy. He wished to avoid conflicts with Vienna. He published *Kelet Népe* (People of the East) to air his views. He was first a member of the House of Magnates in the diet but in 1847 he became the delegate for Moson County in the Lower House. After the March 1848 revolution he welcomed the laws assisting civic progress, which were endorsed by the ruler as well. He accepted the portfolio of transportation and public works in the Batthyány government (until September 11, 1848). Under the impact of the deteriorating condition of the country he suffered a mental breakdown and went to the Döbling Mental Hospital in Vienna for treatment. As his condition improved he again engaged in politics and published a scornful polemic essay criticizing the developing authoritarian Bach system (1857). He used the same basic principles in his famous work, *Rückblicken*, published in 1859. He suffered harassment by the police and committed suicide on April 8, 1860. His funeral represented a mute protest against the absolutist system.

Széll, Kálmán (1843–1915). Politician and prime minister. He was a parliamentary representative first of the Deák Party (1869–1875), then of the Liberal Party (1875–1906) and finally of the Constitution Party (until 1911). In March, 1875 he became minister of finance in the new Wenkheim government and he held the same office in the Tisza government until 1878. After this he became one of the founders of the *Jelzálog Hitelbank* (Mortgage Credit Bank) and then its chief executive officer. After the fall of the Bánffy government he became prime minister and also held the interim portfolio of internal affairs (1899). During his tenure, in December, 1902, he resolved the economic issues with the Austrian prime minister, the so-called Széll-Körber Pact. His endeavors for peaceful understanding and conciliation gave his tenure the "Széll silence" designation. His fall in 1903 was due to the obstruction of the opposition in the recruiting issue. During the coalition government he was the president of the Constitution Party.

Szemere, Bertalan (1812–1869). Politician, prime minister, and writer. During the Age of Reform he was one of the leading members of the young parliamentarians at the diet and endorsed the introduction of liberal reforms. Then he entered public service and became district administrator and then deputy lieutenant of Borsod County (1841–1867). At the last diets of the Age of Reform he was one of the leaders of the opposition (1843–1844 and 1847–1848). In the Batthyány government, established after the revolution, he became minister of the interior and was also elected to the National Defense Committee. During the fighting he was the national commissioner plenipotentiary of Upper Hungary. After the dethronment of the House of Habsburg he became prime minister and also held the portfolio of internal affairs. After the collapse he was forced to emigrate and was sentenced to death in absentia. Later he turned against Kossuth and favored reconciliation with Austria (after 1860).

Szende, Pál (1879–1934). Politician, minister of finance, and writer on economics. Secretary of the National Hungarian Commercial Association (OMKE) and later its general secretary (1908–1918). He was also a member of the organization gathered around the publication of *Huszadik Század* (Twentieth Century) as well of the radical movement led by Oszkár Jászi. He became the secretary of state for finance and then minister of finance in the Károlyi government established after the Fall Aster Revolution. After the collapse of the regime he emigrated to Vienna, in May 1919, where he joined the Social Democrats and published numerous articles.

St. (Saint) Stephen (967 or 977–1038). King of Hungary (1000–1038). Began his rule after the death of his father Prince Géza in 977, first as a prince and, after 1000, as Hungary's first king. In order to consolidate his rule he had to defeat the insurgent tribal leaders and he accomplished this with the assistance of the Hungarian leaders and German knights. The confiscated lands of the defeated tribes were the basis for his organizational arrangements for both state and church. He was the founder of the creation and expansion of Hungary's statehood. After his death there was a struggle for succession. He was made a saint in 1083.

Szentgyörgyi, István (1881–1938). Sculptor. He started his studies as a stone carver in Zurich and then became a student at the Budapest College of Applied Arts. He then became a student of van der Stappen at the Brussels Academy (1905–1910). Returning home he created a number of busts and in 1925 he started teaching at the College of Fine Arts. He is considered one of the outstanding representatives of the neoclassic style.

Szilágyi, Dezső (1840–1901). Politician and minister. After the Compromise he worked in the Ministry of Justice as a secretary to the minister and also taught at the University of Budapest. He was a parliamentary representative, first with the Deák Party and then as a member of the Liberal Party. Later he became one of the leaders of the United Opposition (after 1877). Rejoined the Liberal Party and became minister of justice in the Tisza, Szapáry, and Wekerle governments (1889–1895). He then became the president of the House of Representatives (1895–1898).

SZŰRÖS, MÁTYÁS (1933). Politician and diplomat. Worked at the Ministry of Foreign Affairs (1959–1962) and then served in various diplomatic missions abroad and as ambassador to Moscow (1978–1982). At the time of the change of regime he was a representative of the Reform Communist wing of the Party. And was elected president of the National Assembly in 1989. On October 23, 1989, he proclaimed the Hungarian Republic in Parliament and then became interim president of the republic until May 1, 1990. As a member of the Hungarian Socialist Party he became a parliamentary representative (1989). Vice president of the National Assembly until 1994. In 2002 he was a candidate for the New Left. In 2003 he joined the "historic" Social Democratic Party and was elected its president. He resigned in 2005.

TELEKI, PÁL (1879–1941). Politician, prime minister, and geographer. At the beginning of his political career he was a parliamentary representative of the Constitution Party (1905–1918). During the Soviet Republic he worked with the anti-Bolshevik Committee in Vienna and then became minister of culture and minister of foreign affairs in the Gyula Károlyi government (May–August, 1919). As a member of the Hungarian delegation he was in Paris to receive the peace term of the Peace Conference and, after returning home, he was the minister of foreign affairs in the Simonyi-Semadam government (1920–1921) and, for a short while prime minister. In 1926 he became a member of the government party and of the newly established Upper House of parliament. He was involved in the franc-forging scandal in 1925. He founded a number of institutes, such as the Sociographic Institute, the Political Science Institute, the Hungarian Revisionist League, and the Hungarian Geographic and Population Research Institute. He was the major patron of the Hungarian Boy Scout movement and a leader in the revisionist movement. He became the minister for religion and public instruction in the Imrédy government in May, 1938 and became prime minister in February 1939. It was during his tenure that Hungary joined the Anti-Comintern Pact and withdrew from the League of Nations. In foreign policy he supported the concept of armed neutrality, welcomed the Polish refugees and signed an eternal friendship pact with Yugo-slavia. He was opposed to assisting the Germans in their attack against Yugoslavia and when he saw that it was inevitable, committed suicide on April 3, 1941.

Tersánszky, Józsi Jenő (1888–1969). Writer. At the beginning of his career Ernő Osváth recognized his ability and his first major success was the novel based on his wartime experiences, *Viszontlátásra, drága...* (Au Revoir, my Dear....) After July 1922 he was a principal contributor to *Nyugat* (West). During these years he published a series of novels. *Kakuk Marci ifjusága* (The Youth of Marci Kakuk) was the first in a series Kakuk Marci novels which are considered to be his finest works. Theaters staged a number of his plays and he established his own theater in 1932, the *Képeskönyv Kabaré* (Picture Book Cabaret). In order to make a living during the 1930s he wrote and published a number of entertaining stories and detective novels. During World War II he became a correspondent of *Híd* (1940) and was active in providing forged documents for those needing them. During the Rákosi era, after 1950, he was not allowed to publish and during this period he wrote a number of fairy tales. It was only in 1955 that he was allowed to publish a collection of essays. He received many honors, including the Baumgarten Prize, and several Kossuth Prizes. His work is considered to be one of the outstanding prose contributions to Hungarian literature. It is significant not only for quantity but also for quality.

Tildy, Zoltán (1889–1961). Calvinist pastor, politician, prime minister and president of the republic. Member of the National Independence Party, of the '48-er Peasant Party and then of the Unity Party. One of the founders of the Independent Smallholder Party in 1929 and National Assembly representative (1936–1944). During World War II he became a member of the antifascist Hungarian Front (1944). After the war he was elected prime minister (November 15, 1945–February 1, 1946) and then president of the republic. It was during his tenure that the war crimes trials were held and that the Communists gradually gained ground. Consequently he was forced to resign on July 31, 1948, and was kept under house arrest. At the time of 1956 Revolution he became deputy prime minister in the Nagy government. For this he was sentenced to prison and was rehabilitated only in 1959.

Tisza, István (1861–1918). Count, politician and prime minister. The son of Kálmán Tisza. Liberal Party representative after 1886 and then prime minister (1903–1905). During his tenure he opposed the obstructionist opposition forces, the workers' movements and the agrarian socialists. Because of his policies the government party lost the 1905 elections and was disbanded. In 1910, assisted by the old liberals, he established the National Party of Work and was elected the president of the House of Representatives in 1912. Prime minister again in 1913. After the Sarajevo murders he was opposed to the war but following its outbreak he firmly supported the alliance with Germany. Opposed to the modest reforms of the new king, Charles IV, he resigned in May, 1917. During the start of the Fall Aster Revolution soldiers murdered him as a "war criminal" (October 31, 1918).

Tisza, Kálmán (1830–1902). Count, politician and prime minister. At the time of the War of Liberation he was an assistant clerk in the Ministry of Religion and Public Instruction. After the collapse he emigrated. One of his first political activities was the stand he took against the Protestant Patent in 1859. Later on he rejected the October Diploma and thus again became an opposition member. At the 1861 National Assembly he was the deputy president of the House of Representatives joining the "Decision Party" which was in opposition to Deák. After László Teleki's suicide he became the president of that party. As one of the leaders of the left-center group he opposed the Compromise in its final form. Later, having made peace with the government party he became one of the leaders of the Liberal Party and as such first became minister of the interior and then prime minister. He also held a number of other portfolios. He was the prime minister for a long time, until 1890, and this is considered to have been the most stable period of the Dualist era when the civil administration and the modern governmental system were established. His fall was due to the acceptance of the Defense Act but in fact he resigned because of the problems with Kossuth's citizenship issue. He remained a prominent member of his party and was referred to as the "General."

Tito, Josip Broz (1892–1980). Yugoslav politician and head of state. A member of the Yugoslav Communist Party since 1920 and was elected to the Central Committee of the Party in Vienna in 1934. Subsequently he became a functionary in the Moscow Comintern (until 1936). He performed important organizational activities in the Spanish

Civil War and, returning home, established the Slovenian and Croatian Communist Parties and became the principal secretary of the illegal Yugoslav Communist Party in 1937. During World War II he was the leader of the partisans. In 1945 he formed a government and became prime minister until 1963. He broke with the Soviet Union in 1948 and relied on the Western powers even though his regime continued to be socialistic and he was the center of a significant cult of personality.

Torgyán, József (1932). Jurist, politician, and minister. At the time of the 1956 Revolution he was a member of the Újpest Revolutionary Committee and therefore was expelled from the Bar Association in 1958. He then worked on the Újpest Attorney Board (1959–1990). In 1990, after the change of regime he became a parliamentary representative for the Independent Smallholder Party and leader of the party's parliamentary representatives. After 1991 he was the president of the party until 2002. Being dissatisfied with the changes made by the Antall government, the party, under his leadership, left the coalition. He was elected to the presidency of the Anti-Communist League (1992–1993). Later he became minister of agriculture and minister of rural development in the Orbán government (1998–2001). He resigned in 2006 and created a new party, called the Magyar Megújulás Mozgalom (The Hungarian Renewal Movement).

Tormay, Cecil (1876–1937). Writer. Early in her career she was a correspondent of *Virágfakadás* (after 1904). Her first novel *Emberek a kövek között* (Men among the Rocks) was published in 1911 and gained her recognition even abroad. Her novel *A régi ház* (The Old House) was awarded the Péczely Prize by the Hungarian Academy of Sciences. She was one of the most popular writers of the Horthy era who also became active in public affairs. She was one of the principal organizers of the National Association of Hungarian Women and in 1922 she founded the literary journal *Napkelet* (Sunrise) which was right wing in its policies.

Ungvári, Lajos (1902–1984). Sculptor. He studied at the Budapest College of Applied Arts as a pupil of Lajos Mátrai and Imre Simay (1921–1926). He became a member of the Spiritual Artists' Alliance and of the Association of New Artists. He was one of the founders and a resident of the artists' settlement on Százados Road (after 1945). He received many awards , such as the Szinnyei Society Prize and the Kossuth Prize. He is considered a conservative artist in whose works tectonic unity, stylistic simplicity, and plastic balance are manifest.

Vadász, György (1933). Architect. He started his studies at the Architectural College of the Budapest Technical University (until 1957) and then became a student in the master program of the Hungarian Architects' Association, where his masters included Jenő Szendrői, János Böhönyei, Károly Weichinger, and Károly Dávid (1958–1961). He started his career at the Budapest Urban Architecture Planning Institute (1957–1985) and then established the Artunion Széchenyi Architect Studio. He eventually established his own firm, Vadász és Társai Építőművész Kft. In 1985 he was honored with an appointment as titular university professor and he is considered the most outstanding Hungarian architect of the last few decades. He was first in the competition for the plans to rebuild the National Theater in 2000. At the beginning of his career he endeavored to enliven the rigid structures with the vivid mobility of masses and their rhythmic structure, complementing the creation with touches of the painter. In his later works he shows the maximum compatibility of material and architectural possibilities and the Bauhaus type pure special structures which also show Japanese influences.

Vadász, Mihály (1900–1967). Architect, father of György Vadász. He started his studies at the Budapest Technological University's School of Architecture and then began working in the office of Emil Bauer (after 1926). Following this his work was linked to the activities of Gábor Preisich and together they were responsible for a number of major buildings (1930–1940). In their designs the effects of the Weimar Bauhaus and of the work of Corbusier can be seen. After World War II he started to teach at the Department of Design of the College of Architecture of Budapest Technological University.

Varga, Imre (1923). Sculptor. Studied art at the Hungarian Fine Arts College (1950–1956) as a pupil of Sándor Mikus and Pál Pátzay. He was also parliamentary representative (1980–1990), vice president of the Patriotic Peoples' Front and the president of the Fészek artists' club. He became known in artistic circles in 1965 with his chrome and steel statue, *Prometheus*. He worked in all branches of sculpture and, in addition, did decorative panels, graphics and Gobelins. His statues depict the outstanding figures of Hungarian history, culture, and art.

VARGA, TAMÁS (1953). Sculptor. He studied art at the Budapest Fine Arts and Applied Arts High School (1967–1971) and then at the College of Fine Arts as the pupil of Sándor Mikus, Tamás Vigh, and Imre Varga (1971–1975). Following this he received a scholarship to study at the Hungarian Academy in Rome (1982). His sculptural activities extended over all sculptural areas, small plastics, medals, reliefs, and public square figures which were mainly of bronze and stone. His activities are characterized by ironic, grotesque and surrealistic modes of presentation.

WEKERLE, SÁNDOR (1848–1921). Politician and prime minister. First an official in the Ministry of Finance (1870) and then became state secretary for finance in the Kálmán Tisza government (1886) and then minister of finance (1889–1892). His most important action was the introduction of the gold currency in 1892. He became minister of commerce in the Szapáry government in 1892 and then became the prime minister of a new government (until 1895). The ecclesiastic laws were introduced during his tenure and his fall was due to the rejection of his proposal for mandatory civil marriage. In 1906 he joined the National Constitution Party in order to be able to direct the coalition government. He also held a variety of portfolios in his own government. His second turn as prime minister (1906–1910) meant that the former opposition came to power which meant its essential disappearance. After István Tisza resigned, Wekerle became prime minister for the third time (1917–1918) and this was the last Hungarian government in the history of the Austro-Hungarian Monarchy. During the Horthy era he was busy in economic matters and was also a director of the Hungarian Academy of Sciences after 1914.

WELLISCH, ALFRÉD (1854–1941). Architect. He started his studies in Karlsruhe and then studied in Vienna and Paris. Returning home he became a sought after architect. He was a member of the National Public Building Council and was also instrumental in creating a number of benevolent and cultural activities.

Weltner, Jakab (1872–1936). Publicist and political writer. Because of his left-wing views he became a member of the Carpenters' Labor Union in the 1890s and was elected to the leadership of the Social Democratic Party in 1896. After 1898 he became the central secretary of that organization. He was also one of the editors of Socialist daily *Népszava* (after 1909). During the Fall Aster Revolution he became the president of the Newspaper Workers' Union and was a member of the National Council as well. After the fall of the regime he was forced to emigrate. Returning home in 1924 he again became the editor of *Népszava* and also became a parliamentary representative in 1931.

Wittner, Mária (1937). 1956 revolutionary and politician. After the outbreak of the revolution on October 23, 1956, she joined the fighters, first tending the wounded in the Corvin Passage and then joining the Vajdahunyad Street group participating in armed fighting. For this reason she was arrested in 1957 and sentenced to death. The sentence was commuted to life in prison. She was released in 1970 and started to become involved in anti-Communist activities at the time of the change in the regime. Her activities were largely limited to work with various 1956 organizations. She later became a parliamentary representative for Fidesz in 2006 and became a member of the Employment and Occupational Committee of the National Assembly.

Wlasics, Gyula (1852–1937). Baron, jurist, civil law writer, and minister. He first worked as a judge and then became an official in the Law Drafting Division of the Ministry of Justice (from 1877). He was also a tax attorney in Komárom (1896), assistant prosecutor in Budapest and later royal prosecutor (from 1896). He also taught law at the University of Budapest (1890–1895). As a politician he was a representative of the Liberal Party after 1892 and later joined the government party (1905). Became minister of religion and public instruction in the Bánffy government (until 1903). During his tenure he supported free religious practice and the emancipation of the Jews. He also worked hard for educational programs for the workers and was instrumental in the creation of the Museum of Fine Arts. Subsequently he was the president of the Hungarian Royal Administrative Court (1906–1933) and president of the Upper House of parliament (1927–1935). He was deputy president of the Hungarian Academy of Sciences (1898–1901).

Zala, György (1858–1937). Sculptor. He started his artistic studies at the Budapest Design School and then he went to Vienna where he was a pupil of Edmund von Hellmer. He continued at the Munich Academy where his masters were Max Witmann and Michael Wagmüller and where he was also influenced by Belgian and French artistic trends. He was a dominant figure of the official art circle during the Francis Joseph era as the most important representative of the neobaroque memorial statue sculpture. The principal characteristics of his work were superb technical knowledge, a baroque style with great plasticity, pathos, and pictorial quality. In recognition for his accomplishments he was elected an honorary member of the Hungarian Academy of Sciences in 1930.

Zichy, Jenő (1837–1906). Count, writer, and politician. As a politician he was first with the Deák Party (until 1870) and then independent and finally Liberal Party parliamentary representative (until 1903). He was also the president of the National Industrial Association (1881–1906). It was during his tenure that a system of instruction in industrial skills was established and he was also instrumental in organizing and implementing the national exhibition in Székesfehérvár in 1879. Studying the origins of the Hungarians he led a number of exploratory expeditions to Russia and Asia. He gathered a number of artifacts and created a significant private collection in Budapest which he then bequeathed on the capital city. In recognition of his scientific activities he was elected an honorary member of the Hungarian Academy of Sciences in 1899.

Zsedényi, Béla (1894–1955). Professor of law and president of the Provisional National Assembly in Debrecen. He was first county recorder in Komárom (after 1919) and then became a full professor at the Evangelical Law Academy in Miskolc (after 1925). He was also an associate professor at the University of Pécs in 1928. In addition he was the editor in chief of *Felsőmagyarországi Reggeli Hirlap* (Morning News of Upper Hungary). He became the president of the Provisional National Assembly established at the end of World War II (December 1944) and then he was elected president of the National Supreme Council in May 1945. He was also the president of the National Assembly until the end of 1946. He was later accused of antistate activities and was sentenced to prison in June 1950.

PHOTOGRAPHS

The Physical Topography of the Square

Aereal photograph of Kossuth Square, 1932
(Photo by Béla Vitán)
Hungarian National Museum Historic Photo Gallery

Coffeehouse terrace on Kossuth Square, about 1940
(Photo by Ernő Vadas)
Hungarian National Museum Historic Photo Gallery

The Parliament from Géza Street, about 1896
(Photo by Mór Erdélyi)
Kiscelli Museum of the Budapest Historic Museum

Kossuth Square on a map of 1896
Budapest Capital City Archives

Kossuth Square on a map of 1963
Budapest Capital City Archives

Kossuth Square from the south with the Rákóczi Statue, about 1940
(Photo by Ernő Vadas)
Hungarian National Museum Historic Photo Gallery

Alkotmány Street with the Parliament in the background, 1900s
(Photo by unknown)
Capital City Ervin Szabó Library
Budapest Collection

The south side of Parliament Square with the Andrássy Statue, 1910s
(Photo by unknownphotographer)
Kiscelli Museum of the
Budapest Historic Museum

Automobiles on the square about 1920
(Photo by Unknown Photographer)
Kiscelli Museum of the Budapest Historic Museum

The Symbolic Square

Demonstrators on Parliament Square, September 15, 1905
(Photo by unknown photographer)
Hungarian National Museum Historic Photo Gallery

The *Andrássy* statue, about 1910
(Photo by Unknown Photographer)
Kiscelli Museum of the Budapest Historic Museum

Multitude at the proclamation of the republic, November 16, 1918
(Photo by unknown photographer)
Hungarian National Museum Historic Photo Gallery

Miklós Horthy enters the Parliament Square, November 10, 1919
(Photo by unknown photographer)
Hungarian National Museum Historic Photo Gallery

Festive mass to initiate the year of St. Stephen, March 30, 1938
(Photo by Sándor Bojár)
Hungarian National Museum Historic Photo Gallery

Funeral of Albert Apponyi. The delegation from his district in the funeral procession, February 1933
(Photo by unknown photographer)
Hungarian National Museum Historic Photo Gallery

A soldier of the Red Army raises the Soviet flag on the Parliament, January 1945
(Photo by Yevgeny Haldey)
MTI Photo

The festive transfer of the new buses, March 1947
(Photo by Unknown Photographer)
Hungarian National Museum Historic Photo Gallery

Demonstrating multitude in front of the Parliament. Evening of October 23, 1956
(Photo by unknown photographer)
MTI Photo

A demonstrating multitude listens to Imre Nagy's speech in front of the Parliament in the evening of October 23, 1956
(Photo by Sándor Mező)
MTI Photo

Demonstrating multitude before the Parliament, October 23, 1956
(Photo by Sándor Mező)
MTI Photo

October 25, 1956
(Photo by unknown)
MTI Photo

October 25, 1956
(Photo by unknown)
MTI Photo

Soviet tanks and peaceful demonstrators in front of the Parliament, October 25, 1956
(Photo Unknown Photographer)
MTI Photo

Fusillade scatters the crowd, October 25, 1956
(Photo by unknown)
MTI Photo

Commissioning on Constitution Day, August 20, 1977
Photo by Géza Szebellédy)
MTI Photo

Protest demonstration against the damming of the Danube at Gabčikovo (Bős) and Nagymaros, September 12, 1988
(Photo by Imre Prohászka)
Hungarian National Museum Historic Photo Gallery

Policemen at the educators' demonstration
December 19, 1988
(Photo by Imre Prohaszka)
Hungarian National Museum Historic Photo Gallery

Funeral of József Antall, December 18, 1993
(Photo by Imre Földi)
MTI Photo

Building sand castles on Children's Day, May 30, 2004
(Photo by Márta Hegedűs)
Márta Hegedűs

Puppet show on Children's Day, May 30, 2004
(Photo by Márta Hegedűs)
Márta Hegedűs

Campers on the Kossuth Square, September 21, 2006
(Photo by György Sárközi)
Hungarian National Museum Historic Photo Gallery

The Spiritual Square

Kálmán Széll welcomes Francis Joseph at the unveiling ceremony of the *Andrássy* statue, December 9, 1906
(Photo by Gyula Jelfy)
Hungarian National Museum Historic Photo Gallery

The unveiling of statue design for "The Work" by János Istók, May 1, 1919
(Photo by Unknown Photographer)
Hungarian National Museum Historic Photo Gallery

The *Kossuth* statue at the end of the 1930s
(Photo by unknown photographer)
Hungarian National Museum Historic Photo Gallery

Participants of an international congress at the *Rákóczi* statue. Second half of the 1930s
(Photo by Schäffer Photo Studio)
Hungarian National Museum
Historic Photo Gallery

Martyrs of the Nation 1918–1919 Memorial, about 1935
(Photo by unknown photographer)
Hungarian National Museum
Historic Photo Gallery

Unveiling of the *Kossuth* statue, November 6, 1927
(Photo by unknown photographer)
Kiscelli Museum of the Budapest Historic Museum

Gyula Gömbös speaks at the dedication of the *István Nagyatádi Szabó* statue, November 20, 1932
(Photo by the Schäffer Photo Studio)
Hungarian National Museum Historic Photo Gallery

The unveiling of the *Rákóczi* statue, May 2, 1937
(Photo by Magyar Filmiroda)
Hungarian National Museum Historic Photo Gallery

Crown Guards at the unveiling the *Rákóczi* statue, May 2, 1937
(Photo by Gárdonyi Photoriport)
Hungarian National Museum Historic Photo Gallery

The *István Tisza* statue in front of the north entrance to the Parliament, 1938
(Photo by unknown photographer)
Hungarian National Museum Historic Photo Gallery

Destruction of the Martyrs of the Nation Memorial, 1945
(Photo by Sándor Bojár)
Hungarian National Museum Historic Photo Gallery

The unveiling of the *Kossuth* statue, September 19, 1952
(Photo by Rudolf Járai)
MTI Foto

Model of the *István Tisza* statue, about 1933
(Photo by Mór Erdélyi)
Hungarian National Museum
Historic Photo Gallery

The *Mihály Károlyi* statue, about 1975
(Phoyo by Gyula Eötvös)
Hungarian National Museum
Historic Photo Gallery

The *Béla Kovács* statue, February 2008
(Photo by Balázs Mohai)
Hungarian National Museum
Historic Photo Gallery

The *Attila József* statue, February 2008
(Photo by Balázs Mohai)
Hungarian National Museum
Historic Photo Gallery

The *Imre Nagy* statue, March 2008
(Photo by Balázs Mohai)
Private Collection of Balázs Mohai

PRESS REPORTS

The Szigetszentlőrinc delegation in front of the Parliament, 1904
(Photo by unknown photographer)
Hungarian National Museum Historic Photo Gallery

March 15 festivities in the 1930s
(Photo by unknown photographer)
Hungarian National Museum Historic Photo Gallery

The Holy Crown is taken into the Parliament, June 8, 1896
(Photo by György Klösz)
Kiscelli Museum of the Budapest Historic Museum

Kálmán Széll and Ignác Darányi going to the Parliament, 1903
(Photo by Rudolf Balogh)
Hungarian National Museum Historic Photo Gallery

Ferenc Kossuth leaving the House of Representatives, 1909
(Photo by Gyula Jelfy)
Hungarian National Museum Historic Photo Gallery

Gyula Justh, at the head of the opposition representatives, on his way to a session of the House, June 1912
(Photo by Unknown Photographer)
Hungarian National Museum Historic Photo Gallery

Soldiers on the steps of the Parliament at the time of the demonstration, May 23, 1912
(Photo by unknown photographer)
Capital City Ervin Szabó Library—Budapest Collection

Multitude on Parliament Square looking at the weapons captured from the Russians, about 1915
(Photo by unknown photographer)
Hungarian National Museum Historic Photo Gallery

Guns captured from the Russians, about 1915
(Photo by János Müllner)
Hungarian National Museum Historic Photo Gallery

Suffragettes demanding the vote, June 1917
(Photo by Gyula Jelfy)
Hungarian National Museum Historic Photo Gallery

The proclamation of the republic by Mihály Károlyi on the steps of the Parliament, November 16, 1918
(Photo by unknown photographer)
Hungarian National Museum Historic Photo Gallery

Funeral for the victims of counterrevolution, June 29, 1919
(Photo by János Müllner)
Hungarian National Museum Historic Photo Gallery

Béla Kun speaks from the steps of the Parliament on the occasion of the reconquest of Kassa, June 7, 1919
(Photo by Gyula Jelfy)
Hungarian National Museum Historic Photo Gallery

Mátyás Rákosi and Béla Vágó leaving the Party congress, June 12–14, 1919
Photo by unknown photographer)
Hungarian National Museum Historic Photo Gallery

Commissar of Military Affairs Rezső Fiedler inspecting the international regiments, April 1919
(Photo by János Müllner)
Hungarian National Museum Historic Photo Gallery

People suspected of counterrevolutionary tendencies and interned in the Parliament are taken to lunch, April 1919
(Photo by János Müllner)
Hungarian National Museum Historic Photo Gallery

Romanian soldiers in front of the Parliament, August 4, 1919
(Photo by Gyula Harsányi)
Hungarian National Museum Historic Photo Gallery

Mass in front of the Parliament. Albert Apponyi stands on the right. Beginning of the 1920s
(Photo by János Müllner)
Hungarian National Museum Historic Photo Gallery

Parade of the National Labor Center, about 1935
(Photo by the First Budapest Christian Photo Laboratory)
Hungarian National Museum Historic Photo Gallery

Gyula Gömbös's funeral, October 10, 1936
(Photo by Schäffer Phtoto Studio)
Hungarian National Museum Historic Photo Gallery

The reliquary of the Holy Right Hand on Kossuth Square at the opening of the Year of St. Stephen, May 30, 1938
(Photo by Károly Kredátus)
Hungarian National Museum Historic Photo Gallery

The funeral of Count Pál Teleki, April 7, 1941
(Phote by Schäffer Photo Studio)
Hungarian National Museum Historic Photo Gallery

Funeral of István Horthy, August 27, 1942
(Photo by unknown photographer)
Hungarian National Museum Historic Photo Gallery

Mourners at István Horthy's catafalque, August 27, 1942
(Photo by Hungarian Photoreport Office)
Hungarian National Museum Historic Photo Gallery

Funeral of Endre Bajcsy-Zsilinszky, May 27, 1945
(Photo by unknown photographer)
Hungarian National Museum Historic Photo Gallery

Opening of the Kossuth Bridge, January 15, 1946
(Photo by unknown photographer)
Hungarian National Museum Historic Photo Gallery

Participants at the opening of Kossuth Bridge, January 15, 1946
(Photo by Alfréd Pobuda)
Hungarian National Museum Historic Photo Gallery

Participants at the opening of Kossuth Bridge, January 15, 1946
(Photo by Alfréd Pobuda)
Hungarian National Museum Historic Photo Gallery

Welcoming Mihály Károlyi. May 1946
(Photo by Sándor Bojár)
Hungarian National Museum
Historic Photo Gallery

Lajos Dinnyés welcomes Josip Broz Tito, December 1947
(Photo by Károly Escher)
Hungarian National Museum
Historic Photo Gallery

Guests at the presentation of the Medal of Hungarian Freedom, September 15, 1946
(Photo by Kálmán Szöllősy)
Hungarian National Museum Historic Photo Gallery

Mátyás Rákosi speaks at the mass meeting of the Hungarian Women's Democratic Alliance, August 1947
(Photo by Kálmán Szöllősy)
Hungarian National Museum Historic Photo Gallery

The March 15 mass meeting, 1948
(Photo by Magyar Képszolgálat)
Hungarian National Museum Historic Photo Gallery

The delegates going to the Unification Congress, June 12, 1948
(Photo by unknown photographer)
Hungarian National Museum Historic Photo Gallery

May Day, 1953
(Photo by Dániel Kéri)
Hungarian National Museum Historic Photo Gallery

Electoral mass meeting, May 10, 1953
(Photo by Tamás Horváth)
MTI Photo

Electoral mass meeting, May 10, 1953
(Photo by Ernő Vadas)
MTI Photo

Pioneers place wreaths at the *Kossuth* statue, March 15, 1956
(Photo by Ferenc Vigovszki)
MTI Photo

A group of French tourists, June 1956
(Photo by unknown photographer)
Hungarian National Museum Historic Photo Gallery

Actor Imre Sinkovits recites at the demonstration in front of the Parliament on the Kossuth Square on the evening of October 23, 1956
(Photo by Tamás Farkas)
MTI Photo

Lighting the memorial candles for the dead, November 2, 1956
(Photo by Ferenc Kovács)
MTI Photo

Festivity on the fifteenth anniversary of the establishment of the Hungarian Pioneer Organization, July 1961
(Photo by Ferenc Vigorszki)
Hungarian National Museum Historic Photo Gallery

The funeral of Mihály Károlyi, March 18, 1962
(Photo by Tamás Fényes)
MTI Photo

Soviet soldiers removing snow, February 1963
(Photo by Antal Wormser)
Hungarian National Museum Historic Photo Gallery

Raising the National Banner, August 19, 1972
(Photo by Andor Tormai)
MTI Photo

Torchlight mass meeting in front of the Parliament in honor of the Tenth National Peace Conference, October 26, 1984.
(Photo by Zoltán Pólya)
Hungarian National Museum Historic Photo Gallery

Victor Orbán speaks in front of the *Kossuth* statue, March 15, 1989
(Photo by Imre Prohászka)
Hungarian National Museum Historic Photo Gallery

President George Bush, at the *Kossuth* statue July 12, 1989
(Photo by Imre Prohászka)
Hungarian National Museum Historic Photo Gallery

Honor Guard at the visit of President George Bush, July 12, 1989
(Photo by Imre Prohászka)
Hungarian National Museum Historic Photo Gallery

Mátyás Szűrös at the proclamation of the republic, October 23, 1989
(Photo by Tamás Székely)
Hungarian National Museum Historic Photo Gallery

The funeral of János Kádár, July 14, 1989
(Photo by Imre Prohászka)
Hungarian National Museum Historic Photo Gallery

October 23, 1989
(Photo by Margit Wagner)
Hungarian National Museum Historic Photo Gallery

Celebrating multitude, October 23, 1989
(Photo by Imre Prohászka)
Hungarian National Museum Historic Photo Gallery

Árpád Göncz elected president of the republic, August 3, 1990
(Photo by Tamás Szigeti)
Hungarian National Museum Historic Photo Gallery

Taxi driver protest demonstration, October 23–28, 1990
(Photo by Imre Prohászka)
Hungarian National Museum Historic Photo Gallery

Demonstrators protesting the raising of gasolin prices, October 27, 1990
(Photo by Zoltán Fejér)
Hungarian National Museum Historic Photo Gallery

Demonstration of the workers of the Ikarusz bus factory, December 14, 1990
(Photo by Imre Prohászka)
Hungarian National Museum Historic Photo Gallery

"NO GOD, NO HOMELAND": Anarchist demonstration, December 13, 1991
(Photo by Zoltán Fejér)
Hungarian National Museum Historic Photo Gallery

"WE DEMAND A DECENT EXISTENCE": Antipoverty demonstration, May 24, 2000
(Photo by Csaba Habik)
Hungarian National Museum Historic Photo Gallery

The new president, Ferenc Mádl, and the former president, Árpád Göncz (on the right), August 4, 2000
(Photo by Tamás Szigeti)
Hungarian National Museum Historic Photo Gallery

Demonstration by the fire fighters, November 8, 2001
(Photo by György Sárközy)
Hungarian National Museum Historic Photo Gallery

Temporary skating rink on the square, January 2, 2002
(Photo Szilárd Koszticsák)
MTI Photo

Farmer demonstration with tractors, March 2, 2005
(Photo by Márta Hegedűs)
Private Collection of Márta Hegedűs

The police barrier, September 20, 2006
(Photo by György Sárközy)
Hungarian National Museum Historic Photo Gallery

A night in the tent, September 21, 2006
(Picture by György Sárközy)
Hungarian National Museum Historic Photo Gallery

The right-wing extremist György Budaházy speaks, September 23, 2006
(Photo by György Sárközy)
Hungarian National Museum Historic Photo Gallery

Still life on the Kossuth Square, September 26, 2006
(Picture by Péter Gyula Horváth)
Hungarian National Museum Historic Photo Gallery

Parliamentary Representative and Fidesz President Viktor Orbán dismantles the police barrier, March 19, 2007
(Photo by András Péter Németh)
Hungarian National Museum Historic Photo Gallery

Details from the Studio 73 Limited's prize-winning plan for the reconstruction of the Kossuth Square

NAME INDEX

A

Achim, András, 120, 247
Aczél, György, 85–86, 247
Ádámfy, József, 63, 67
Áder, János, 247
Adulyadedj, Bhumibol, 201
Ady, Endre, 135–136, 247
Andrássy, Countess Géza, 123
Andrássy, Count Gyula, Sr., 18, 26–27, 31, 49, 50–56, 58–59, 61–65, 68, 71, 77–79, 84–86, 94, 113, 116–117, 121–124, 148, 159, 166, 180, 248, 252, 254–255, 258, 265, 270, 276
Andrássy, Count Gyula, Jr., 248, 258
Andrássy, Countess Sándor, 123
Andrássy, Count Tivadar, 123
Andrássy, Katinka, 85
Andrássy, née Ilona, 123
Andrew II, 249
Andrew III, 249
Andropov, Yuri, 260
Anjou dynasty, 248
Antall, József, 210–211, 213–214, 248
Apponyi, Count Albert, 67, 116, 159, 171–172, 248
Aradi, Nóra, 85
Árpád dynasty, 248–249
Árpási, Zoltán, 85
Attila, József, 17
Augusta, pincess, 159, 268

B

Bach, Baron Alexander, 168, 294
Bácskai, Vera, 2
Bajcsy-Zsilinszky, Endre, 17, 187–188, 249
Balassi, Bálint, 7, 15, 249
Balázs, Ferenc, 202
Balogh, Péter István, 100
Bálint, architect, 148
Bánffy, Dezső, 282, 295, 303
Bárczy, István, 75
Barkács, Gyula, 100
Barry, Charles, 26
Báthory, Stephen, 7, 24, 42, 70, 92, 107, 114, 117, 135, 249
Batthyány, Count Lajos, 57, 65, 250, 254, 256, 271–272, 279, 293–295

Batthyány, Count Tivadar, 125
Batthyány, Countess Lajos, 123
Battiz, Gyula, 155
Beatrix of Aragon, 253
Béla III, king, 261
Béla IV, king, 249
Bem, Józef, 282
Bene, László, 243
Beöthy, Algernon, 108, 250
Bereczky, Vilmos, 203
Berinkey, Dénes, 251, 259
Bernáth, Aurél, 278
Berza, László, 77
Berzeviczy, Albert, 73–74, 109, 250
Bethlen, Count István, 17, 68–69, 78, 168–169, 173, 177, 179, 250–251, 261, 265, 283
Bey, Noureddin Ferouh, 174
Biermann, István, 151, 251
Bihari, Mihály, 41
Bilik, Károly, 144
Bíró, Dezső, 134
Blasek, Lajos, 152–153
Blitz, Miksa, 14
Boda, Dezső, 107
Bodrero, Emilio, 174
Böhm, Lajos, 126
Bőhm, Vilmos, 125, 251
Böhönyei, János, 301
Bolberik, Pál, 213
Bokányi, Dezső, 114, 119, 128, 130–131, 134, 136, 145, 147, 150, 251
Borbás, György, 49
Boros, Géza, 89, 93
Brezhnev, Leonid, 291
Bródy, Sándor, 17
Büchler, József, 140, 252
Buckler, József, 126
Budaházy, György, 223, 227
Budai, Gusztáv, 150
Budavári, Benő, 205
Bukovics, Gyula, 10, 251
Bülow, Bernhard Ernst von, 124
Bush, George Herbert Walker, 33, 198, 204, 252
Buzáth, János, 171, 172

C

Callmeyer, Ferenc, 91
Charles Robert (king of Hungary as Charles I), 248
Charles IV, 248, 268, 299
Chernenko, Constantin, 260
Ciano, Count Gian Galeazzo, 252
Corvin, János, 253
Corvinus, Matthias, 253, 256, 265
Csabi, Gábor, 100
Csáky, Count Albin, 110, 253
Csánk, Elemér, 12
Csaplár, Péter, 188
Csepely-Knorr, Luca, 100
Csőr, István, 152, 153
Csordás, Lajos 93
Csurka, István, 216, 253
Czinege, Lajos, 194–197, 253

D

Dálnoki Miklós, Béla, 187–188, 254
Darányi, Kálmán, 181
Dávid, Károly, 301
Deák, Ferenc, 49, 52, 59, 65, 121, 195, 248, 254–257, 265, 271, 295–296, 299, 304
Delvecchio, Ferenc Devecis, 7
Demszky, Gábor, 223, 237, 254
Déry, Attila, 2
Dessewffy, Count Aurél, 109
Deutsch, János, 150, 152–153
Deutsch, Tamás, 222
Dézsi, Mihály, 215
Dinnyés, Lajos, 255
Dizsóry, László, 185
Dobi, István, 269
Donáth, Gyula, 12
Dovcsák, Antal, 139
Durski-Trzaska, Karol, 174

E

Elek, Artúr, 74
Elizabeth, Queen, 257
Eörsi, László, 42
Eötvös, Baron József, 66, 255, 276, 293
Eötvös, Baron Károly, 107
Erkel, Ferenc, 188
Erkel, Lajos, 119
Erszinger, József, 126
Eszterházy, Prince Pál, 66, 256

F

Fabó, Beáta 9
Fadrusz, János, 12, 256
Falk, Miksa, 7, 15, 257
Faragó, Géza, 148
Farkas, István, 125
Farkas, Zoltán, 74, 76
Farkaslaky, Erzsébet, 2
Fehérvári, 109
Fejérváry, Baron Géza, 288
Fényes, László, 126, 257
Fehér, Artúr, 140
Fekete, József, 54
Ferdinand V, 65, 257
Ferenczy, Béni, 278, 289
Ferkai, András, 2
Fittle, Kamill, 54
Fischer, Ágoston, 80
Foerk, Ernő, 58, 72
Fónay, Jenő, 204, 208, 258
Francis Joseph (Ferenc József), 5, 10, 12, 29, 49, 58, 65, 67 189, 257, 263–264, 268, 288, 290, 304
Frederic, Archduke, 107
Freidrich, István, 159–160, 164, 258, 268, 277, 283, 287
Fricsay, Richárd, 129
Füredi, Richárd, 70, 258

G

Gábor, Eszter, 10, 16
Gádor, Endre, 47
Gál, Zoltán, 212, 216–217
Gál, Zoltán, Sr., 258
Garami, Ernő, 134, 259

Garbai, Sándor, 125–126, 129, 131, 145, 150–151, 154, 259
Gergely, Antal, 100
Gergényi, Péter, 233
Gerő, András, 2–3, 54, 79
Gerő, Ernő, 43, 189, 259
Gerő, István, 14
Géza, Prince, 296
Gisella, Princess, 268
Goldschmiedt, Sári, 140
Gombár, Csaba, 209, 260
Gömbös, Gyula, 69, 73, 75, 105, 177–181, 260, 269
Gömbös, László, 90, 261
Göncz, Árpád, 90, 211, 219, 261
Gorbachev, Mikhail Sergeyevich, 204, 260
Görgey, Artúr, 224, 272
Görgey, Gábor, 224, 261
Gosztonyi, Gyula, 152
Grespik, László, 223
Grosics, Gyula, 209, 241
Gross, Mór, 152–153, 278
Gulási, Gusztáv, 152–153
Gyáni, Gábor, 2, 9, 34
Gyalokai, Lajos, 114
Gyenes, Lajos, 14
Gyenis, Géza, 150, 152-153
Gyüre, Borbála, 100
Györgyi, Dénes, 75
Győri, Béla, 210
Gyurcsány, Ferenc, 230–231, 233, 235, 240–241, 262

H

Haász, Gyula, 278
Habsburgs, 79, 167–168
Halápi, László, 81
Halász, Hajnal, 75
Hamburger, Jenő, 150
Hanák, Péter, 3
Hankiss, Elemér, 209, 262
Haubrich, József, 150
Hauszmann, Alajos, 11–12, 19, 62, 262, 266, 275
Havas, Henrik, 98
Haypál, Benő, 144
Hegedűs, András, B., 41
Heitler, László, 88
Héjjas, Iván, 265
Helfy, Ignác, 22, 262
Hellmer, Edmund von, 256, 304
Heltai, Viktor, 130
Hennig (Hemin), Mihály, 150, 152–153
Hentzi, Heinrich, 129, 131, 263
Herczeg, Ferenc, 71, 263
Hildebrand, Adolf, 271
Hiller, István, 228
Hitler, Adolf, 188, 287
Hock, János, 144
Hollósi, Simon, 270
Hóman, Bálint, 76, 263
Homann, János, 100
Horger, Antal, 267
Horn, Gyula, 214, 264, 275
Horthy, Miklós, 29, 35, 37–40, 65, 67–69, 71, 75, 77–78, 84, 88, 157–166, 178, 183, 250, 260, 263–264, 268,

273, 277, 282, 286–287, 300, 302
Horthy, István, 185, 264
Horvát, Boldizsár, 11, 265
Horváth, Gyula, 107
Horvay, János, 64–67, 80–81, 265
Hübner, Tibor, 14
Hugo, Victor, 205
Hültl, Dezső, 14, 266
Hunyadi, János, 111, 114, 149, 188, 253, 265
Huszár, Károly, 258, 283

I

Imrédy, Béla, 297
Ivanov, B. P., 196

J

Jakabffy, Ferenc, 52
Jacob, 156
Jadwiga, (Hedvig) of Anjou, 248
Maria, of Anjou, 248
Jagiellon dynasty, 253
Jámbor, 148
Jászai, Samu, 155
Jászi, Oszkár, 126, 134, 266, 296
Jellačić, Josip, 271
John Sigismund, 249
Jókai, Mór, 108, 267
József Ágost, Archduke and Palatine, 69, 71, 128, 178, 268
József, Attila, 267
Jungfer, Gyula, 15
Justh, Gyula, 115, 124, 268

K

Kádár, János, 40, 43, 84, 86, 93, 199–200, 237, 268, 280, 284–285, 291
Kállai, Gyula, 188, 269
Kállay, Miklós, 186, 269
Kamermayer, Károly 286
Kampfl, József, 91
Karátsoni, Countess Jenő, 123
Károlyi, Count Alajos, 85, 124, 269
Károlyi, Count Gyula, 261, 297
Károlyi, Count Mihály, 36–37, 40, 62, 71, 84–85, 88, 94, 105, 126, 132, 135–136, 190–191, 228–229, 257–259, 261, 267–268, 270, 276, 280, 296
Kárpáti, Aurél, 76
Kárpáti, Ferenc, 200, 202
Katona, Csaba, 75
Kazai, Barna, 194, 196–197
Keglevics, Count István, 110
Keller, László, 235
Kemény, Lajos, 188
Kendeffy, Countess Katinka, 53
Kernstock, Károly, 133
Khrushchev, Nikita, 279, 292
Kiczkó, Kálmán, 129, 131
Király, Albert, 155
Kisfaludi Strobl, Zsigmond, 12, 80, 270–271,

Kiss, Ernő, 114, 271
Kitajka, Lajos, 129, 131
Klárik, Ferenc, 129
Klauzál, Gábor, 66, 271
Klobusitzky, János, 110
Kő, András, 42
Kocsis, András, 80, 271
Kodály, Zoltán, 252
Kölcsey, Ferenc, 293
Kollár, József, 14–15
Kolonics, Sándor, 144
König, Otto, 291
Korbély, Ferenc, 150, 152–153
Körber, Ernst von, 295
Kornidesz, Mihály, 86
Mihály, Kornidesz 86
Korvin, Ottó, 275
Kósa, Miklós, 152–153
Kossuth, Ferenc, 116, 123, 271
Kossuth, Lajos, 2, 4–5, 7, 9, 11, 13–17, 20, 27, 29, 30–31, 33–35, 37–38, 40–45, 48, 52, 54–55, 62–68, 74–77, 79–83, 88–95, 97, 99–101, 167–179, 181–182, 184–186, 189–190, 193–195, 197–199, 201, 203, 206, 210, 213–215, 217, 221–224, 226–227, 229–239, 241–242, 256, 262, 271–272, 299
Kovács, Ákos, 75
Kovács, Béla, 31, 93–94, 273
Kovács, Dénes, 54
Kovács, Ferenc II, 144
Kovács, Imre, 188, 273
Kovács, Pál, 215–216
Kövér, László, 241
Kozma, Lajos, 15, 273
Krassó, György 204, 274
Krecsányi, Kálmán, 119
Kresner, József, 144
Krúdy, Gyula, 62
Kubinyi, András, 2
Kúdos, 114
Kun, Béla, 145–146, 150, 154, 270, 274, 293
Kuncze, Gábor, 219, 235, 274
Kürthy, Baron Lajos, 109
Kuti, Zalán, 100

L

Ladislaus V, 266
Lajkó, Ferenc, 152, 153
Lajta, Béla, 273, 278
Landler, Jenő, 150, 275
Lassen, John, 275
Lázár, György, 278
Lechner, Jenő, 70, 100, 275
Lechner, Ödön, 278
Lékai-Leitner, János, 126, 275
Lenin, Vladimir Ilyich, 62, 149, 275, 290, 293
Liber, Endre, 47, 63, 66, 68, 70
Liebknecht, Karl, 62
Liebmann, Katalin, 214
Lőwy, Béla, 150, 152–153
Lónyay, Menyhért, 17, 276
Loránfi, Antal, 270
Louis I, The Great, 248
Lovászi, Márton, 125, 134, 276

Lugossy, Mária, 90, 214, 277
Lyka, Károly, 61, 66

M

Madách, Imre, 17
Magyar, Bálint, 224
Maier, József, 174
Makovecz, Imre, 89, 222, 277
Maléter, Pál, 284
Málnai, Béla, 15, 278
Malvin, Albrecht, 14
Maria Theresa, 256
Martinovics, Ignác, 149
Marton, László, 87–88, 278
Marx, Karl, 62
Mátrai, Lajos, 270–271, 282, 300
Mayer, János, 69, 179
Mécs, Imre, 90, 211, 278
Medgyessy, Ferenc, 289
Medgyessy, Péter, 224, 227, 262, 278
Melegh (Meleg), János B., 150, 152–153
Mészáros, János, 183
Mészáros, Lázár, 279
Mészáros, Lajos, 65
Meszlény, Lajos, 109
Metternich, Prince Klemens Wenzel von, 169
Mezőfi, Vilmos, 120, 279
Miagray, József, 139
Miklós, Ödön, 109
Mikó, Árpád, 48
Mikó, Sándor, 15
Mikoyan, Anastas, 279
Miksa, Falk, 158
Mikus, Sándor, 261, 301–302
Milošević, Slobodan, 218
Mock, Alois, 264
Mohácsi, Sándor, 100
Molotov, Vyacheslav, 287, 290
Müller, Ernő, 139

N

Nagy, Ferenc, 190–191
Nagy, Feró, 209
Nagy, Imre, 38, 41, 91, 93, 144, 192–193, 204, 269, 273, 280, 285, 298
Nagy, Lambert J., 42
Nagy, Zoltán, 85
Nagy, Zsigmond III, 144
Nagyatádi Szabó, István, 31, 68, 69, 70, 92, 177, 178, 280
Nákó, Count Kálmán, 109
Németh, Miklós, 264, 278
Nickel, Christa, 85
Nopcsa, Baron Elek, 109
Null, Eduard van der, 290

O

Obersovszky, Gyula, 204, 281
Ólmosi, Zoltán, 75
Orbán, Antal, 72, 179, 281
Orbán, Viktor, 219, 221–222, 225, 230, 239–240, 281, 300
Orosz, József, 98

P

Paar, Count, 121
Pacelli, Eugenio, 183–184, 281
Pál, Mihály, 78
Pálffy, Gyula, 126
Pálffy-Daun, Vilmos, 109
Pallavicini, Marquess Sándor, 110
Pálóczy, Antal, 55, 57, 100
Palotás, János, 206
Pásztor, János, 75–76, 271, 282
Pásztor, Mihály, 2
Pásztor, Mrs. János, 75
Pátzay, Pál, 261, 278, 289, 301
Pécsi, Máte, 100
Peidl, Gyula, 258–259, 283
Perczel, Dezső, 108, 282
Péter, János, 85
Péterdi, Andor, 129
Péterfy, Sándor, 281
Pető, Gyula, 150, 152–153
Petőfi, Sándor, 66, 127, 185, 205, 210, 223, 263, 267, 282
Petrényi, József, 233
Peyer, Károly, 155–156, 175–176, 251, 282–283
Pigécz, István, 150, 152–153
Pintér, Béla, 14, 283
Pintér, Klára Katalin, 100
Pius XI, 281
Pius XII, 281
Podmaniczky, Baron Frigyes, 50–51, 129, 283
Pogány, Gábor O., 80
Pongrátz, Gergely, 208–209, 217, 283
Potlák, Rudolf, 139
Potó, János, 47, 78
Pozsgay, Imre, 87, 237, 284
Preisich, Gábor, 15, 284
Preusz, Mór, 129, 131, 138–140
Prohászka, László, 47, 73, 78, 81
Prónay, Baron Dezső, 109, 265
Propper, Sándor, 139
Provalov, K. I., 194
Pugin, A. W. N., 26
Puky, Endre, 173
Putnoki, Móric, 180

R

Rabinovszky, Márius, 72
Rácz, Laci, 147
Rácz, Sándor, 205, 285
Ráday, Mihály, 2
Räde, Károly, 100
Radetzky, Joseph von Radetz, 113
Radices, Mónika, 100
Radnai, Béla, 271
Raffay, Sándor, 180
Rajk, László, 270
Rajna, György, 47, 83
Rákóczi, Ferenc I, 285
Rákóczi, Ferenc II, 36, 74–76, 79, 88–89, 94, 100, 180, 182, 195, 226, 235, 285
Rákosi, Mátyás, 38, 42, 82, 84 150, 259, 285, 298
Ráth, Károly, 110, 286
Ravasz, László, 186
Reagan, Ronald, 204

Révész, Sámuel, 14–15
Réti, Miklós, 209–210
Révai, József, 81–82, 286
Ribbentrop, Ullrich Friedrich von, 287, 290
Ripka, Ferenc, 65, 169, 287
Róna, József, 12, 287
Rothermere, Lord Harold Sidney Harmsworth, 288
Rózsa, Gyula, 88, 93
Rudas, László, 150
Rudnay, Béla, 107, 114, 288
Rudolf, Archduke, 267, 288

S

Sadeczky, Alajos, 100
Saint (St.) Stephen, 31, 59, 183, 249, 287, 296
Schickedanz, Albert, 53–54 289
Schmidt, Friedrich von, 27, 290
Schönberger, Emil, 119
Semmelweis, Ignác, 61
Senett, Richard, 36
Sengei, Károly, 12
Serédi, Prince Primate Jusztinian, 184
Shevkun, Nikolay, 197
Siccardsburg, August von, 290
Siege, Maria von, 27
Sigismund of Luxemburg, 265
Siklóssy, László, 2, 6
Silchenko, Nikolay, 197
Simay, Imre, 300
Simonyi-Semadam, Sándor, 297
Singer, Vera, 126
Sinkó, Katalin, 48
Sipőcz, Jenő, 67, 172, 289
Skalnitzky, Antal, 289
Smarilla, Géza, 155–156
Somogyi, Árpád, 82, 289
St. Ladislaus I, 249
Stalin, Josip Vissarionovich, 38, 79, 193, 230, 274, 279–280, 286, 289–290
Steindl, Imre, 19–20, 23, 25–27, 29, 40, 290
Steiner, Rudolf, 277
Stemenko, Sergei M., 196
Straub, Bruno F., 198, 200, 291
Stróbl, Alajos, 52, 270, 291
Sugár, Sándor, 126
Suslov, Mikhail, 291
Sütő, András, 213, 292
Szabad György, 212–213, 292
Szabó, András, 189, 197
Szabó, B. István, 188
Szabó, Endre, 234
Szabó, István I., 150, 152–153, 178
Szabó, János ("Uncle"), 204
Szakasits, Árpád, 176, 188, 292
Szalay, László, 7, 24, 293
Szamuely, Tibor, 62, 145
Szántó, Béla, 145, 150, 294
Szapáry, 296, 302
Széchenyi, Count István, 7, 15, 29, 40, 66, 257, 262–263, 272, 277, 279, 294
Székely, Andor, 148
Székely, András, 85

Széll, Kálmán, 59, 121–123, 295
Szemere, Bertalan, 65, 120, 276, 295
Szemere, Miklós, 120
Szende, Pál, 125–126, 295
Szendrői, Jenő, 301
Szentgáli, Ferenc, 150, 152–153
Szentgyörgyi, István, 69, 296
Szépvölgyi, Zoltán, 88
Szilágyi, Dezső, 11, 296
Szluha, István, 110
Szőnyi, István, 278
Szokoli, József, 150, 152–153
Szory, István, 150
Szűcs, György, 48
Szűrös, Mátyás, 201–202, 237, 297

T

Teleki, László, 299
Teleki, Pál, 184, 261, 297
Tersánszky, Józsi Jenő, 67, 298
Thököly, Imre, 285
Thurmer, Gyula, 232
Tibor, Szamuely, 293
Tildy, Zoltán, 32, 188–190, 273, 298
Tilgner, Victor Oscar, 256
Tisza, Count István, 71–74, 77–78, 84–85, 94, 108, 126, 129, 131, 179–180, 229, 250, 256–258, 268, 275, 282, 302
Tisza, Count Kálmán, 5, 17–18, 111, 149, 298–299, 295–296, 302
Tisza, Lajos, 23
Tito, Josip Broz, 299
Tőkés, László, 237
Torgyán, József, 207–208, 300
Tormay, Cecil, 38, 163–164, 300
Tóth, Dezső, 86
Tóth, Zoltán I., 82

U

Ullmann, Vilma, 13
Ungvári, Lajos, 80, 300

V

Vadász, György, 87, 301
Vadász, Mihály, 15, 284, 301
Vadjiralongkorn, Maha, 201
Vágó, Béla, 154
Vámbéry, Rusztem, 74
Vanczák, János, 139
Várady, Gyula, 284
Varga, Imre, 85, 302
Varga, László, 42–43
Varga, Tamás, 91, 302
Várkonyi, Balázs, 214
Vayer, Lajos, 67
Vécsey, 114
Velasquez, Diego, 61
Verő, Mária, 10, 16
Víg, Imre, 144
Vigh, Tamás, 302
Vincze, Sándor, 150
Vix, Fernand, 270

Vladislas II, 253
Vladislaus I, 265
Volkay, János, 100
Vörös, Boldizsár, 62
Vörös, Károly, 2

W

Wagmüller, Michael, 304
Wagner, Richard, 144
Wehner, Tibor, 48
Wałesa, Lech, 239
Weichinger, Károly, 301
Wekerle, Sándor, 121, 124, 128, 272, 302
Wellisch, Alfréd, 13, 15, 302
Weltner, Jakab, 303
Wenckheim, Béla, 256
Werner, Antal, 54
Wesselényi, Miklós, 256
Windischgraetz, Prince Alfred I, 169
Winkler, Franz, 178
Witmann, Max, 304
Wittner, Mária, 205, 303
Wlassics, Baron Gyula, 159, 173
Wright, Buttler, 173
Wright, Frank Lloyd, 277

Y

Ybl, Ervin, 72, 76
Ybl, Miklós, 283, 289–290

Z

Zala, György, 12, 49, 53–55, 57–58, 61, 72, 78, 85, 123–124, 179, 281, 304
Zacsek, Gyula, 209, 217
Zeidler, Miklós, 83
Zichy, Count Géza, 109
Zichy, Count Jenő, 110, 304
Zola, Emile, 133
Zrínyi, Ilona, 285
Zsedényi, Béla, 187, 304
Zumbusch, K., 291

ABOUT THE AUTHOR

ANDRÁS GERŐ is professor of history, and chairman of the Department of Economic and Social History, Eötvös Loránd University, Budapest. He is also professor of history at Central European University, and the director of the Institute of Habsburg History. He has published widely in Hungarian, as well as in English and German. His recent English-language publications include: *The Hungarian Parliament (1867–1918): A Mirage of Power*; *Emperor Francis Joseph, King of the Hungarians*; *Imagined History. Chapters from Nineteenth and Twentieth Century Hungarian Symbolic Politics*; and *The Jewish Criterion in Hungary*.

BOOKS PUBLISHED BY THE CENTER FOR HUNGARIAN STUDIES AND PUBLICATIONS

CHSP Hungarian Authors Series:

No. 1. *False Tsars*. Gyula Szvák. 2000.

No. 2. *Book of the Sun*. Marcell Jankovics. 2001.

No. 3. *The Dismantling of Historic Hungary: The Peace Treaty of Trianon, 1920*. Ignác Romsics. 2002.

No. 4. *The Soviet and Hungarian Holocausts: A Comparative Essay.* Tamás Krausz. 2006.

CHSP Hungarian Studies Series:

No. 1. *Emperor Francis Joseph, King of the Hungarians*. András Gerő. 2001.

No. 2. *Global Monetary Regime and National Central Banking. The Case of Hungary, 1921–1929*. György Péteri. 2002.

No. 3. *Hungarian-Italian Relations in the Shadow of Hitler's Germany, 1933–1940*. György Réti. 2003.

No. 4. *The War Crimes Trial of Hungarian Prime Minister László Bárdossy*. Pál Pritz. 2004.

No. 5. *Identity and the Urban Experience: Fin-de-Siècle Budapest.* Gábor Gyáni. 2004.

No. 6. *Picturing Austria-Hungary. The British Perception of the Habsburg Monarchy, 1865–1870.* Tibor Frank. 2005.

No. 7. *Anarchism in Hungary: Theory, History, Legacies.* András Bozóki and Miklós Sükösd. 2006.

No. 8. *Myth and Remembrance. The Dissolution of the Habsburg Empire in the Memoir Literature of the Austro-Hungarian Political Elite.* Gergely Romsics. 2006.

No. 9. *Imagined History. Chapters from Nineteenth and Twentieth Century Hungarian Symbolic Politics.* András Gerő. 2006.

No. 10. *Pál Teleki (1879–1941). A Biography.* Balázs Ablonczy. 2006.

No. 11. *The Hungarian Revolution of 1956. Myths and Realities.* László Eörsi. 2006.

No. 12. *The Jewish Criterion in Hungary.* András Gerő. 2007.

No. 13. *Remember Hungary 1956. Essays on the Hungarian Revolution and War of Independence in American Memory.* Tibor Glant. 2007.

No. 14. *Reflections on Twentieth Century Hungary: A Hungarian Magnate's View.* Baron Móric Kornfeld. 2007.

No. 15. *Ideas on Territorial Revision in Hungary 1920–1945.* Miklós Zeidler. 2007.

No. 16. *Hungarian Illusionism.* András Gerő. 2008.

No. 17. *Romanians in Historic Hungary.* Ambrus Miskolczy. 2008.

No. 18. *The Kingdom of Hungary and the Habsburg Monarchy in the Sixteenth Century.* Géza Pálffy. 2009.

No. 19. *A Possible and Desirable Pension System.* József Banyár and József Mészáros. 2009.

No. 20. T*he Austro-Hungarian Monarchy Revisited.* Edited by András Gerő. 2009.

No. 21. *Public Space in Budapest. The History of Kossuth Square.* András Gerő. 2009.